OUTREACH

Annie Oakley of the Wild West

ANNIE OAKLEY

OF THE

WILD WEST

by Walter Havighurst

Introduction to the Bison Book Edition
by Christine Bold

University of Nebraska Press
Lincoln

Copyright © 1954 by Walter Havighurst
Introduction copyright © 1992 by the University of Nebraska Press

First Bison Book printing 1992
Most recent printing indicated by the last digit below:
10   9   8   7   6   5   4   3   2

Library of Congress Cataloging-in Publication Data
Havighurst, Walter, 1901–
Annie Oakley of the Wild West / by Walter Havighurst; introduction to
the Bison Book edition by Christine Bold.
p.   cm.
Originally published: New York: Macmillan, 1954. With new introd.
"Bison."
Includes bibliographical references (p.   ) and index.
ISBN 0-8032-7253-7
1. Oakley, Annie, 1860–1926.   2. Shooters of firearms—United
States—Biography.   3. Entertainers—United States–Biography.
I. Title.
GV1157.O3H3   1992   91-41864
799.3'092—dc20   CIP
[B]

To Colonel and Mrs. John R. Simpson

CONTENTS

ILLUSTRATIONS

INTRODUCTION

By Christine Bold

The spectacle of Annie Oakley in the ring of Buffalo Bill's Wild West show is alive with suggestive paradoxes. The girlish figure, demure and petite, embodied femininity and fragility. Brawny frontiersmen and Native Americans towered over her, miming the most violent struggles and depredations of the savage frontier. Yet her skillful act with firearms denoted control, mastery, a nerveless intimacy with the instruments of destruction: she blasted glass balls a handful at a time with revolver and shotgun, sighted in a mirror to shatter targets behind her, and swung her rifle at clay pigeons from the back of a galloping horse, all at top speed. The very incongruity of her presence enchanted audiences, who showed her an adulation that equaled, and at times surpassed, that accorded Bill Cody himself. Partly in response to her popularity, the managers of the Wild West ensured her prominence on billboards and in the entertainment, often scheduling her act immediately after the opening Grand Review. The girlish figure who seemed least typical of Wild West violence thus occupied the show's rhetorical center. This intriguing conundrum is brought to life in Walter Havighurst's 1954 biography, still the most thorough account of Annie Oakley's life available.[1]

This scene of female power is especially poignant in the context of our emerging appreciation of women's multiple roles in developing and popularizing the western frontier. Only recently has scholarship challenged the dominant male myth of the frontier, responding to the muffled voices and teasing glimpses of western women and to fissures in the received stereotypes of passive female captives and frontier wives driven mad by isolation. We are beginning to forge a much richer sense of female ranchers, settlers, politicians, prostitutes, authors, artists—as well as the unhappy helpmeets who unquestionably existed—not silently "standing by their men" but creating a diverse culture at times in accord with, often in opposition to, male pursuits.[2]

At least part of the value of Annie Oakley's story is its contribution to this new and exciting narrative—more correctly, narratives—of the frontier West. Yet it is an incomplete story in many ways, peppered with contradictions and gaps. Writing in a celebratory more than analytical vein, Walter Havighurst does not solve the enigma of Annie Oakley, but he does bring the performer to life with so much detail and contemporary shading that we can hypothesize about the symbolic meanings of her life.

Those meanings are centrally bound up with the significance of the Wild West show in the late nineteenth and early twentieth centuries. Although Annie Oakley did have a professional life before and after her seventeen years with Bill Cody—as Havighurst details—her fame, then and now, rests on her starring role in the Wild West. That show codified frontier violence and white American suppression of "natives," American and foreign, as a heroic game. The "mythic space" of the Wild West rewrote American history triumphantly in an age complicated by the closing frontier, crises in urbanization and industrialization, and aggressive extracontinental expansion. Thus the show boosted public morale and resolved ritualistically some of the contradictions of the new American imperialism. The rhetoric of frontier imperialism redoubled when the Wild West toured Europe, incorporating symbolic types—from French chasseurs and Russian Cossacks to the crowned heads of several countries—into its display. Shadowing the United States' ascension to world power, Buffalo Bill held the might of Europe under his sway.[3]

In this rhetorical context, Annie Oakley clearly shared some qualities with her fellow performers. Her youth and dexterity could easily represent the youthful superiority, the self-reliance and democratic individualism of the new republic. The conjunction of such an innocent figure with firearms—as with Johnny Baker, "the Cowboy Kid," her fellow marksman—gave a favorable gloss to the violence visited by the dominant, white American culture on Native Americans, Philippinos, Chinese Boxers, and other foes inside and outside the ring. These intimations of moral purity seem to account partly for Annie Oakley's enthusiastic reception within and beyond America.

Yet her public presence also suggests a cluster of gender-specific connotations. The youthfulness that was insisted on in her perennial epithets "Little Missie" and "girl of the plains" had a maiden, virgin-like cast. Carroll Smith-Rosenberg has said: "Victorian America was a society of infinite sexual complexity. It simultaneously spawned both the loose and vigorous sexuality of the frontier and the repression of Edith Wharton's New York."[4]

From Oakley's entrance in the Wild West in 1885, she embodied this combination precisely, with her stetson hat, fringed outfit, and militaristic medals, all tempered by the tailoring of blouse and skirt to Victorian modesty—never a glimpse of breast nor knee—and the girlish swath of hair fanning around her shoulders. Her marriage to Frank Butler was never advertised by the show's management and seems to have been suppressed during the European tour. Although he appeared with her in the ring, as assistant and target-holder, her girlish persona, plus his ten years' seniority—and the fact that he looked his age—would have suggested more a paternal than a conjugal relationship. The importance of this maiden quality is suggested by the fate of Lillian Smith, a rival shot who joined the Wild West the year after Oakley. Smith's sensuality was written in the lines of her body and the expressions of her face; although her shooting matched Oakley's and her youthful achievements were even more striking, she lasted only two years in the show and faded fast from public memory.

The enduring female performer was desexualized both by infantilization and by domestication. Publicity for the show made much of the homeliness of Oakley's canvas quarters, heightened by the flowers she always grew on any extended engagement. Her compassion for children generally and orphans specifically was broadcast loudly: her complimentary tickets to those in a Staten Island orphanage supplied Major John Burke, the show's public relations man, with priceless publicity; he proceeded to institutionalize such periodic invitations to disadvantaged children as "Annie Oakley Days." In London, she was acclaimed for hosting teas for English mothers and children outside her reception tent and for introducing them to Native American children.

This affiliation with women and children fulfilled a particular function in the ring. Oakley's early slot in the show was partly designed as gentle preparation for the explosive violence to follow: by feminizing shooting and destruction, she helped the less sturdy members of the audience to negotiate the thrilling horror of the noise, speed, potential injury, and simulated death. By extension,

Annie Oakley feminized America's "gun culture" at a crucial moment in its formative stage.[5] Frontier violence and its technology were under hot debate in the 1880s when she joined the Wild West (*cowboy* was an ambivalent term at best; the postmaster general was busy banning violent stories of western outlawry from the mail); her act may well have helped to tip the balance toward the embrace of guns as heroic inventions. Her female purity sanctioned firearms.

The roles made viable for Oakley by the Wild West publicity machine were maidenhood and surrogate motherhood, without intervening adulthood. In an era when American women were denied the vote, severely limited in their ability to hold property, and hedged about in their choice of profession, this public construction of Oakley smacks of lip service to the powers of womanhood. On the one hand, she defeated men with her skill, speed, and nerve; but this display of prowess was framed by pseudo-chivalric intimations of the virgin maiden and codification of her power as ultimately located and contained within the home. That uneasy yoking of images recurs in representations of womanhood throughout the nineteenth century; Annie Oakley is unusual only in the startling incongruity with which these meanings collide. The same imagery attended her public appearances outside the Wild West: in theatrical melodramas such as *The Western Girl*, in shooting contests against eminent marksmen, and in exhibitions before military and royalty across Europe. Her appearance in vaudeville, to which she had recourse every time the family purse ran low, was framed more tellingly yet; Havighurst reports:

> In February she appeared again at Tony Pastor's Opera House, climaxing a bill that included Samson, the Strongest Man on Earth; the Ossified Man whose torso gave back a stony sound when struck with a hammer; the Elastic Skin lady, contortionist extraordinary; a one-armed juggler, and a troop of musical artists. (p. 160)

In other words, Annie Oakley as freak.

Most posthumous treatments of Annie Oakley have capitalized on her image as paragon, a "straight shooter" in all senses. From the 1935 film *Annie Oakley*, directed by George Stevens and starring Barbara Stanwyck, to the 1946 Rodgers and Hammerstein musical *Annie Get Your Gun,* composed by Irving Berlin and originally starring Ethel Merman, and the 1950 Metro-Goldwyn-Mayer film of the musical with Betty Hutton, the youthful shot is spunky and virtuous. Her heroism is especially stressed in inspirational writings for young readers, often to patriotic effect: "As the nation developed and prospered, so did Annie. Her story, like the country's, was one of struggle and triumph; her spirit of energy, ambition and optimism that of America's golden era."[6] The 1976 Robert Altman film, *Buffalo Bill and the Indians; or, Sitting Bull's History Lesson,* catches more of the paradox inherent in Annie Oakley representing an America that denied her, as woman, many of its rewards. Altman's Annie (played by Geraldine Chaplin) is a shooting automaton, an innocent, well-meaning naïf cheated by everyone from the scheming, sodden Buffalo Bill to her adulterous husband.

The complications in the triumphant Oakley legend multiply when we reflect on its production. On the information available, it seems a myth largely constructed by men but willingly sustained and in some ways finessed by Annie Oakley. She was no mere victim of the male gaze, but neither was she an autonomous being. Annie was originally self-denominating: she changed her name from the hated Phoebe Ann Moses to the catchy Annie Oakley, taking her surname from a suburb of Cincinnati: the location of her first shooting triumph, against her future husband, according to one biographer.[7] But thereafter, men named her and positioned her: Bill Cody christened her "Missie"; ringmasters announced her as "the little girl of the western plains"—a diminutive echoed by British royalty; Sitting Bull adopted her as his daughter, with the name "Little Sure-Shot"; and even her husband seems to have apostrophised her as "my little girl," in verse and prose. Will Rogers, homespun western philosopher, named her saintliness in writing her obituary:

> She was not only the greatest rifle shot for a woman that ever lived, but I doubt if her character could be matched anywhere outside of a saint. . . .
>
> I had heard cowboys who had traveled with the Bill Show speak of her almost in reverence. They loved her. She was a marvelous woman, kindest hearted, most thoughtful, a wonderful Christian woman.[8]

As Carroll Smith-Rosenberg tells us, these are the classic virtues of the sentimental Victorian heroine, here articulated in the folksy accents of the westerner circa 1926.

Her husband was her primary tutor, teaching her to read, educating her in world affairs, and coaching her in the shooting tricks that made her fame: in Havighurst's words, "father, brother, husband, in one changing man" (p. 22). But Annie had been earlier educated by her mother and her female employers in the womanly art of sewing, and biographers agree that hers was an exceptional skill which she used in service of her stardom, designing and producing all her own costumes. At that level, at least, she was responsible for the amalgamated image of frontier modesty. These costumes also sustained the illusion of her girlishness, right into her forties, as did her consistent lies about her age, in public speeches and autobiographical notes. And it was she who dyed her white hair back to chestnut, at the age of forty-two, to star in the melodrama *Western Girl*.

Her identification as a westerner seems to have been the concoction of Burke and Cody, a necessary fiction to ensure a nice fit between her shooting skills and the western rhetoric of their show. Although Annie was never west of the Mississippi until 1896, there is no evidence that she demurred. And indeed, her origins seem to have been lowly enough to qualify as "frontier": brought up in a one-room log cabin in Ohio, poverty led her to hunt for food and so hone her shooting talent. This past also provided raw material for a recapitulation of the hunter figure: note that where James Fenimore Cooper's heroic Leatherstocking, for instance, hunts for his own survival, Annie Oakley was celebrated for hunting in support of the domestic circle.

Perhaps the most disturbing aspect of this constructed image is its apparent seamlessness. The reader who is interested in Oakley's personal life—as distinct from her public persona—must look hard to discover much more than inconsequential details, gaps, and silences. Biographers seem to assume that Oakley's person and persona were indivisible, that the public construction cost the private person nothing. No complex being emerges from behind the simple, serene, unruffable markswoman who concentrated her life on the perfection and repetition of shooting glass balls. Courtney Riley Cooper's early, hagiographical account makes the assumption explicit in her characterization of Oakley as "wholly without ego."[9] Havighurst is nowhere so blithe, but his narrative method—which appropriates Oakley's thoughts and re-actions, invents dialogue for her, and generally folds her voice into his—perpetuates the seamlessness of the portrait.

For the contemporary, more skeptical reader, however, questions abound as to how much was sacrificed to the public image and how far Annie Oakley's arrested development extended beyond the circus ring. What does the lack of children or marriage to the paternal Frank Butler say about the eternally youthful Missie? A later, female biographer suggests Oakley's extreme propriety:

> All her life Annie had been a modest person, and this feeling extended into her funeral preparations. She wanted a woman embalmer. Miss Louise Stocker . . . was called to the residence in October 1926. Calmly, Annie outlined her wishes.[10]

How did this physical shrinking accord with the exhibitionism of cartwheels and handstands—however muffled by leggings and skirts—before millions of male and female spectators? Her vaunted generosity and affection to her family seem not to have survived the stresses of circus life. Dexter Fellows, one-time publicity man for the Wild West, speaks of her extreme miserliness. She seems to have regarded the other white female performers in the Wild West, introduced on the heels of her success, as rivals to be vanquished, not sisters to be embraced. And what should we make of the parenthesis in Oakley's diary entry ruminating on her meeting with the emperor of Austria in 1890:

> I really felt sorry when I looked into the face of the Emperor of Austria. . . . his face looked both tired and troubled. I then and there decided that being just plain little Annie Oakley, with ten minutes work once or twice a day, was good enough for me, for I had, *or at least I thought I had,* my freedom. [my emphasis][11]

Even these speculations are thin, eked out from contradictions and hints in the received story of Annie Oakley. Her surviving auto-biographical notes only compound the mystery: she misrepre-sented her birthdate there, too; doctored clippings that contradicted her own dramatic stories about herself; and generally delivered a mishmash of fact, memory, and invention.

But if the telling details of Oakley's private life are beyond recall, their very absence speaks volumes to the contemporary reader. Feminist thinkers have emphasized that the two-dimensional, purified woman set on a pedestal for public worship is as much the victim of dehumanization and objectification as the vilified slave. Oakley's agency in such a process does not contradict the thesis, but rather suggests how deeply the effects can bite. Did her visible centering in the western frontier myth entail the marginalization of her personhood, the suppression of her maturation? Can we say of Annie Oakley what Eric Mottram says of the western hero: "Conditioned action, mythicization and addiction enclose a man in a required role that requisitions his liberty"?[12] Certainly all we seem able to grasp from this distance is a cardboard figure, exhilirating and inspiring from one angle—she beat men at their game, she pulled herself out of poverty, she won public status—but dark and disturbing from another.

These reflections are not, of course, Walter Havighurst's. He wrote in the 1950s, an age generally less skeptical of cultural icons than Robert Altman's or ours, and with a profoundly different construction of womanhood. While Havighurst does interrogate the fictions in Oakley's own account, his primary thrust is the celebration of a figure and an era. During the Cold War 1950s woman's place in the home was underwritten by advertisers, Hollywood filmmakers and public figures with a desperate need for consensus and contained order. Small wonder, then, that Havighurst did not hesitate to speak for Oakley, nor felt my compulsion to plumb the paradoxes of a story so nicely uplifting. The Cold War also galvanized the search for distinctive marks of American democracy, among which the frontier was paramount. Havighurst's account came only four years after Henry Nash Smith's ground-breaking *Virgin Land: The American West as Symbol and Myth*, the seedbed of contemporary analyses of popular western culture. Havighurst tackled material omitted by Smith—although *Virgin Land* presents Buffalo Bill and dime-novel heroines, among others, as literary productions, it comments not at all on the Wild West show nor Annie Oakley—but he proceeded from a similarly optimistic interpretation of the frontier as axiomatic to America's national consciousness. Achieving access to both documents and surviving relatives and acquaintances of Annie Oakley, Havighurst minutely tracked the movements of the woman and the show that defined her. However we read his narrative—whether with or against the grain—we must be grateful for the vast canvas that he painted, fascinating in its detail and its sweep. He gives us an Annie Oakley whom we can recuperate and puzzle over, if never quite understand.

NOTES

1. Additional biographies include Clifford Lindsey Alderman, *Annie Oakley and the World of Her Time* (New York: Macmillan, 1979); Courtney Ryley Cooper, *Annie Oakley, Woman at Arms* (New York: Duffield, 1927); Charles Parlin Graves, *Annie Oakley, The Shooting Star* (Champaign, Ill.: Garrard Press, 1961); Isabelle S. Sayers, *Annie Oakley and Buffalo Bill's Wild West* (New York: Dover, 1981); and Annie Fern Swartwout, *Missie: The Life and Times of Annie Oakley* (Blanchester, Ohio: Brown Publishing, 1947).

2. Important recent work on the women's West includes Susan Armitage and Elizabeth Jameson, eds., *The Women's West* (Norman: University of Oklahoma Press, 1987); Anne M. Butler, *Daughters of Joy, Sisters of Misery: Prostitutes in the American West, 1865–90* (Urbana: University of Illinois Press, 1985); Annette Kolodny, *The Land before Her: Fantasy and Experience of the American Frontiers, 1630–1860* (Chapel Hill: University of North Carolina Press, 1984); Vera Norwood and Janice Monk, eds., *The Desert Is No Lady: Southwestern Landscapes in Women's Writing and Art* (New Haven: Yale University Press, 1987); Glenda Riley, *The Female Frontier: A Comparative View of Women on the Prairie and the Plains* (Lawrence: University Press of Kansas, 1988); and Lillian Schlissel, *Women's Diaries of the Westward Journey* (New York: Schocken, 1982).

3. See Richard Slotkin, "The 'Wild West,' " in *Buffalo Bill and the Wild West* (Brooklyn, N.Y.: Brooklyn Museum, 1981); Christine Bold, "The Rough Riders at Home and Abroad: Cody, Roosevelt, Remington and the Imperialist Hero," *Canadian Review of American Studies,* 18 (1987): 321–50. Slotkin's larger argument about the frontier's symbolic functions is stunningly documented in *The Fatal Environment: The Myth of the Frontier in the Age of Industrialization, 1800–1890* (New York: Atheneum, 1985).

4. Carroll Smith-Rosenberg, "Sex as Symbol in Victorian America," in *Prospects: An Annual of American Cultural Studies,* ed. Jack Salzman

(New York: Burt Franklin, 1980), p. 51. Smith-Rosenberg expands her thesis in *Disorderly Conduct: Visions of Gender in Victorian America* (New York: Oxford University Press, 1985).

5. See Eric Mottram, " 'The Persuasive Lips': Men and Guns in America, the West," *Blood on the Nash Ambassador: Investigations in American Culture* (London: Century Hutchinson, [1989]).

6. Alderman, p. 83; see also Jan Gleiter, *Annie Oakley* (Milwaukee: Raintree Children's Books, [1987]).

7. Sayers, p. 7.

8. Quoted in Alderman, p. 82.

9. Cooper, p. 9.

10. Sayers, p. 86.

11. Quoted in Sayers, p. 42.

12. Mottram, p. 30.

Annie Oakley of the Wild West

A crowned queen was never treated with more reverence than was I by those wholesouled cowboys. For seventeen long years I was just their little sister, sharing both their news of joy and sorrow from home.

—From ANNIE OAKLEY's *Autobiography*

CHAPTER 1

A Girl from Darke County

> Wild turkeys, wild geese, pigeons, grouse, and quail
> were plentiful, and every Sunday game would be found
> on the table. . . . Lots of coons, minks, foxes, muskrats,
> rabbits, and squirrels in all parts of the county, and their
> hides could be seen nailed to every barn.
>
> —GEORGE W. CALDERWOOD: *Darke County Boy*

GREENVILLE, in the prairie and woodland of western Ohio, was
already an old town in 1876. Some of the first Ohio memories were
centered there—St. Clair's defeat by the Indians, Mad Anthony
Wayne's lean men driving back the Shawnees and Miamis, the Great
Council in 1795 when a thousand chiefs and warriors met the treaty
makers in the trampled compound of Fort Greene Ville. Though
the big stockade was gone, the trenches still showed beside Greenville Creek and under the elms of Third Street. But the memories
were distant. The border men had gathered here in coonskin caps,
tricornered hats, and eagle feathers—William Henry Harrison, Isaac
Zane, Meriwether Lewis and William Clark, Little Turtle, Black
Hoof, Leatherlips, Buckongehelas, and the Big Wind himself, Anthony Wayne; but they seemed as remote as English yeomen on the
green banks of Runnymede.

Since that meeting of the captains and the chiefs, Greenville had
become the seat of Darke County and it was more aware of the
future than of the past. The main street was hopefully named Broadway; there was a new stone courthouse beyond a busy market square.

Four times a day a train puffed past on the Dayton & Union Railroad. Men talked about another railroad, the Cincinnati, Hamilton, & Dayton, and survey crews were already hacking through Darke County brush—though the farmers loafing in Weston and Ullery's Hardware Store said a good plank road to Cincinnati would put all the railroads out of business. There was timber enough in Darke County, they agreed, to lay a mud-proof road all the way from the Ohio River to Lake Erie. From Broadway came the rattle of harness and the creak of wagon wheels—another four-horse team hauling a load of hoops and staves from the hickory groves up north. In four days the load would arrive at Cincinnati, eighty miles away, pulling up at the big cooper shops beside the breweries and packinghouses.

Like any town in America, Greenville was inhabiting the future. New sawmills snarling at the edge of the timber; new shops turning out staves, tubs, pails, broom handles, trunk slats, spokes, chairs, singletrees, axles, and wheels; new flouring mills grinding Darke County wheat; new drying barns hung with broad brown leaves of tobacco; a new broom factory beside the old icehouse on Tecumseh Creek. Now men talked about a new railroad to hoot at the barges on the canal that skirted the eastern border of the county.

Meanwhile cows plodded down Broadway to drink at Greenville Creek. Teams were hitched in front of Fitts' Tavern, and farmers filled their kerosene cans at the Katzenberger Brothers' general store. After supper children shouted around the town square, playing London Loo in the tangy October dark. Hallowe'en gangs pushed over wooden privies and tossed wagon wheels onto the roofs of barns. On election night the whole town stood around the courthouse in the light of leaf fires. Up in Weston and Ullery's hall old Aaron Quick played his fiddle, *Rosin the Bow* and *Jennie Put the Kettle On* for the weekly dance. Every day in the fine October weather farmers rocked into town on mounds of fresh-husked corn and ragged loads of broom brush. Twice a year old "Coonskin" Brown tramped in, with an even hundred coonskins lashed to his plodding horse. He tied old Nell to the Broadway hitching rack and sold his skins to Frenchy La Motte.

Frenchy, dark-eyed, with a short red beard and quick movements, his hands always in the air, had a wild and wary look like an uncaught fox. He talked about times when beaver were thick as squirrels around Loramie's Lake and a man could take a bale of mink and marten from the St. Mary's marshes. He sold gun shells, lanterns, axes, traps, harness, saddles. In front of his shop crouched a pile of dusty pelts; in the back room he sorted out skins and tied them into shaggy bundles for shipment to St. Louis. He cared less than nothing about plank roads, railroads, shingle mills, and broom factories. He could remember that room stacked to the roof with bales of raccoon, mink, muskrat, and deer skins; his father was known as a fur trader all the way to Sandusky-on-the-Lake.

To his dim shop, with the wood stove winking in the corner, came mud-stained men from the marshes and the bottom timber. They had no money in their pockets; they traded skins for traps and knives and lantern oil. Occasionally another trader came, so quietly that sharp-eared Frenchy La Motte looked up startled from his bench by the stove.

She was a slight figure in a worn woolen skirt beaded with stick-tights and cockleburs. From under a boy's faded cap chestnut hair spilled down to her shoulders, and she walked noiselessly in a boy's heavy shoes, too big for her trim ankles and tiny feet. She had gray eyes, clear as light, that looked at things directly. She always brought a bundle wrapped in gray-green swamp grass.

Quiet and small, childlike in her too big clothing, she brought a feeling into the dusty shop. She made Frenchy La Motte think of things far away from Greenville; he remembered his father talking of the leafy streets of Paris and the bare Dakota plains. The slouching men watched across the room while Frenchy handed her a rifle. "All fixed now. Good as new." She studied the brightly filed gunsight, swung the stock to her shoulder, and sighted down the barrel. She had a quick wide smile that made her look older. Then she remembered the grass-wrapped bundle. "For you, Mr. La Motte."

"Who was that?" someone asked when she was gone.

Frenchy's dark eyes came up. "You don' know Annie Mozee from North Star township? She's shy little thing, like pigeon dove. But she's good hunter."

"North Star— Rough country up there."

"She takes plenty birds—pigeons, grouse, quail. Charlie Katzenberger sends her game to Cincinnati. Hotel people like to serve her birds." He unrolled the long strands of marsh grass, still moist and sweet-smelling, and lifted a plump grouse by its feathered legs. "See —shot through the head. Like always."

*   *   *

Annie rode out of town on an empty grain wagon, swaying on the high seat beside a young farmer.

"You sell your birds, Annie?"

"Yes. And they gave me a letter at the post office." She fumbled inside her shirt.

"Better keep it there."

They rumbled through the covered bridge and past the schoolhouse where children were streaming out the door. Some began skipping rope on the playground and others raced toward a pile of leaves under the big maple tree. Annie watched until the wagon rattled around a bend.

The driver sat silent, the reins in his brown hands, the horses jogging loosely and their harness jingling. He felt his jacket pocket. "I got a letter myself. You recollect my brother Jim?"

She remembered the tall lean man tramping the stubble fields with a gun on his shoulder. "Where did he go to?"

"He's out in Kansas, fighting the Indians. He had friends in Custer's regiment. They all got wiped out, he says, on the Little Big Horn."

"Who killed them?"

"Sitting Bull and those varmints."

Her gray eyes roved the autumn pastures. "Is it a far-off place?"

"What place?"

"Where they fought the Indians."

"Yes, it's far off. Way out in Kansas, and beyond there to the Black Hills and the Sioux country."

They passed through the scattered village of Dawn. At the crossroad a homemade sign pointed east toward Versailles, Frenchtown, and Russia, and north toward Brock, North Star, and Celina. Though Annie couldn't read the sign she knew what it said, and she felt the distance in those Darke County names.

The driver slapped the reins. "I'd ruther be here," he said as though he had decided something. "I'd ruther live in North Star township."

North Star—it was only a cluster of houses around a store, a church, and a blacksmith shop. It was a mixture of people, a family from Kentucky (they said "Kaintuck"), a family, like Annie's own people, from Pennsylvania, the family of an Irishman who had dug the canal at Piqua and had driven mules on the towpath between Dayton and St. Mary's. Old Hieronymous Star had built the first cabin at the crossroads, but Annie felt the place was named for something mysterious and distant like the clear star glittering over the northern woods. One of its farmers had gone to fight the Indians in far-off Kansas, and all its people had come from distant places.

As the sun touched the western woods the stubble fields turned golden. She gave up the picture of North Star and watched her long shadow, perched on a high wagon behind long-legged horses, sliding over rank grass at the roadside. Ahead rose the wooden church steeple at Brock, though the houses were hidden in trees. Sunlight touched the stones in the little graveyard.

She didn't wait for the crossroad. "I'll light down here. I'll cut through the woods and across the fields."

"Pick you up a rabbit on the way home?"

"Might be."

She took her gun from the gunny sacks and jumped down. "Thanks for the ride."

Then she was alone, scuffing through dead leaves in the little cemetery where under a wooden headboard her father lay buried. A few scarlet leaves still burned in the sumach bushes, and wild clematis climbed over the old gravestones. She waited there a little, not a house in sight, hearing the wind rattle the cornstalks beyond the fence row and watching for a rabbit in the wheat stubble. Finally she put the gun to her shoulder and drew the sights together. She found a walnut hanging at the end of a bare branch. Her finger pressed and the walnut fell. Frenchy had done a good job.

She went on home in the sunset—over the ridge, through leaf-strewn woods, down the rough pasture slough. She stepped across Swamp Creek—only a trickle at that season—and came out on the section road. There was a pale patch there, and it always gave her a silent, solemn feeling. She had seen the farmers digging gravel from a mound above Swamp Creek and throwing it on wet places in the road. The gravel was full of human bones—Indian skeletons, her mother said—soon ground white under the wagon wheels. She had seen other mounds, green and silent, beside the creeks of Darke County. Sometimes she wondered about the people who had lived and died here in the forgotten times.

When the sun was gone the quick October dusk came down. The first white stars were showing when she saw the lamplight in the kitchen window.

Her mother spoke in her soft Quaker voice. "Is thee tired, child? It's a long trip to Greenville."

"Matt Hawkinson brought me to the corners."

"Tha'll be hungry."

They kept asking about Greenville—her brother John, her little sister Hulda, her stepfather with his dim eyes and rumbling voice—and supper was over when she remembered the letter. She reached inside her woolen shirt. "A letter they gave me at the post office."

Susan Moses held it to the lamp. "Why—it says Annie Moses. It has tha name, child."

"Read it to me."

Annie bent over the table, studying the page her mother spread in the lamplight.

"It's from sister Lyda. She wants tha to come to Cincinnati to live with them."

"To Cincinnati—"

Her mother turned the page and went on reading. " 'It is good for a girl to see the way people live in the city and not be always hunting in the woods. A girl can go to school here, even learn to make dresses and play the piano. Joe has a good job and we are in a nice house with a spare room for a little sister. You are sixteen now and ready for new things. Have mother write us when to meet the train.'"

When her mother looked up the light was bright in her eyes. "I'm glad for thee, Annie. Tha can learn reading at last, and music, and sketching." Susan Moses did pencil and crayon sketches and still dreamed of the time when she could take up painting. One of her sketches hung on the kitchen wall—a cabin with the winter snow around it and smoke feathering from the chimney.

From the shadows, rocking in his chair, the old man now remembered the city, and his voice began to rumble.—It was a fine place, Cincinnati. Long streets and great houses, horsecars and carriages, big steamboats on the river. Fine people—

Annie sank down beside the rocking chair. "I don't want any other people." She felt homesick already.

He put a hand on her head. "You can come back and tell us."

"Yes, I will." She jumped up and ran to her mother. "I'll come back often."

Her mother nodded. "This will be tha home but not tha bondage." She touched Annie's flushed cheek. "Young girl tha still be, but tha learns quickly. Tha'll do well, I know."

That night, with moonlight falling across the bed, Annie could not sleep. To leave Darke County—she had never thought of it. She got out of bed, hugged the blanket around her, and crouched at the window. For a long time she looked at the moon-paled pasture, the vague spread of the cornfield, and the deep dark woods beyond. All her memories were here. She needed to draw them around her, like a blanket, even the painful ones, before she let them go.

*   *   *

The winter day had almost passed, and they stared out at the furious snow while the burning logs licked at the hearth. At last the wagon came, a blurred gray shape in the swirl of white, with a ghostly figure huddled on the seat. When the traces were freed the horses went on to the stable, but they had to lift her father down from the wagon and carry him into the house. The wind cried all that night, and her father talked brokenly about Pennsylvania, the people on the roads, the grinding of the summer's grain. Though the room was cold, he kept throwing off the covers and his thin face glistened in the lamplight. At last the wind went down and the voice was still. But Jacob Moses did not leave his bed. For weeks he lay there while snow deepened in the woods. When the warm wind came, the creeks ran full and pools of sky-blue water dotted the pasture. But it was a false spring. While another snowstorm buffeted the house, Jacob Moses moaned again in his fever. After the storm had gone, the house was desolate as the frozen fields. Annie remembered, as close as yesterday, though it was twelve years past, her mother standing lost and distant before she drew the sheet over the quiet face. She sat beside the bed, looking as though no one could ever reach her, while the cold dusk filled the room.

At the moonlit window Annie hugged the blanket close. Her parents must have been lonely in the Ohio woods. They had come from a bustling place, a wagoners' inn on a highway in Pennsylvania. Sometimes Susan Moses talked about the great wagons and the high-slung stages, teamsters clumping in from the stable yard, and families warming themselves at the fire while supper was laid on the long table. Always people, voices, the rattle of harness and the great wheels rumbling, bells jangling from the collars of the six-horse teams. It was like living in a strong river of life. But when the tavern burned, Jacob Moses did not stand staring at the ashes. The road was there, with life flowing westward. When the stagecoach came he lifted his wife and two small daughters into the open door. Like countless families before them, they were going west. Jacob Moses had a Quaker's soft speech, yet he loved horses and hunting.

So Annie Moses was born in the woods of Darke County on the far edge of Ohio. Her first memories were gathering hickory nuts and red haws, digging calamus root and ginseng, stripping the bark of sassafras and slippery elm. With her three older sisters she hunted fox grapes in the woods and crayfish in the creek. Her childhood belonged to the open—running over grassy tussocks in the slough, lugging yellow pumpkins from the tattered corn rows, gathering windfalls under the apple trees, trying to milk the stray cow, Old Black, that wandered half wild through the woods.

After her husband's death Susan Moses became district nurse, and her children were scattered. Little John and Hulda were taken by neighbors. Nine-year-old Annie went to the County Home, where the children taunted her with a singsong *Moses Poses!*—she would never forget that humiliation. A year later she was taken by a farm family who promised to give her care and schooling, a promise soon forgotten. She was a virtual slave in a heartless household; at the end of her life Annie Oakley wrote with pent-up feeling in her fragmentary autobiography, "The man was a brute and his wife a virago." After two years she ran away. Back in North Star township she found her mother remarried. Her older sisters, Lyda, Sarah Ellen, and Elizabeth, were married and gone, but the younger children were at home. Her new father, Joseph Shaw, looked at her from dim eyes and spoke in a gentle, rumbling voice. He wanted Susan Moses' children around him.

In the reunited family Annie was the oldest child. She rode the roan pony around the rail-fenced pasture. In the woods she learned the habits of quail and the feeding places of grouse. She trapped rabbits in figure 4's of binder twine and caught quail in cornstalk traps covered by brush and baited with grains of corn. She never tired of the ragged meadows and the encircling woods.

To Ohio twenty years before, Jacob Moses had brought a long-barreled cap-and-ball Pennsylvania rifle. It was taller than Annie when she first took it down from the wall, but it felt alive in her hands. She polished the long blue barrel and rubbed the stock till it shone like silk. When she raised it to her shoulder and drew the sights together, the gun seemed to belong to her. Soon she was hunting in the corn rows, in the woods, over the tawny pastures, and across the snowy fields. Before she was fifteen Frenchy La Motte was buying her pelts and Charlie Katzenberger was sending her dressed game to Cincinnati. That rifle paid off the mortgage on the half-wild little farm.

Hunched at the window Annie pictured the road her stepfather had told about—the long road that led over the low ridges and past the scattered woods toward the Ohio River where the hills of Kentucky rise across the water. All roads are one road, he had said in his deep soft voice, leading to distant places. Across the moonlit pasture came a windy flutter of wings. In spring the fall and migrant birds roosted there—robins, blackbirds, vireos, swamp sparrows. You wouldn't know they thronged the branches until some creeping fox disturbed them. Out of silence came that stormy rush of wings. They swirled up, dimming the silver moon. Then they settled again in the cedars, and the night was still.

The girl crept back to bed, but still she did not sleep. Into the room came the moonlight and the night. She saw the pale star twinkling in blackness over the north timber. She closed her eyes, and her mind filled with things she would always remember—the horse trough at North Star lined with green moss soft as a kit fox pelt, the clang of the anvil in Will Pierson's shop, the arch of trees where the dusty road dropped down to Greenville Creek, white apple blossoms in the orchard, the cornstalks rattling and birds flying in a windy sky, yellow lamplight in the kitchen window as she came home at dusk. Faintly across the fields came the whistle of the midnight train. By morning it would be in Cincinnati.

CHAPTER 2

View from Shooter's Hill

Erected in 1851 to house a Baptist seminary, the
ornate three-story building became noted as a beer-garden
and shooting resort in the 1860's and 1870's. In 1888 it
was destroyed by fire.

—Cincinnati: A Guide to the Queen City

IN THE 1870's a thin, myopic little man, the son of a Greek girl
and an Irish army officer, born on an Aegean island and destined to
die in Japan, was living on the Cincinnati riverfront and writing
feature stories for the Sunday Enquirer. Lafcadio Hearn prowled the
dark alleys of the lower city. He peered into courtyards and doorways
and sat in tavern rooms with the city's riffraff. Fascinated by the life
of the levee, he wrote about the big white packets and the grimy
barges, about Rat Row and Sausage Row, about squalid Bucktown
between Broadway and the Culvert, about Gamblers' Row on Fourth
Street, about voodooism and vagabonds and the wild dances of the
rivermen. Everywhere he looked his half-blind eyes saw strangeness
and drama.

On a summer day in 1876 he climbed the spire of St. Peter's
Cathedral, clinging to the shoulders of a steeplejack, in order to
describe the city from that height. At the tip of the spire he hung
onto the cross and looked downward. He could not see the city
whose sounds came up to him like echoes from another world. He
crept down the ladder and inside the spire. But back in the newspaper office he wrote all night under a flaring gas jet, describing what

he had not seen. "From that great height, every portion of the city encircled by the hills was distinctly visible. . . . All the Plum Street canal bridges from the elbow eastward were plainly visible, Mill Creek shimmered with a golden gleam in the west, and the Ohio curved in blue serpentine in the south."

In those years Cincinnati was one of the most vivid cities in America. From the great sickle of the Ohio to the crescent of its highlands the city spread across the basin. The river was alive and musical with steamboats, their bells ringing above the rumble of the levee; one big packet had five hundred silver dollars melted in its bell metal to give a lingering tone. Above the waterfront stood hotels and boardinghouses, huge public markets, the stockyards and packing plants of "Porkopolis." Horsecars clanked past the splendid Burnet House, "the grandest hotel in America," the faro games on Fourth Street, Fountain Square with its encircling trees and plashing waters, the huge new Music Hall seating eight thousand persons, and Pike's Opera House with its marble lobby and a stairway whose balustrades gleamed like gold. Through the city snaked the tawny Miami and Erie Canal and the commerce of sand boats, pork boats, ice boats from Lake Erie, lumber boats, whisky and beer boats, boats bringing hay and corn and carrying away famous Cincinnati hams and Cincinnati furniture—all drawn by mule teams with their trace chains jangling. Beyond the canal was "Over the Rhine," rich with the smells of German cooking and hearty with the strains of German bands. The big friendly Coliseum at Twelfth and Vine offered a German chorus between acrobatic acts and demonstrations of trick shooting, while the patrons washed down hasenpfeffer, sauerbraten, wienerschnitzel with mugs of malty beer.

Celebrated restaurants overlooked the city. The Highland House on Mount Adams accommodated eight thousand in its dining rooms, beer gardens, and pavilions. Here Theodore Thomas led orchestral concerts while people strolled the promenades above the city and the river. Lookout House, at the head of Main Street on Mount Auburn, was perched above the German settlement; it had its own German band and Swiss yodelers. On the brink of Clifton Heights stood Bellevue House, offering food, drink, dancing, and a sweeping view of

the city. The hilltop at Fairmount was crowned by the pleasure resort of *Schuetzenbuckel*—"Shooter's Hill"—with its rambling pavilion; on the days of *Schuetzenfest* a concert band played German
waltzes between the target matches.

Cincinnati was the Queen City of the West, full of music, gaiety,
Gemütlichkeit. It was just eighty miles from Greenville, but to a girl
from Darke County it was another world.

*   *   *

On a bright November day when the last yellow leaves were fluttering from the trees on Grand Street, Lyda Stein led her sister up the
steep streets of Fairmount. From the ridge Annie saw Cincinnati
spreading across the basin and the hills of Kentucky rising beyond the
river.

"Not much like North Star, is it?" Lyda kept pointing over the
city as though she could gather it all in one avid gesture. She hated
the memory of Darke County, the lonely back roads, the empty
marshes, and the dark line of the woods. "Oh, Annie, I'm glad you
came. Everything is different here."

Annie asked gently. "Don't you ever get homesick?"

Lyda shook her head. For bare feet and tattered clothing? For
digging potatoes and hoeing weeds? No, she never got homesick for
that. "And you won't either, Annie. You don't belong there. The way
you talk, the way you smile, even the way you walk—you don't belong
to the country. I remember even when you were a baby you looked
different. And you did things better. Like cutting out paper dolls—
you made them with more life and spirit. You know, Annie, I've had
feelings about you."

"But Lyda, I can't even read yet. Not even a child's book."

"That's why you're here! You'll learn all kinds of things. You'll be
different here."

"I don't think I could ever forget Swamp Creek and the pasture
slough."

"Pasture—you've had enough pasture." She pointed again. "See where the river curves away. We almost went to live in that part of the city, in Oakley or Hyde Park."

"Oakley—" Annie said. "That's a nice name."

"See that building, like a castle above the river. It's the Highland House. Joe wants to take you there."

"What for?"

"Music and dancing and the sight of all the boats on the river. And we'll go to the other places, Lookout House and Bellevue." She pointed again. "Right here on the hilltop is Schuetzenbuckel."

Annie looked at the painted balconies and cupola towers. "What did you call it?"

"Schuetzenbuckel. It's a German name for a shooting club."

Schuetzenbuckel, Annie repeated to herself as they went home to Grand Street. *Schuetzenbuckel*.

Joe Stein wanted to show the city's night life to his wide-eyed sister-in-law. "Vine Street," he said, as they stepped off the horsecar. "There's no gayer street in America."

He was a tall man with a naturally ruddy face that even the gaslights could not pale. His long stride kept Annie stepping quickly.

They passed the Burnet House with its lights and music. They watched people streaming into the gleaming lobby of Pike's Opera House. They wandered through the Emery Arcade and came out on the street where wienerwurst men, mustard men, oyster peddlers, hotcorn men were shrilling their whistles and blowing their horns. It was a street of wonders—the Atlantic Gardens, the Pacific Gardens, the London Concert Hall, the Melodeon, Kissel's Concert Hall, Wiswell's Art Gallery. They saw the horrors in a waxworks museum, a huge panorama of the Battle of Sedan, the wild animals in the basement of Robinson's Opera House.

Across the canal they were never out of sound of music. Schickling's, Schuler's, Wielert's, the Coliseum—they were all places of sawdust floors, singing waiters, bands playing German waltzes. When they were on the street again Annie heard the sharp sound of rifle fire.

"Where's the shooting?"

He pointed to a row of lighted windows over a beer garden. "It's the Germania Schuetzen Association. They're crazy about target shooting."

"Could we go there?"

"No, but we can go to Charlie Stuttelberg's. Come on."

The shooting gallery was idle, with guns on the counter and Stuttelberg sitting under a gas flare reading the *Cincinnati Abend Post*. At the end of the range gas jets fluttered over a row of metal ducks, another row of big-eared rabbits, and a bull's eye of concentric rings.

Joe picked up a rifle. "I used to be a good shot." He banged away six times, and two ducks fell over in the middle of the line. He handed a gun to Annie. "Try it."

She weighed the gun in her hands and glanced along the barrel. "Do they give prizes?"

Charlie Stuttelberg didn't look up from his paper. "No charge if you ring the bell five times."

"What bell?"

"In the bull's-eye," Joe said.

She swung the gun to her shoulder. The first shot drew a *bong!* from the bull's-eye. Charlie looked up from his paper. She pumped a new shell in. Then she fired fast. The target sounded like an alarm gong, and when she put the gun down the metal still rang with vibration.

Joe stared down at her, and Charlie Stuttelberg jumped up from his chair.

"Lyda told me you hunted quail in the country," Joe said.

She nodded. "Quail are harder to hit than a tin target."

Charlie Stuttelberg picked up another gun. "Try it again. No charge."

She swung the gun up and fired. The bell was silent, but six ducks fell over like a row of dominoes on the metal track.

Charlie Stuttelberg looked at the girl with two braids of hair down her shoulders and her feet tapping the rhythm of the German band across the street. "You don't look like a marksman, but I'll bet you can outshoot Frank Butler."

"Who's he?"

"He's the shooting star at the Coliseum. You been on the stage, Miss?"

"Oh, no."

"Where did you do your shooting?"

"At home, in the country. I shot birds for Mr. Frost's hotel."

"Jack Frost—at the Bevis House. That's where Frank Butler's stopping." When he took off his hat his head shone in the gaslight. He was a small man with a large and drooping mustache. He picked up another gun. "Try one more."

She brought the sights together on the bull's-eye—*bong, bong, bong* —and swung down to the row of rabbits. The two end ones fell over, and the last shot dropped the rabbit in the middle.

Charlie Stuttelberg clapped the derby on his bald head. "Come on over to the Bevis House."

"What for?"

"Tell Jack Frost his quail hunter is in town."

On the southwest corner of Court and Walnut, a short block from the canal, stood the four-story Bevis House with the office of the Bevis Coach Line in its cluttered and friendly lobby. Thirty years before it had been a busy packing plant; in its deep storerooms Cincinnati hams and sides of bacon were chilled with ice brought down from Lake Erie. When the packing firms moved to Mill Creek valley the solid building became a hotel, operated by Martin Bevis and W. H. Ridenour. In 1865 young Thomas Alva Edison lived there while working as an operator in the new Cincinnati telegraph exchange. In the middle seventies it came under the management of John B. Frost, who later changed its name to the Globe Hotel.

Jack Frost was an Englishman from the lake country of Cumberland. When he tired of his small farm near the foot of Skiddaw Mountain, he brought his family to America. They tried homesteading in Kansas, but because the lonely life there gave him a hunger for cities and people he came to Cincinnati and the Bevis House. His casual English manner attracted theatrical people, and soon his hotel was a meeting place of singers, actors, musicians, entertainers.

One of the Frost children was a slender dark-haired girl who went to school in Cincinnati as Sarah Frances Frost. She had a natural voice and a natural bearing. At twelve she sang with a juvenile opera company in *H.M.S. Pinafore* and *The Chimes of Normandy*; then she joined Miss Josephine Riley's traveling company, taking her mother's name, Fannie Brough. In 1887, while "Annie Oakley" was being cheered by thousands in Madison Square Garden, she appeared on the New York stage as "Julia Marlowe."

*   *   *

When Charlie Stuttelberg had identified Annie Moses, tall John Frost leaned across the desk. "So you're the hunter from Darke County. You're not as big as my girl Sarah, and she's gone to bed already." He turned to Stuttelberg. "You wouldn't believe it, Charlie —those birds are all shot through the head. We never have our guests spitting out bird shot. You wouldn't think—"

Charlie nodded vigorously. "I believe it. I believe she can outshoot Frank Butler."

Frost's eyes began to twinkle. "Frank thinks well of himself. You know, he shoots the center spot out of a five of spades. He shoots the flame off a candle."

"I've seen him shoot. I'll match this girl."

The hotel man tapped his fingers on the desk. "He's Irish, you know. Jaunty Irish. It might be interesting. You sure she'd have a chance?"

"I'll put fifty dollars on her."

"We might arrange a match at one of the clubs—the Cincinnati Schuetzen Verein or the Germania Schuetzen Association."

Joe Stein said: "Or at Fairmount. That's where we live."

Frost nodded. "Shooter's Hill."

"Schuetzenbuckel," Annie said. It was her first speech.

Jack Frost slapped the counter. "All right, Fairmount. We'll match this little girl against Frank Butler."

*   *   *

On the wooded St. Clair Heights above the Mill Creek valley the Cincinnati Baptists had built a seminary, but it never attracted more than a handful of students. After the Civil War the rambling frame building was decked with porches and flower-lined balconies and a flagpole was raised above the cupola tower. Rich German food was served in the big dining room, beer was brought to the outdoor tables, and from a balcony a band played between rounds of the schuetzenfest. Eventually the building burned, but flags were whipping in the November air when little Annie Moses arrived for a shooting match with the professional Frank Butler.

It was all strange and exciting to a girl from Darke County—the big lounge with antlers over the fireplace, the long dining room looking over the city, the view of a profile Sphinx on the edge of Pancake Hill. Before she had stopped wondering she was led to the target range. There stood a ruddy man, big, blue-eyed, smiling, with a shotgun cradled in his arm. He wore a belted shooting coat and a soft green hat with a jutting feather.

"Mr. Frank Butler—your challenger, Miss Annie Moses."

The marksman stared at her. "This girl—I thought you said—"

"I said there was a crack shot from upcountry. Here she is."

This time his smile was for her, a smile of interest and surprise, of warm and friendly pleasure. She had never seen a man so handsome. He lifted his feathered hat. "It's a pleasure, Miss Moses."

Annie bobbed her head. "Same here," she managed.

Together they went to the shooting station, and Annie was offered her choice of guns from a rack. She lifted a polished gun, balanced it, glanced along the barrel. "All right," she said.

Frank Butler won the toss and took his position.

"Pull!" he called.

The bird sailed out and the gun swung to his shoulder.

"Dead!" cried the referee.

As Annie took her station, she felt lost. A strange place, a strange crowd, a strange gun, a strange man smiling at her. She had never shot clay targets from a mechanical trap; she had never seen a shooting range like this. The gun began shaking in her hands. She brought it to her shoulder, then she lowered it to her waist, and still her hands trembled.

The gallery was dead silent as she waited. She tried to think of the target, but her mind was full of the silent men behind her and the money that hung on her shooting. She wanted to put the gun down, to go home to Darke County. If she were in the woods, watching a covey of quail burst up—then she remembered how they flew. She had told herself many times, and now she told herself again: *You don't sight them. You just swing with them, and when it feels right, pull.* Quail were swifter than clay targets. *When it feels right—*

She forgot all but the gun in her hands and the trap where the clay bird would rise. The wind whipped her skirt and tugged at the ribbon on her hair. She stood lightly balanced, her eyes waiting.

"Pull!"

When the bird arced up the gun rose with a single motion to her shoulder. Her cheek pressed the gunstock, her eyes caught the sailing target. Her finger pressed.

"Dead!" cried the referee.

They were two experts, the big smiling man and the grave small girl, both shooting with instinctive skill. *Pull . . . Dead, Pull . . . Dead, Pull . . . Dead,* the call went on unchanging, until the last shot of the twenty-five.

"Pull!" called Frank Butler. The target came up steeply and quartering to the right. It was an instant longer before the gun sounded. The target sailed on in the sunlight.

"Miss!" the referee cried.

Annie balanced herself, ready to swing from the waist, holding the gun lightly.

"Pull!"

Up came the barrel, her cheek snuggled to the wood. In an instant she corrected for the target's flight. While the gun was swinging her finger pressed.

All her life she remembered the view from Shooter's Hill, wide-spreading and distant, full of light and color, with the far hills hazy in the sun; and all her life she remembered the referee's high-pitched cry. A year later she was Frank Butler's wife. Two years later she was his partner on the stage. Six years later she was a shooting star and Frank Butler was her manager. Eleven years later she was followed by crowds through the streets of London. She never stopped wondering that it all began with the cry of *Dead!* and the smell of gun smoke on the autumn wind.

CHAPTER 3

Circus in the Rain

"BUTLER and Oakley" the gun case read. "Butler and Oakley" was lettered on the battered costume trunks. Month after month, season after season, Butler and Oakley were on the road. "Annie Oakley"— the name pleased her. It had a firm sure finished sound, like a gun barrel locking, like a cartridge sliding into a chamber. All her life she resented the family name, foolishly remembering the singsong taunt from her childhood, *Moses Poses! Moses Poses!* After Frenchy La Motte called her Annie Mozee she always said her name that way; years later she changed *Moses* to *Mozee* in the family Bible, and she tried to persuade her brother John to change his name legally. Only once, on her marriage certificate, did she sign as Annie Moses. She became Annie Oakley to herself as well as to the audiences in halls and theaters.

For five years they traveled the Midwestern circuit—Ohio, Michigan, Indiana, Wisconsin, Illinois—living in drab hotels and actors' boardinghouses, practicing new shooting acts in the theater alley, changing costumes in drafty dressing rooms, coming on stage after the jugglers and before the dog and pony show. For Annie Oakley they were years of schooling. "Jimmy" read to her—newspapers, books, magazines—while she sewed her costumes. When she put the sewing down he read slowly, moving a finger along the printed line—*Work on the Museum of Art in Central Park is going on rapidly during the present winter. . . . No snowstorm so severe as the recent one in March has been known in the West since the construction of the Union Pacific Railroad. Many lives were lost and sheep and cattle in great numbers perished.* Then he waited for her to read it alone.

That was one kind of schooling, and there was another. On the make-believe stage of a hotel room she went through her act, over and over—making her entry, timing her action, jumping the table and seizing a new gun while her eyes followed a falling target, doing her comical little dance step before she ran to the wings. Again he was a schoolmaster. *Practice, practice, practice.* He was never satisfied. New costumes, new novelties, new action, with Annie always at the footlights when the act was ended. "Butler and Oakley" the showbill said, but it was Annie Oakley who drew the curtain calls. Marksmen were commonplace; hundreds of professional shots were on the circuit. But a girl just under five feet and a hundred pounds, in a pleated skirt and a crisp embroidered jacket, shooting coins out of a man's hand and cards in the air, turning flips and cartwheels beside her gun table, running to the footlights with her friendly girlish smile—that was magic even to people who had never lifted a gun.

Back and forth across the Midwest states they rode in jerky trains. Outside passed the shocked autumn cornfields, the gray winter pastures, the plowfields where black furrows shone in April sunlight. Especially in spring she grew homesick. Years later in her sentimental autobiography she recalled that yearning for "the fairy places, the green moss, the big toadstools, wild flowers, baby rabbits, squirrel and quail." Frank, too, had memories. Left in Ireland when his parents came to America, he had worked his passage to New York in 1863. He drove a milk wagon, cleaned stalls in a livery stable, sold newspapers, and tried to learn the glass-blowing trade. For two years he worked on a fishing boat out of New York harbor. He trained a pair of dogs and got a few stage engagements in Brooklyn, New York, and Philadelphia. After strenuous practice he learned trick shooting, and with another marksman, Billy Graham, he played all the way from the Bowery Theater to the Mississippi. But in Cincinnati he acquired a new partner. "Little Annie," he called her, "Little Girl." He wrote verses and sketches for her to put away in the dented costume trunk, and saved her clippings from the newspapers. He was ten years older, and all his life he called her his little girl. Sometimes he threw back his head in boyish laughter, sometimes he was lost in thought and memory. She had never had a father; now she had father, brother, husband, in one changing man.

It was a satisfying life. They were together, using their skill, saving money (they would be frugal all their lives), everywhere applauded. It might have gone on and on. But on a wind-stirred April day in 1884 a stranger came to their dressing room. Could Annie Oakley ride a horse? Could she shoot from horseback? Could she do in a circus ring the tricks she did on the stage? Would she sign a contract for forty weeks with Sells Brothers Circus, the Biggest of all Big Shows?

Frank looked at her—already she was the one who made decisions. It was spring, with the circus season just beginning and the vaude-ville season near its end. Through the open stage door came a blare of band music and the clatter of hoofs in a street parade. When Lewis Sells spread a contract on the dressing table, Annie nodded.

The Sells brothers were Ohio men from the village of Dublin on the Scioto River; it had once been chosen for the site of Ohio's capital. But the capital went to Columbus and Dublin remained a crossroads, and the restless Sells boys became roving circus men. The chief of the four brothers—Lewis, Ephraim, Allen, and Peter—was Lewis Sells, a big bald man with grizzled mustache and bearded chin. When he was thirty, in the winter of 1871, he organized a show which held its first performance in Columbus in the spring of 1872. At that time two hundred circuses roamed the roads of the Midwest and there was no great need of another. It was easy to pun on the name of the new show, and rival outfits got Ohio villagers to repeating: "Sells is a Sell. . . . Sold on Sells." The first season was a dismal failure. But stubborn Lewis Sells borrowed money from his father, insisting that all the show needed was a new name and an elephant. In 1873 they acquired a "ponderous pachyderm" and traveled under a spangled name, "Paul Silverberg's Great Circus." Business picked up, and in the third season the brothers went back to their own name. In the spring of 1878 they left their creaking wagons in the winter lot on the Olentangy River just north of Columbus and loaded the show on railroad cars.

By 1884 when Annie Oakley and Frank Butler joined the organization it was billed as "The Biggest of all Big Shows, requiring three immense railroad trains. Its parade a plume-topped tidal wave of splendor. Its menagerie filled with the finest collections of Carniverous and Herbivorous animals ever seen anywhere. Under its big top one hundred superior and startling acts at every performance."

Some of the acts were grandiose, some were skilled and daring, some were pure sham. Mr. Orrin Hollins, world-vanquishing Spanish equestrian; Prince Fokio, the Japanese juggling marvel; the Boneless Man of Leipsic, Herr Delhauer; fifty double somersault leapers, including High Tom Ward who leaps over fourteen elephants; the Flying Fairy, Viola Rivers; educated giraffes and zebras and the world's only performing hippopotamus; a telescope chariot carrying aloft in mid-air a living elephant and on its back Lola, the Princess of India. To this roster was added the peerless Annie Oakley, world's champion markswoman, breaking targets from the back of a galloping horse.

Now it was not Butler and Oakley; it was Annie Oakley and her husband. Frank Butler did not complain. He was ready to be her manager, to load her guns, to set up the shooting table and throw the targets, to wait outside the ring while the audience called her back. The routine grew familiar—the band playing, the long procession, crowds under the big canvas, the performance in the sawdust ring. Through the summer months they crossed and recrossed the midland states, and when autumn came Lewis Sells had a better idea than heading for the winter lot at Sellsville on the edge of Columbus. All over the country newspapers were heralding the World's Fair and Cotton Centennial Exposition to open in December at New Orleans. Railroads advertised excursions to the Crescent City, steamboats offered special rates for the winter season. Crowds would pour into New Orleans from December until March. That was the place for the Biggest of all Big Shows. When the Ohio cornfields withered and the woods were bare and geese passed over in their honking wedges, Lewis Sells took his outfit south.

*   *   *

During the winter of 1884-1885, people in Darke County read in the Greenville weekly *Advocate* about the World's Industrial and Cotton Exposition in New Orleans—"The Biggest Exhibit, the Biggest Building, the Biggest Industrial Event in the World's History." On December 16th, in his office in Washington, President Arthur pressed a button and at Audubon Park on the Mississippi the huge gates swung open. Crowds streamed through the groves of live-oak and orange trees, past acres of blooming gardens, along landscaped lakes and lagoons. Above the splashing of fountains came the boom of cannon from the parade ground and the pealing of bells from Exposition Hall. By telegraph wire and cable the word was flashed around the world.

In the farmhouse at North Star they read about these wonders. "Thee can hardly realize," Susan Moses said, "that Annie is there."

Lafcadio Hearn was there, writing a series of impressions for *Harper's Weekly*. The myopic little man heard Colonel Breaux read President Arthur's message in the vast hall, and what he could not see he could feel and imagine—"beneath those acres of roofing, in the bewildering vistas of pillars, before that ocean of faces." Exposition Hall, with thirty-three acres under a single roof, had been designed by the Swedish architect Torgerson and built by three thousand laborers. Its Renaissance façades rose up to bannered towers, and around its great Machinery and Music halls hung miles of balconies. Lafcadio Hearn loved color. He squinted up at the "snow-white slopes of its sanded roofs gleaming between the blue of the sky and the gray-green tint of the walls." Scattered about the lagoons were a dozen other domed and towered buildings—art galleries, pavilions, restaurants, amusement halls. At sundown forty miles of electric wire burst into light; electric illumination was as great a wonder as any exhibit in the great hall. When Hearn went home to the dim streets of the French Quarter, he was still marveling. "Never did the might of machinery seem to me so awful as when I first watched that enormous incandescence."

The Centennial Exposition celebrated the hundredth anniversary of the export of Louisiana cotton, but its exhibits included the silk of Japan, the porcelain of China, the silver and leather of Mexico, the big trees of California, the bison of Dakota, the yellow corn of Nebraska—shaped into a lofty statue of Liberty. It was expected to draw a million visitors to New Orleans. New wharves had been built on the river and a railroad short line had been laid to the exposition grounds. Tall-stacked steamboats smoked above the levee where silk-hatted Negroes guided gleaming carriages between buckboards, carts, and wagons. Every day brought new representatives from foreign governments and newspaper men from the cities of the North. Just after Christmas, Richard Watson Gilder, editor of the Century, arrived to write up the spectacle for his magazine.

Two other shows had set up in New Orleans, hoping to trade on the Exposition crowds. Sells Brothers' big tent occupied a field beyond Audubon Park and near the river. Buffalo Bill's Rocky Mountain and Prairie Exhibition, grandfather of the rodeos, used the old Metairie Race Track on the city's northwestern fringe.

To draw visitors to New Orleans the railroads offered "the cheapest rates of travel ever known in the annals of transportation." But January brought gray skies and an endless sullen rain. Week after week the rain kept falling. Banners dripped from the Exposition towers, and ponds collected in the gardens. The excursion trains never ran, the crowds did not come. Annie Oakley was the only visitor from Darke County to wander through the echoing exhibition hall. After forty-four days of sodden weather the New Orleans bankers and cotton merchants dug into their pockets to pay for their lavish fair.

In the circus the performers went unpaid. Salaries were canceled till the stands should fill again. The wrinkled little paymaster went from one gloomy tent to another telling about hardships over at the Metairie Race Track where Buffalo Bill's Indians and cowboys were camped in the rain. —There, he declared, shaking the water off his soggy hat, was some real calamity. On the way to New Orleans they had a steamboat wreck and Buffalo Bill lost half his show in the river. Animals, wagons, equipment. They had nothing left but a battered stagecoach and some bucking horses. Buffalo Bill was trying to get new animals on credit. Everybody knew they had lost $60,000 last season.

The paymaster looked out at the river fog and turned back to

Annie Oakley and Frank Butler. —That Wild West outfit had to play in the weather, not even a canvas over their heads. It never was much of a show and now it was going under. Major North, Buffalo Bill's ranching partner, was in a hospital somewhere and Captain Bogardus was pulling out.

He put on his hat, turned up his collar, and sloshed off in the rain.

When he was gone Frank Butler picked up a damp folder from the floor. He began to read:

Buffalo Bill's Rocky Mountain and Prairie Exhibition

The grassy sward our carpet,
heaven's azure canopy our canvas.

A Year's Visit West in Three Hours

A company of recognized historical scouts, led by America's most renowned Frontiersman, monarch among celebrities of the plains, late Chief of Scouts, U.S. Army

Hon. W. F. Cody
Buffalo Bill

Major Frank North, Commander U.S. Indian Scouts, Captain David C. Payne, "The Oklahoma Raider," Captain A. H. Bogardus, magic manipulator of the shotgun, for 13 years Recognized Champion of the World, and his four marksmen sons

Eugene Bogardus
Edward Bogardus
Henry Bogardus
Peter Bogardus

Annie sat up on her cot. Frank said, "You can outshoot him and all his sons together."

She tossed her embroidery hoop onto the table. "Let's go over and see their outfit."

The Race Track oval was a field of mud. At one end of the grandstand around a huddle of tepees Indians squatted over smoking fires. A line of horses stood dripping in a muddy corral. A cowboy splashed past in a mud-stained slicker and disappeared into a long tent where a harmonica wheezed and a flat voice was singing "—ten-dollar horse and a forty-dollar saddle." In the opening of the next tent stood a big man in a fringed jacket. From his broad-brimmed hat hair fell to his shoulders. He was smoking a cigar.

Frank Butler said, "You're Mr. Cody."

"No," he boomed. "Bill Cody hasn't been on the lot for a week. I'm Major Burke, Arizona John, press agent and manager. Come in out of the wet." He held back the soggy canvas.

Inside it was comfortable—a wooden floor, table, lamp, couch, brass spittoon. He pulled up canvas chairs to a Sibley stove with red sparks sifting down to the ash pan.

"You wanted to see Bill Cody?" he asked, and went on talking. "He might be downtown at the St. Louis Hotel or at the Monteleone bar, or he might be somewhere else a long way from here. He got disgusted with the weather. Said Fate is against him and he's an Ingersoll man from now on. Can't blame him; we have had bad luck." He put a fresh match to his cigar and began recounting their misfortunes—how Pony Bob Haslam, an old friend of Cody's from the Pony Express days, now advance agent for the show, had hired a river boat at Cincinnati to transport the outfit to New Orleans. It was a cheerful voyage, heading into warm weather and thinking about the big Exposition crowds. They played a few towns on the way down. Just below Vicksburg, in the middle of the river and the middle of the night, they had a collision. The cowboys swam horses ashore and a barge picked people out of the water, but they lost their steers and buffalo and all their equipment. Some of the Indians headed back to Dakota. Still, the show opened in New Orleans two weeks after the wreck. They had twenty-five Indians in the saddle, seven Mexicans, eight cowboys. Some new Indians and buffalo were coming from Nebraska; they got some steers right out of the New Orleans stockyards.

Arizona John pushed back his big hat. —Then came a new blow. Major Frank North was Cody's ranching partner on the Dismal River in Nebraska; they had scouted the Sioux country together years ago. In the show all last season he had paced the Pawnees in their war dance and led their attack on the Deadwood stage. At Hartford, Connecticut, his saddle girth broke and he fell under the horses. They had to leave him in a Hartford hospital. By Christmas he was well enough to go west to recruit new Indians for the New Orleans engagement; a week later he was dead. That damped Cody more than the rain.

Major Burke tossed his cigar into the mud.—This rain couldn't last forever and the show would get rolling again. It was too good a show to go under. Nothing like it anywhere.

Annie said, "It's the kind of show I'd like to go with."

"Doing what?"

"Shooting."

The burly man stared down at her. "You mean—target shooting?"

Frank Butler said, "My wife is the best marksman in America— target shooting, trap shooting, trick shooting. I'd like to match her against Captain Bogardus."

"Bogardus—" Arizona John shook his big head. "He's gone too. Couldn't stand the weather, said he wanted to put his boys in school. Young Johnnie Baker is practicing to take their place. He's fourteen, been with the show since it started in Nebraska two years ago. He ought to be out there practicing now. Let's see how he's doing."

They didn't find Johnnie Baker, but at the target range Annie Oakley gave a demonsration that kept Arizona John exclaiming: "Just a girl! A graceful little girl! And she shoots like magic! A heroine of the plains!" Cowboys and Indians stood around grinning, and Annie grinned back. She was ready to join them now.

Major Burke hesitated. —Cody was off somewhere, and Salsbury, his partner, was raising money in the West. When they were both on hand, with new Indians, horses, and buffalo, things ought to pick up. It couldn't rain forever. The schedule would take the show to Birmingham and other Alabama towns before the winter was over. The summer tour would begin in Louisville the last week of April. If Annie Oakley still wanted to join up then, she'd know where to find them. But why did she want to leave Sells Brothers?

Frank Butler explained that in a circus shooting was like walking a tightrope or juggling ten pins, but this looked like a show where marksmanship meant something.

This, Arizona John declared, was an exhibition of the Great West, where shooting fast and shooting straight were the first and second commandments. He looked down at Annie. "I could write a lot of stories about you. Try us at Louisville in April. We'll have a new name then. Going to call it Buffalo Bill's Wild West. Maybe that'll change our luck."

CHAPTER 4

Myth on Wheels

A visit West in three hours to see scenes that have cost thousands their lives to view.

—*Buffalo Bill's Wild West*

SPRING comes early to the Ohio valley. By mid-April lilacs are blooming in the farmyards, dogwood bursts white in the woods, and redbud makes a ruby haze along the hills. After the crest of water has passed, the Ohio becomes again the wide slow river of the West. The April sun is warm almost as summer; in the bluegrass pastures horses seek the thin shade of the new-leafed sycamores.

At Louisville in April, 1885, workmen were putting a new coat of paint on the green and white clubhouse at Churchill Downs—already, since its building ten years before, a famous race track. Grass was green in the big oval, and stable hands took thoroughbreds around the track, getting ready for the Derby in the first week of May. But another event was coming. On Thursday morning, April 23rd, people opened the *Courier-Journal* to a picture of mounted horsemen, Indian wigwams, and a file of covered wagons diminishing over a distant plain. Louisville was used to grooms and jockeys, but these were horsemen of a different color—an Indian in feathered headdress, a plainsman with a broad-brimmed hat and hair falling to his shoulders.

Louisville Base Ball Park, three afternoons only, April 24, 25 &
26, reconstructed, enlarged, improved, the only original

BUFFALO BILL'S
WILD WEST

America's National Entertainment
including two hundred Indians, Scouts, Cow Boys, Mexicans,
Herds of Buffalo, Elk, Steers, Ponies, etc. One hundred and
twenty days at the New Orleans Exposition. Street Parade Friday
morning.

On the morning of April 24th a horse made a hollow sound on the
cobblestones of Walnut Street. Up on the box a colored driver
hummed in the morning sun, a deep lazy note like the low string on
a guitar, and in the cab Frank Butler let down the glass. From the
river came a long-drawn whistle. All of spring was in that voice, a
bass undertone with a treble vibrating in it, a contentment and a
restlessness. Down the river Louisville sent tobacco, hemp, whisky,
nails, gunpowder; up the river came sugar, rice, and coffee. Again
the deep voice sounded.

Annie breathed the spring and peered out the cab window. Past
them moved the neat brick houses with their stone trim scrubbed
to a frosty white and the red brick sidewalks swept and washed. In a
side street pigs grunted along the drainage trench and lay blissful
in the sun. Above the steady *clop-clop, clop-clop*, the driver answered
hm-umm, hm-umm. For a moment the river glinted at the end of
a street, with the green hills of Indiana beyond. Then a barn closed
the view, and a big colored poster showed a big man in a big hat,
mounted on a white horse; beyond him a mass of buffalo darkened
a rolling plain. BUFFALO BILL'S WILD WEST. *America's Greatest
Entertainment.*

"Won't we ever get there?" she asked. "We must be on the wrong
street, Jimmy."

He knocked on the ceiling. "How much farther to the ball park?"

The humming stopped. "A short piece, Cap'n. A short piece more."

They were silent amid the rattle of hoofs and rumble of wheels.
Behind them lay years of restless trouping, the variety shows and

exhibition halls, the county-seat opera houses and makeshift theaters, and the final dismal winter in dripping circus tents. Ahead loomed uncertainty—a new show, new people, a strange new outfit from a western country they had never seen.

When Annie sat back her feet did not quite touch the floor. She had a straight nose, a firm wide mouth, direct gray eyes set far apart. There was something else, like the tension of a fine steel spring beneath her girlish quiet, that made her different from her husband. He sat relaxed, his long legs stretched across the gun trunk on the floor, a big, ruddy, boyish-looking man. All his strength was outside, but she had something hidden. Her hands were small and strong, a square palm with lean firm fingers. Now they kept pleating the fold in her skirt.

The *clop-clop* softened and the wheels left the cobblestones. "Whoa!" the driver called.

Frank jumped out and lifted her down beside him. The driver helped him with the trunks. "Thank you, thank you, Cap'n." The cab rolled away.

Across the green field beyond the rows of bleachers stood a cluster of wigwams, an empty picket-pole corral, a long mess tent with open sides and wood smoke sifting out of a chimney in the canvas roof. A man in a white apron looked up from a long table.

"Where's everybody?" Frank called.

"In the parade. You're three hours early for the show."

Annie drew a breath. "That's good, Jimmy. I need to practice. I haven't seen a target for ten days."

He opened the gun trunk, set up the little table with its green velvet cloth and laid the guns across it. He took his place at the portable trap.

She lifted a gun from the table. "Pull." The gun fired and the target sailed on unbroken. He pulled the lever again, and again the target got away.

He shook his head. "This light. You're not used to it. Try again with the sun behind you."

She shot with the sun over her shoulder, and again she missed. From the cook tent came a burst of laughter.

Frank took the gun out of her hands. "You're tired. All this travel, and the noisy hotel last night. Tomorrow we'll try again, in a proper costume. We shouldn't have come in street clothes."

"Clothes don't matter," she said in a low voice. "Clothes don't break a target." She walked back to the gun table, thinking of all her years of shooting, in the woods of Darke County, on theater stages, in the circus ring—and of Frank Butler teaching, timing, encouraging, making her try again and again. *Practice, practice, practice. And believe in yourself. Practice and believe.*

"We'll try tomorrow," he repeated.

She took a gun from the table. "Throw another, Jimmy."

Up came the target and her gun raised with it. She followed its flight for an instant and her finger pressed. The target shattered in its climb.

"Throw a pair."

Twice the gun sounded and both disks pulverized in air. She laid her gun on the table and walked off twenty paces.

"Throw the glass balls."

As the balls went up she ran across the grass. Light as the glass globes she leaped over the table and grasped the gun. Before the stock was against her shoulder she began firing. The four balls vanished.

"Mirror," Frank said.

He took his place, holding up a clay disk. Twenty steps away, with her back to him and a rifle over her shoulder, she sighted in a hand mirror. When she fired the target was dust in his hand.

"Remarkable shooting! Remarkable!"

Across the grass came a slender, quick-moving man in a derby hat, a cutaway coat, and striped trousers. He took off his hat. "I am Nate Salsbury—Mr. Cody's partner. Major Burke told me about you." He turned to the girl with the gun faintly smoking in her hands. "I have never seen a better display of marksmanship. Can you ride a horse? Can you shoot from horseback? Can you be in costume for today's performance? I'll want some photographs for posters. Now I'll find you a dressing tent."

An hour later the parade came into the grounds—whooping Indians in feathered bonnets, Mexicans in vivid serapes and huge sombreros, weathered cowboys, long-horned steers, shaggy buffalo, a file of pack mules with their ears flopping, light-stepping horses ahead of the battered stagecoach with a bearded driver and two Indian children on the swaying seat. It was not like a circus parade, with peeling mirrors and molting plumes and dull dead faces of the performers. This procession was alive. The cowboys fogged their ponies across the field and leaped to the ground. With grunts and cries the Indians herded horses into the corral. When saddles were pulled off them the pack mules brayed, kicked at each other, and rolled on the grass. The steers began bawling, and an old bull buffalo lowered his massive head and pawed the ground. A bugler in cowboy clothes tilted up his horn and sent an answer to the call of a steamboat across the fields. Someone cried, "When do we eat?"

Nate Salsbury led the newcomers to the cook tent, explaining that Cody had stopped off downtown at the Galt House with some race-track people. At the long table Major Burke appeared. He pushed his big hat back on his long hair and boomed down at Annie: "You know when you come on? First thing after the grand entry."

Nate Salsbury propped a program against a pitcher of milk. He explained with obvious satisfaction that the Wild West was not a circus. No gilt and spangles, no sideshows, no games of chance, no freaks and monstrosities, but an honest and dramatic picture of American life beyond the Missouri. As he talked he kept jabbing at the program: *A company of recognized historical characters . . . including Captain David C. Payne, the Oklahoma Raider; Buck Taylor, King of the Cowboys; Con Groner, Sheriff of the Platte, the nemesis of the lawless; and Mexican vaqueros, Wichita Indians, Pony Express riders, and Captain A. H. Bogardus, magic manipulator of the shotgun—* He took a pencil from his striped vest pocket, drew a line through the last name, and wrote in "Annie Oakley." Her act would come early, he said, following the grand circuit of the arena, before the ride of the Pony Express and the attack on the wagon train.

The Wild West was more than a business with Nate Salsbury. Forgetting his pie and coffee, he talked about his first meeting with

Cody. Two years ago, when he was playing in Chicago with his musical company "Salsbury's Troubadours," he went out to Humboldt Park to see Cody's exhibition, then on its first tour. He had expected some horse racing, but what he saw took him straight to Cody's tent. Before he left he had bought a half-interest in the show. Since then the Wild West had been improved and expanded, but there were greater things ahead. They had only scratched the surface of the life, lore, and history of the West.

He called the performers over—handsome Frank Richmond, master of ceremonies, lanky Buck Taylor, hulking Con Groner, the half-breed Bill Bullock, and the bearded old squaw man John Nelson, who preferred his Sioux name, Cha-sha-sha-na-po-ge-o—"Red Willow Fill the Pipe." One after another they shook Frank Butler's hand and took off their big hats to Annie. "Glad to see you, Miss. Glad you're with us."

They shuffled out, rolling cigarettes in brown paper, and she looked up at a handsome smiling man in a fringed jacket with a silk neckerchief held by a diamond pin. He had large dark, liquid eyes, a flowing mustache and a pointed beard. While Nate Salsbury introduced Annie Oakley and her husband, Buffalo Bill swept off his broad hat and his hair fell round his shoulders. His strong voice filled the tent. "They've told me about you, Missie. We're glad to have you here."

Missie—now she was named. She would be Missie to the cowboys and the Indians, to the mule drivers and the Mexicans. She would be Missie in New York and London, in Quebec and Montreal, in Paris and Rome. She would be Missie for seventeen years.

An hour later, in a wide-brimmed hat and fringed skirt and jacket, she mounted a calico pony in the shadow of the grandstand. A fanfare of drum and bugle. From his red-covered box in the center of the ring Frank Richmond's voice filled the grounds: "Ladies and Gentlemen: The Honorable William F. Cody and Nathan Salsbury present the feature attraction, unique and unparalleled, the foremost woman marksman in the world, in an exhibition of skill with the rifle, shotgun, and pistol—the little girl of the Western plains— Annie Oakley!"

She looked like a girl but she hit the arena like a veteran. Ahead of her a galloping cowboy threw targets in the air. On the loping pony Annie raised her rifle—the targets shattered as he threw them. To a scatter of applause she leapt off and ran to her gun stand in the ring. Frank Butler was there, juggling two glass balls. She raised a gun. With two reports the balls vanished. Up went three balls. While they floated downward she jumped over the stand, grasped a fresh gun, swung it to her shoulder. The balls never touched ground. She vaulted the table and turned her back on the target. Her left hand held a gleaming bowie knife; over her shoulder she aimed a rifle at a silver disk Frank Butler held above his head. Sighting in the knife blade, she fired. The target spun from his hand.

While the crowd roared she caught her pony, swung into the saddle, and raced out of the ring. At the end of the arena Buffalo Bill sat in an open buggy behind a matched team of mustangs. He waved his hat as she passed him. "Sharp shooting, Missie!"

That was the first appearance, and all the others were like it, but her act never grew mechanical or stale. When the drum rattled and the bugles shrilled, when the Indians fell silent and the cowboys leaned in their saddles and the announcer called her name, she rode into the ring as though she had just arrived from Fort Laramie or Deadwood City. She had never been west of the Mississippi, but by some miracle she was the Western girl. In the arena she was surrounded by a limitless new country, a land of legend and fable. The Wild West was a show, doubtfully successful, $60,000 in debt as it began its third season; it was also the windswept prairie and the flowing plains, the long cattle trail and the buffalo wallows, the Overland Stage and the cavalry station, the Indians creeping up on the wagon train at the fording place. Wherever the show made camp it carried strong illusions. A relay of riders and horses on a race track would be next to nothing, but the enacting of the Pony Express tapped the folk memory, the American feeling. The Wild West changed a ten-acre show lot into the huge harsh country beyond the Missouri. Cody and Salsbury had a myth on wheels. With fifty laconic Indians and cowboys and two cattle cars of stock they carried the epic of the frontier.

It had begun by accident. For the Fourth of July in 1882 Cody staged at North Platte an "Old Glory Blowout," the first of all rodeos, and on that day he got the idea of a traveling Western show. The next spring he borrowed trained horses from Dr. Carver of North Platte and buffalo from Merrill Keith who had a small herd grazing on his cattle range; he hired some Indians from the Pine Ridge Agency and a troop of young cowboys from neighboring ranches. In April he assembled the outfit beside the Union Pacific tracks at North Platte and ran through some riding and roping contests. A month later the "Rocky Mountain and Prairie Exhibition" gave its first performance at the fair grounds in Omaha. They finished the season at Coney Island.

The performers were figures of Western life and folklore, and of the fertile invention of press agent John M. Burke. Buck Taylor, lean, tall, hard-riding King of the Cowboys, was a native of Massachusetts who had worked for Major Frank North and Buffalo Bill on their Dismal River ranch, but according to the program notes turned out by "Arizona John"—himself from Washington, D.C.—Buck Taylor was born in Texas, left an orphan at eight with a ranchman uncle, lived in Taos with leathery old Kit Carson, fought with Crockett at the Alamo, and drove Texas cattle to the plains of Nebraska where he made the acquaintance of Buffalo Bill. Bowlegged, soft-spoken Con Groner, "Cowboy Sheriff of the Platte," had been sheriff of Lincoln County, Nebraska. On a galloping horse he had chased Jesse James over the state boundary. According to Major Burke this nemesis of lawbreakers had caught fifty murderers and countless horse thieves, cattle rustlers, road agents, and outlaws, including the notorious Doc Middleton and his desperate band. (A year later Doc Middleton would travel with the Wild West.) Once the cowboy sheriff had followed horse thieves 1,900 miles through Nebraska, Wyoming, Montana, and Idaho. Captain David C. Payne, "Old Ox-heart," the Cimarron Scout, the Oklahoma Raider, had been a pistol-pointing squatter in Indian territory. Utah Frank, Bronco Pete, Montana Joe, and Blue Hall were veterans of the range who rode wild horses and roped wild cattle. Bridle Bill at each performance took his life in his hands and climbed aboard the murderous mule Suicide. The squaw man John Nelson, who handled the ribbons from the high seat of the Deadwood Stage, had once been a guide for Mormon wagon trains. Swarthy Bill Bullock came from the upper Missouri—the program said he "combined the best blood of the Sioux with the blue blood of the East." Mustang Jack, whom the Indians called Petsze-ca-we-cha-cha, could seize a horse's mane at full gallop and leap astride. Jim Lawson, for years a side-kick of Buck Taylor on the Dismal range, was "a rare combination of plains lore, cow sense, horsemanship, and general Western nerve and knowledge." Bill Halstead of the Rio Grande could throw a thousand-pound steer by the horns or tail, but he was "amiable as a child." Jim Hathaway, who reenacted the Pony Express, was "an aristocratic youth who preferred the danger of the plains to the wealth and society of his own people." The bearded "White Beaver" who led the emigrant wagons was "a reckless adventurer on the boundless prairies, yet in elegant society an aristocrat and a cultured mind." They were all plain laconic Western men, but Major Burke's program made a badlands saga of them. Soon Annie Oakley would be more legendary than the rest.

The best efforts of Arizona John were lavished on his idol, Cody. He had raised so much lore around the name of Buffalo Bill that Cody hardly knew the sober facts of his own life. According to the press agent's fantasy Cody as a boy had saved a wagon train from ambush in the sand hills of Kansas. As a young Pony Express rider he had once covered three hundred miles in two nights and a day, using twenty-one ponies. As a buffalo hunter he had strewn the plains with shaggy carcasses, as an Indian fighter he had taken more scalps than the hairs of his own head. His body bore 193 scars of bullet and arrow. Among all the tribes from the Wichita Hills to the Canadian border he was known as *Pahaska*, the Long-haired One.

Burke himself was a subject for publicity. A big beefy man with fleshy features, a curling mustache, and flowing hair, he had once been a drama critic for a Washington newspaper. In 1869 he went to Dakota on a hunting trip that swung his future in a new direction. There he met Cody "—at sunset out on the Missouri and the light from the river shining straight up into his face. He was on horseback, and he was the handsomest, straightest, finest man I have ever seen in my life." The scout's lithe and powerful physique, his skill and nonchalance, his way with horses and his knowledge of the plains won Burke's unending admiration. Soon the burly drama critic was wearing a Western hat, letting his hair grow long, calling himself Arizona John, and claiming to be a native of Indian territory and a hero of the Sun Dance. On that hunting trip he introduced Ned Buntline, dime novelist, to his new hero. Buntline persuaded Cody, then twenty-seven years old, to come east to appear in a melodrama, *Scouts of the Plains,* and Cody's public life began. John Burke traveled with them as advertising manager. One night during the shabby first season in 1873 Burke said, "I have met a god and goddess in my life." The goddess was Mlle. Morlacchi, a dark-eyed dancer billed as "Pale Dove." The god was Cody. The goddess was soon forgotten, but he had been with Cody ever since.

Another of Cody's idolizers was round-faced Johnnie Baker, just turned fifteen, billed as the Cowboy Kid. His father had settled in 1862 at O'Fallon's Bluffs on the Platte. Three times the Indians drove them off and fired the house; finally Lew Baker moved in to the settlement of North Platte. He had been a wagon driver on the plains trails, and the old-timers stopped there to see him. When Johnnie was nine a big, long-striding man with hair to his shoulders came in to town, and Johnnie followed him like a dog. Cody saw the worship in the boy's eyes. He took the youngster on a sixty-five-mile buggy trip to the Dismal River. While they jolted across the prairie the big man pointed: "There's where the Pawnees use' to have their camp. . . . That white patch out there, like a snowbank, is buffalo bones left by the railroad hunters. . . . There's a draw over beyond the ridge where a party of Sioux ambushed a line of wagons." Then his voice dropped. "But it's all changing, boy. I first saw the site of North Platte when I was with a bull train on the way to Utah. There was a fording place right there, and beyond it the trail swung north to the Bluewater, then west again." He stared off. "Now the trail is grassed over and coyotes bark at the railroad trains."

When Johnnie Baker was ten Cody came back from a winter theatrical tour and built a place outside North Platte—a rambling clapboard house surmounted by an eight-windowed tower and an imposing barn with three spaced cupolas; SCOUT'S REST RANCH was spelled out on the long roof and could be read a mile off. While the first Wild West outfit assembled at North Platte, twelve-year-old Johnnie Baker was underfoot; when they opened at Omaha he was still there, following Cody like a shadow. Then the great man put him in the show. He wore his hair long, continued to idolize Buffalo Bill, and had a passion for guns. Cody was teaching him to shoot.

When Annie Oakley joined the show Johnnie watched her like a coyote and kept a coyote's distance. But one May morning in an Indiana town he turned from shooting at a paper target on a picket stake and found her watching him. While she exclaimed over his silver-mounted rifle, he stared at the ground. When she asked if he had ever shot buffalo, his silence melted. —Yes, he had shot a buffalo, a big bull that broke his leg while they were playing last summer at Prospect Park, New York. But that was not like shooting on a hunt. Buffalo Bill had promised to take him hunting in Nebraska in the fall. Buffalo Bill had been teaching him to shoot, but now he was too busy.

Annie suggested practicing together. They might work up some tricks.

"The knife trick—will you teach me to aim in a knife blade? I'll carry your guns. I'll bring your ammunition from the wagon. Buffalo Bill told me to watch how you swing with a target." Now Johnnie Baker had a god and a goddess in his life, and Annie Oakley had a lasting friend.

The new life fell into a steady pattern. After her performance old Pop Whittaker filled the folding tub in her tent with steaming water. She bathed and rubbed herself with witch hazel; then she lay on her cot, relaxed and still, while Frank read from the local newspaper. An early supper in the big friendly cook tent, and soon the loaded wagons were creaking toward the railroad. She and Frank had a stateroom, not big enough to swing a gun in but snug, clean, and homelike, with sandwiches on the table and a spirit lamp for making tea. By midnight they were under way and the little room held the rhythmic click of rails. At daybreak, unloading in a strange town, the ride to the race track or the fair grounds, the clamor of the roustabouts and canvasmen, the smell of coffee and bacon. An hour of practice behind the grandstand, the street parade, the dinner call at eleven-thirty. By the end of the performance the crews were loading again. *Another day, another dollar,* and a new town tomorrow.

*   *   *

On the 17th of May they unloaded in South Chicago and made camp at the Chicago Driving Park. A decade later the Union Stock Yards would spread over those grassy acres, but then it was the edge of settled Chicago, with the Blue Island marshes ending in open prairie. Canal boats crept by on the South Branch, bound for the Illinois River and the Mississippi. Pale cliffs of lumber, just down from Wisconsin sawmills, lined the levee, and grain elevators jutted above long low slaughterhouses and packing plants. Farm wagons rumbled down Halsted Street and Archer Avenue. From the west came long trains of corn, wheat, barley, and bawling cattle. There, on spacious grounds, with the commerce of the prairies flowing past, the Wild West shook out for a two weeks' stay.

In high spirits the parade moved down Archer Avenue (Archey Road the Irish canal diggers called it) and onto the granite slabs of State Street where crowds lined the sidewalk and leaned from open windows. At the head of the line rode Buffalo Bill, doffing his hat to the cheers. Behind him rolled the band wagon with its six white horses stepping lightly to the strains of *Oh! Susanna, Don't You Cry for Me.* With a rattle on the stones came Chief White Eagle and fifteen Pawnee warriors sitting bareback on their broncos. Grizzled Pack Smiles on a dusty mule led a string of pack mules with flopping ears and dainty feet. A whooping announced the Wichita Indians on their painted ponies, with Chief Dave at the head. The Mexican vaqueros rode with jingling spurs and buckskin strings bouncing above the bright serapes tied behind their saddles; their faces were dark under the wide sombreros and their buckskin jackets were laced with white leather. In a carriage drawn by a team of matched mustangs rode the frontier markswoman, girlish Annie

Oakley. Again a whooping *Ki-yi-yip-a-ou!* and the street was full of cowboys and long-horned steers. The parade ended with the Deadwood Mail Stage, dented with bullets from the desperadoes of the Black Hills, drawn by six black mules. Old Pop Whittaker leaned from one window and his wife, in a ruffled shirtwaist and sunbonnet, peered from the other. On the swaying seat sat wrinkled John Nelson, his long beard blowing.

Back at the lot the horses were bedded in clean rye straw, buffalo browsed on mounds of dried timothy and clover, steers grazed over their hay-strewn corral with a cowboy playing a mouth organ from the top rail. Beyond the cook tent and the bunk tents, opposite the clustered tepees of the Indians, rose two A tents, one for Buffalo Bill and Nate Salsbury, the other for Annie Oakley and her husband. Annie's tent was as neat and homelike as a schooner's cuddy. A pair of chintz curtains framed the opening; inside were two folding cots, canvas chairs, a steamer table, a wardrobe trunk and a gun trunk, a collapsible tub and clean crash towels on a folding rack. The wooden floor was covered by a bright Axminster rug.

The tent was home, and around it lay the life of the West—Indians squatting beside their little fires, cowboys sprawling in the sun, Mexicans napping on the trampled grass. At show time the whole lot came to sudden life. Thousands streamed over the ground and into the long grandstand. Music blared from the arena, and when the cowboy band put down their instruments Frank Richmond mounted his box. *Ladies and Gentlemen*—Buffalo Bill appeared on a prancing stallion, Annie Oakley galloped around the track shooting glass balls out of the air, cowboys roped and threw the wide-horned steers, the Pony Express came dashing to a relay station, Indian hunters rode bareback among stampeding buffalo. When the stagecoach rumbled over the prairie, Indians whooped out from their ambush in the cardboard buttes. In the nick of time Buffalo Bill and his cowboys raced to the rescue. Amid the whizz of arrows and the crack of rifle fire the stage rocked on toward Deadwood City.

They had fine weather and record crowds, and despite the opposition of Chicago's pulpits they packed the stands on Sunday. Said the *Chicago Sun* on Monday, May 25th: "Yesterday afternoon no

less than 20,000 people were present to witness the portrayal of wild
Western life. All classes were represented, from the dirty-faced news-
boy to the club man with immaculate linen." According to the
Chicago Tribune the Sunday crowd was "considerably more than one-
twentieth of the entire population of the city—about 40,000 persons."
And the papers promised a new feature for the coming week: Major
Burke had offered $1,000 to any local rider who would mount a
bucking pony that had been sent in from the Chicago Stock Yards.

In the cook tent they talked about the season ahead of them—
Buffalo, Boston, Portland, then the cities of Canada. Nate Salsbury
was sure that Canada would welcome the Wild West; he had scheduled a tour from Montreal to Windsor. But now they were settled,
like a ship in harbor. When the red dusk darkened over the prairie
and the lights of Chicago made a glow in the night sky, it was good
to wander over the grounds, hearing the canal horns and seeing the
lighted train windows diminishing in darkness, or to drive in a
carriage along the lake shore and watch the moon rise out of the
water. To a girl from Darke County there was a never ending wonder
about the meeting of sky and sea.

Cody was in high spirits. Riding around the arena on a white horse
with silver-mounted saddle, he beamed at the crowds. After the show
he met reporters in his tent, gave them "a glass o' greetin'," and
showed them through the Indian village and the stock corrals. In
a cutaway coat and pearl gray Stetson he drove off to dinner with
his new Chicago friends, the railroad men, the meat packers, the
Gold Coast women with bare shoulders and trailing gowns. He came
back after midnight, smelling of cigar smoke and brandy. Still restless, he strolled the sleeping show grounds, clinking silver dollars in
his slanting trouser pockets, humming his favorite song: *Tenting tonight, tenting tonight, tenting on the old camp ground.*

In the headquarters tent a lamp was burning and Nate Salsbury
bent over a mound of papers on the table. When his partner came in,
Nate looked up, his lean face deeply lined in the lamplight. He had
some question, about figures, about personnel, about organization.
Cody liked to be consulted on anything—except business. He would
consider gravely Johnnie Baker's problems about sighting a falling

target or Chief Red Eagle's desire for a new blanket. But when Nate Salsbury questioned how the show could be improved and enlarged for the new season, Cody shrugged his broad shoulders. The show was doing fine. Why, it was just two years ago, here in Chicago, that he and Salsbury had first met. It was less than two years since a young German lawyer, John Peter Altgeld, drew up the contract that made them partners and co-owners of the Wild West. Since then they had weathered calamity and disaster—sunk in the Mississippi River, rained out of New Orleans, $60,000 in debt. But now the show was bigger than ever, the safe was bulging with money, and the crowds kept coming. Everybody loved it. Everybody.

He strode out again where moonlight paled the wagons and the tepees threw sharp shadows on the ground. The ponies pointed their ears at his passing, the steers and the buffalo munched their hay. *Tenting tonight, tenting tonight, tenting on the old camp ground.*

After the lamp was out Nate Salsbury lay sleepless on his cot. A pony whickered from the corral and an old buffalo snorted. Then the lot was silent. Far off a whistle quavered. The roar of the train gathered and faded and the night was still again. Cody began snoring in the darkness, but Nate Salsbury's mind was busy with a new idea.

Before the show moved on to the East, Major Burke took a train from the big sooty Union Station between the black Chicago River and the canal. He was on his way to Indian country, to the Sioux reservation at Grand River in Dakota Territory where the great chief Sitting Bull was brooding on the downfall of his people.

CHAPTER 5

Daughter of Sitting Bull

Tatanka Iyotake—He came into our midst, strong as
a buffalo bull, and sat down.

WHILE the show moved east, playing one-day stands through Indiana and Ohio in fine June weather, Major Burke was on the high Dakota plains. At Fort Yates, in the office of the Standing Rock Agency, the summer wind smelled of grass and distance, and Arizona John was restless to be outside. But Indian Agent James McLaughlin, a strict straight Scotsman, did a thorough job with the paper work before he was ready. With two interpreters, William Halsey and Joseph Primeau, they climbed into a box wagon and rattled through the stockade gates. They swung southwest, away from the gaunt gorge of the Missouri, over the ocean of grass and the blowing June flowers.

At the end of the second day they pulled up at a scattering of lodges on Grand River. Smoke seeped from the supper fires, and dogs sniffed at a pile of dried cattle bones. Arizona John got down stiffly. The dogs yapped around him till an Indian youth drove them away. The burly visitor took off his Stetson, removed three hairpins from his knotted hair, and raised a hand in greeting. He was at the camp of the villain of Custer's Massacre, the infamous *Tatanka Iyotake*, Chief Sitting Bull.

The next day Major Burke had a meeting with the somber chief. Sitting Bull, fifty-one years old, stood five feet eight inches, with a massive head and bull-broad shoulders, a tapering waist and neat small feet. His stern face was pitted with smallpox scars from an epidemic in his youth. They were two big men, Burke and Bull, and both were fond of ceremony. Arizona John spoke of his great gratification at meeting a chief whose fame was known afar. While the interpreter put that into Sioux, the chief stood impassive. He had risen to leadership of the Hunkpapa people, the most powerful tribe of the Sioux nation. He had killed his first buffalo at ten, his first enemy at fourteen. He had annihilated Custer's Cavalry on the ancient Sioux hunting grounds of the Little Big Horn. Since then he had endured exile, starvation, imprisonment. Now he lived with his two wives and ten children on the reservation.

Finally he spoke. In a deep, deliberate voice he welcomed the visitor with flowing hair. But what had the white man to do with a chief now confined like a horse on tether to the agency lands?

Major Burke put his proposal. He wanted Sitting Bull and a party of Sioux warriors and their women to travel with the Wild West show. They would be well paid, well fed, well treated. They would see the cities and towns of the white men, they would have fresh beef in their tepees and fine horses to ride. At the end of the summer they would be brought back on the railroad to their camps in Dakota.

Sitting Bull led the way to his tepee. Inside they sat on a buffalo robe with the interpreter between them. Through the open flap came the smell of cooking where the women bent over the scattered fires. The sun sank in a rosy haze over the buttes and the long summer twilight softened the plain. They ate their supper and lighted their pipes, and still *Tatanka Iyotake* did not give his answer.

*   *   *

Sitting Bull was not a novice in business matters. In his boyhood his first nickname meant "slow." Now he was too shrewd to make a quick agreement. Ever since the summer day of 1876 when Custer's regiment was slaughtered, Sitting Bull had been a famous man.

On September 5, 1883, when the cornerstone of the Dakota capitol was laid in Bismarck, the Territorial town was full of celebrated guests. Four special trains on the newly completed Northern Pacific had brought an impressive gathering: General Grant, Carl Schurz, the British and German ambassadors, newspapermen Joseph Pulitzer, Joseph Medill, and A. H. McClure, railroad builders Henry Villard and James J. Hill, the governors of six neighboring states, Marshall Field, Noah Brooks, and Viscount James Bryce, who was gathering impressions of the West to use in his projected book on America. At the head of this parade of notables marched a powerful, deep-chested Indian with pock-marked face and braids of hair swinging at his waist.

In *The American Commonwealth* Viscount Bryce described the decorated town and the gathering of visitors, all of whom were over-shadowed by *Tatanka Iyotake*. "By far the most remarkable figure was that of Sitting Bull, the famous Sioux chief, who had surprised and slain a detachment of the American army some years before. Among the speeches made, in one of which it was proved that Bismarck was the center of Dakota, Dakota the center of the United States, and the United States the center of the world, and that Bismarck was destined to be 'the metropolitan hearth of the world's civilization,' there came a short but pithy discourse from this grim old warrior, in which he told us, through an interpreter, that the Great Spirit moved him to shake hands with everybody." After the ceremonies at the cornerstone Sitting Bull did a profitable business selling his photograph from the tail of a wagon. He had already learned the value of the white man's silver.

A year later, in September, 1884, Sitting Bull began a more extensive public life. With a party of Sioux he was taken on a tour of the Eastern states, "for exhibition, observation, and instruction," and to the profit of an ex-army man, Colonel Alvaren Allen of the Merchant's Hotel in St. Paul. This dubious project was authorized by Henry M. Teller of Colorado, Secretary of the Interior, who had as little conception of the Indian's dignity as most men of his time. Sitting Bull joined the tour because he was promised an interview with the President in Washington—though he was cheated in this as in other agreements.

Under the management of Colonel Allen the Sioux party was exhibited at the Minnesota Agricultural Fair during the first week of September. Crowds pressed around the platform to see Sitting Bull. Through an interpreter he made a speech, saying that when he returned to his people he would raise corn like the prize samples at the Fair. On Sunday he consented to attend a high mass at the St. Paul Cathedral.

From Minnesota Colonel Allen took his Indians east. They arrived in New York on September 11th—Sitting Bull, Long Dog, Spotted Horn Bull, Crow Eagle, Flying By, Good Sounding Iron, Gray Eagle, Sitting Bull's wife Seen-by-her-Nation, his sixteen-year-old niece Princess Red Spear, and two other squaws, along with interpreters Louis Primeau and Paul Blum and Harry McLaughlin, the son of the agent at Standing Rock. A reporter from *Harper's Weekly* met the party at the station and accompanied them to the Grand Central Hotel. He wrote that Sitting Bull wore a calico shirt, blue trousers with white stripes, beadwork leggings and moccasins, and a heavy otter-tail headdress. Twin braids of hair tied with rawhide hung to his waist. On a rawhide thong around his neck he wore a crucifix given him by the priest at Standing Rock. The reporter noted that at their first dinner in New York the Sioux delegation put away seventeen bowls of soup, fifteen plates of fish, twenty-one large sirloin steaks, and numerous helpings of tapioca pudding, ice cream, cake, and coffee.

They were in New York to fulfill a contract with the Eden Musée a newly opened exhibit of waxworks and novelties on West 23rd Street. This establishment advertised a Nevada Silver Mine in Complete Operation, a Chamber of Horrors, the Last Days of Livingstone, the Death of the Prince Imperial, and concerts, afternoon and evening, in the Winter Garden. In mid-September, 1884, among wax images of presidents, kings, and criminals, the museum offered in flesh-and-blood reality "the famous Chief Sitting Bull with his wives and warriors." The crowds came. After a month at the Eden Musée, Colonel Allen took his band to Brooklyn; from October 20th to 25th they were on exhibit at the Music Hall on Flatbush and Fulton Avenues. Then, without a visit to the Grandfather in Washington, the Sioux were hurried back to Standing Rock, where the first snow of November was blowing across the plains.

* * *

Now, under the tall blue sky of June, 1885, the box wagon rattled back to Fort Yates, with Major Burke jostling among Sitting Bull and eight of his warriors. In the Agency House, where the windows looked out at the upthrust Standing Rock, he sat at a pine table and wrote out a contract:

> This Agreement entered into this sixth day of June, 1885. . . . I, John M. Burke, do hereby agree to pay Sitting Bull Fifty (50.00) Dollars per week, to be paid weekly every Saturday night; Five (5) Indians at Twenty-five (25.00) Dollars per month each, paid monthly; three Indian women at Fifteen (15.00) Dollars per month, to be paid monthly; and William Halsey Interpreter to be paid Sixty (60.00) Dollars per month. . . . Sitting Bull and party do hereby agree to travel with the Buffalo Bill Wild West Show . . . for summer season of four months. . . . John M. Burke does also agree to pay all expenses . . . of the party from the Show to Standing Rock at expiration of this contract.

While the interpreter read this document, following the lines with a blunt forefinger, Sitting Bull scowled in silence. Arizona John dipped the pen and waited for his signature. But there was another agreement the chief wanted. He spoke to the interpreter; the interpreter translated. Major Burke added a line at the bottom of the page:

> P.S. Sitting Bull is to have sole right to sell his own Photographs and Autographs.

When the others had signed—John M. Burke, Business Manager for Cody and Salsbury; James McLaughlin and Joseph Primeau as witnesses, the scowling chief carefully drew his picture of a crouching buffalo and misspelled his name: "Sietting Bull."

Arizona John pushed back his chair and reached into his pocket for cigars. "Let's have a smoke."

Two days later, on the 8th of June, Major Burke led his party aboard a Northern Pacific train at Mandan, Dakota Territory. William Zahn, once a member of Custer's regiment, helped load their equipment, and a mixed crowd of soldiers, railroadmen, and Indians watched the train pull out.

On Friday, June 12th, while the Wild West was making camp at the Driving Park in Buffalo, two cabs rolled out East Ferry Street and pulled up at the arena in a puff of dust. Out stepped Arizona John, beaming with pleasure and calling greetings across the lot. Behind him came the Sioux. William Halsey spoke to them, pointing over the show grounds. They had been bewildered in the cavernous station at St. Paul and the ringing streets of Chicago, but here they were at home. They breathed the smell of dust and horses. They saw smoke sifting up from cooking fires outside a row of Pawnee wigwams. They heard the snort of buffalo in the picketed corral and rifle fire from the practice range. Then came Cody in a white buckskin suit and a cream-colored Stetson. *Pahaska*—Long Hair. He raised a hand and spoke to Sitting Bull. The chief raised a hand, palm outward. They knew each other from past meetings on the plains.

With a canvas chair at the entrance to his tent, Sitting Bull took his ease in the sun, watching the cowboys herd horses at the end of the arena. An hour before show time gates were opened and the grounds filled with people. They streamed past the buffalo and the steers, past the pen of milling ponies, past the tepee where old John Nelson sat smoking beside his Oglala wife and his dark-eyed children. They stopped at the tent that bore the somber and reverberating name of Sitting Bull, the chief who had ambushed the Seventh Cavalry and, so the legend went, slashed off the scalp of General Custer as a trophy of the massacre. They stared at him and the chief stared back; then he went inside his tent for tobacco. He stayed there, sitting on a dusty buffalo robe while the voices rose outside. He did not need an interpreter to understand them.

It was a glum celebrity who sat with Major Burke in an open buggy when Frank Richmond announced—the feared and famous warrior of the Western plains, War Chief of the Fighting Sioux, the one and only Sitting Bull.

Ten thousand people packed the grandstand; while the buggy made its circuit ten thousand voices jeered at the murderer of Custer. Arizona John tipped his hat to the storm of sound, but the chief sat like stone, his head framed in a bonnet of eagle feathers, his dark eyes moving scornfully over the crowd. The buggy pulled up at the end of the oval. Around the track pounded a troop of Mexicans, a file of cowboys, a band of Indians on spotted ponies. While the stands applauded, Arizona John kept pointing and exclaiming, but he might have been talking to a wooden Indian. At that moment the contract signed at Standing Rock seemed as uncertain as a tumbleweed.

Sitting Bull put a brown hand on the buggy wheel and stepped down. He began to walk away, lurching with the old limp left from a battle at Kildeer Mountain in his youth. Major Burke had brought him all the way from the Missouri; now the grim chief was ready to go home.

In the arena Frank Richmond was announcing "—the girl of the Western plains . . . incredible feats with pistol, rifle, and shotgun." Annie Oakley ran on light feet to her gun table while the glass balls sailed upward. She seized a rifle, swung it to her shoulder, and squeezed the trigger. The balls shattered in air.

A grunt of pleasure broke from the chief. His dark eyes watched a galloping cowboy swing a set of targets on a leather thong. Annie Oakley, loping after him on a buckskin pony, snatched a pistol from the ground and shattered the targets, one, two, three. As Frank Richmond announced, "With the target behind her, seeing its reflection in the blade of a hunting knife, Miss Oakley will pierce a playing card held in the attendant's hand," Sitting Bull climbed back into the buggy. At the crack of the rifle the card fluttered to the ground.

Above the roar of the crowd boomed the voice of Sitting Bull: "*Ho! Ho! Was-te! Wa-kán!*" As Annie ran out of the ring the chief jumped down and shambled after her; Major Burke found him at the door of her tent, repeating, "*Wan-tan-yeya Ci-sci-la*"—Little Straight

Shooter, Little Sureshot. From that moment Annie Oakley was a daughter of the storied chief.*

While Cody sat convivially in the barroom of the Iroquois Hotel, the guest of proprietor Monte Gerrans, Nate Salsbury took Annie Oakley and her husband to the office of the Buffalo Courier to see George Bleistein. Besides his newspaper, big bluff George Bleistein owned a circus printing business, the Courier Show Printing Company, the biggest concern of its kind in the country; he printed placards, posters, and programs for the Wild West, Barnum and Bailey, Adam Forepaugh, Ringling, and Cole Brothers. In the Courier studio Annie Oakley posed with a rifle on her shoulder and her hair rippling from a wide hat with a silver star on its uprolled brim. She was just two months short of twenty-five, but she seemed a girl of seventeen. Her costume was simple—tan leggings, pleated tan skirt trimmed in blue, a buttoned tan blouse with blue cuffs—and she faced the camera with an unconcerned and simple beauty. She stood five feet tall and weighed ninety-eight pounds; her eyes were direct and fearless, and the rifle seemed a part of her trim figure. She brought space and wind and open country into a cluttered studio above the noise of Genesee Street.

The bald little photographer ducked out of the camera hood and rubbed his hands together. "Never have I had a better subject. Never." He ducked back again.

When they drove to the show grounds Nate Salsbury had left an order for a thousand posters. Little Sureshot would soon be as familiar as Buffalo Bill.

On June 13th they left Buffalo for a series of one- and two-day stands in Pennsylvania and New York. At every stop reporters came

---

* Writers on Annie Oakley (though none on Sitting Bull) have stated that Annie Oakley and Sitting Bull first met "at a theater in St. Paul." Actually their paths could not have crossed until June 12, 1885, at Buffalo. Sitting Bull appeared at the Minnesota State Fair in 1884, but Annie Oakley was then on tour with Sells Brothers Circus. Annie Oakley's autobiographical sketch does not mention Sitting Bull until he joined the Wild West; then it states: "Sitting Bull had met me in St. Paul in 1882." Throughout 1882 Sitting Bull was a military prisoner at Fort Randall on the Missouri. The Wild West publicity agents played up the friendship of Annie Oakley and Sitting Bull and Annie's adoption by the chief—predating it, for a good story, to an earlier meeting. In her own account Annie Oakley went along with the press agents' story.

to see the infamous Sitting Bull. Burke led them over the grounds, giving a press conference on the way. —There was Cody's horse, the dapple gray, a veteran of the buffalo chase. . . . Wild horses in that corral, better not step too close. . . . Pawnee Indians from Nebraska. . . . The old Deadwood Stage, used to carry gold from Deadwood City to Cheyenne. . . . Sitting Bull's tent—

But the chief wasn't at home. They found him sitting in the doorway of another tent, watching a girl sew fringe on a costume. "How," the chief said to the reporters, and turned back to Annie Oakley.

There, Major Burke observed, was something to write about. The great medicine man of the Hunkpapa Sioux and the champion woman marksman of the world. She could shoot the center spot out of a five of spades dropped from a flagpole, and her favorite reading was the New Testament. The chief was gentle as a grandfather with her, but he had given the U.S. Army its worst defeat in history, setting up scarecrow Indians for Custer's men to shoot at while the Sioux ambushed them from a fringe of trees.

The newsmen scribbled it down and looked around them. They made notes on the furnishing of Annie's tent, the Bible and the basket of crochet work on her folding table, the gun trunk and the embroidered costumes. They made notes on Sitting Bull's brass-studded belt, his crucifix on a rawhide thong, his long hair parted in the middle and hanging in pigtails bound with otterskin. They saw the scars on his chest and his forearms; Burke explained that a hundred pieces of flesh had been cut from him as an offering to the Great Spirit and that he then danced the Sun Dance, hour after hour, until he had a vision of victory for his people.

The chief had just arrived, Arizona John declared, from the high plains country beyond the Missouri. He had joined the Wild West because he wanted to be with Annie Oakley—Little Sureshot, he called her. Two, three years ago he had seen her shooting in a St. Paul theater and had carried a photograph back to the Standing Rock reservation where he kept it in a tin box in his tepee. Now he had adopted her as his daughter. Matter of fact, he liked to adopt people. He might even adopt a newspaper man if he took a notion.

That part of Major Burke's discourse was sober truth. Back on the great grass range above Grand River, Sitting Bull had wives and children, but he had a larger family by adoption. As a young man of twenty-two, far out on the winter plains of Montana, in a raid on the rival Assiniboins, he had adopted a brother. From a tepee beside the frozen Missouri rushed four Assiniboins. Sioux arrows dropped them on the snowy ground—a man, a woman, and two children. One child was left, a frightened boy of eleven, surrounded by his enemies. As their bows were bending he cried to Sitting Bull—"Big Brother!" The young warrior had no brother of his own, but in that cry he found one. He stepped between the boy and the arrows. He mounted his horse, pulled the youth up behind him, and rode away. In the warmth of his tepee he fed his new brother, dressed him in deer-skins, and painted his face. Outside, he gave away a horse in his honor. Ten years later, in 1867, on the edge of the Black Hills, the sacred medicine ground, he adopted another brother, an Oblate missionary, Jean Baptiste Marie Genin, who had become a trusted friend of the Sioux. In the winter of 1869 he found a third brother—a mail carrier captured by the Sioux while crossing their hunting grounds above the Yellowstone. This white man, Frank Grouard, was not entirely white; the son of an American sailor and a woman of Hawaii, he had broad flat features and a swarthy color. Sitting Bull defended him from his captors, led him to his camp, and there adopted him, giving him a Sioux name which meant "Sitting-with-Upraised-Hands." Grouard remained for three years with the Sioux, becoming a skilled scout and hunter. Then he left the Indians, and eventually he turned against them. In 1876, seven years after Sitting Bull had made him a brother, Frank Grouard led Colonel Reynolds and his Third Cavalry against the Sioux in their Slim Buttes camp on Powder River. If the stern chief remembered that treachery it did not diminish his devotion to Wan-tan-yeya Ci-sci-la. She would remain his daughter until the day of his death, five years later, on the bleak Dakota prairie.

Sitting Bull was fascinated by the way the Wild West roustabouts drove tent stakes in the ground. Every morning he took his place in that sweating, swinging circle. He swung a sledge in show lots across Pennsylvania, in the county seats of southern New York, in the towns of Connecticut. These were one-day stands, and the outfit was talking about Boston, where they could shake down for a solid week.

*   *   *

The Old South Meeting House in Boston had seen Puritans in somber cloaks and steeple hats, marching redcoats and defiant Sons of Liberty, feathered figures hurrying to the harbor to dump British tea into the midnight water. Once the hall was filled with hoofbeats; in 1776 the British used it as a cavalry school and served rum in the gallery. On the morning of July 27, 1885, it heard another clatter of hoofs and saw another kind of history. Through winding Washington Street, with music blaring from the cowboy band, came the long parade of the Wild West. Ahead of the band wagon rode Buffalo Bill, raising his hat to solid walls of people. On a spotted pony came Sitting Bull in a war bonnet of eagle feathers; he stared at the gilt weathervane of the Old State House while the Yankees jeered and whistled. From files of Indians—Pawnee, Wichita, Sioux—war whoops quavered in the narrow street. Then came scouts, Mexican vaqueros, Nebraska cowboys, with a creak of saddle leather and a scuffle of hoofs on the granite paving stones. The newest part of America had come to the Old Bay Colony. It passed down Washington Street, up through Scollay Square, under the shadow of King's Chapel and the Parker House, along the Common and the Public Gardens.

On foot, on bicycles, in carts and carriages, crowds followed all the way to the show grounds in Beacon Park beside the Albany Railroad. They streamed past the show train where steers and buffalo were being herded from their slat-walled cars. They swarmed over the ground, past the tents of the Indians and the stockade of wild horses. They pressed around the tent where Sitting Bull was signing a stack of photographs and looked into the tent of Annie Oakley where Johnnie Baker was polishing a rifle barrel. In the headquarters tent Major Burke introduced a line of reporters and Cody called for drinks. Nate Salsbury paced the floor with his quick stride. "We could play here for two weeks," he said to a *Globe* reporter, "with full stands at every performance. Now we'll have to turn people away."

"You seem to regret that, sir, and not just in the line of business."

That was true. Nate Salsbury believed in the Wild West as Yankees believed in Thanksgiving. He thought it made every spectator a better American.

In Boston for the first time the Wild West held night performances, flooding the arena with new calcium flares. Frank Butler worried about the artificial light. At dusk, before the arena was open, he took Annie to the ring. When she broke a dozen targets he was satisfied. "I guess you could do it in the dark, Missie."

While the band played its opening medley crowds poured into the stands. Long lines of carriages arrived at the gate, and people from Beacon Hill strolled past the Indian tepees and the cowboy camp. The Wild West fascinated the residents of Back Bay along with the Irish from South Boston. With fanfare came the grand entry. Buffalo Bill, Annie Oakley, Sitting Bull, Frisking Elk, Buck Taylor, Bronco Bill, Mustang Jack, Tom Clayton, Con Groner— one after another they dashed into the arena and reined up before the stands. Fanfare again, and Annie Oakley ran into the flood-lighted ring, shooting whirling targets out of the air with a revolver. This was Salsbury's shrewd planning. The Wild West was a noisy, fast-paced show, full of hoofbeats, war cries, gunfire. But it began with a girl alone in the huge arena, a magnetic girl in a knee-length skirt and a wide-awake hat. Her action quickened. She threw down the pistols and raised a rifle. She exchanged the rifle for a shotgun. In five minutes she had prepared both the animals and the audience for the explosive sequence of the show. Never in the Wild West did a horse run away or a steer stampede.

Her act was followed by a rodeo of riding, herding, and roping. To the beat of Indian drums the tribesmen stamped out the grass dance, the war dance, the corn dance, the scalp dance. A buffalo hunt took place under the calcium lights, and the Pony Express raced past the stands in a demonstration of "how they brought the mail to old Cheyenne." When the Deadwood Stage rolled up and Frank Richmond pointed to "four young millionaires about to set forth on a perilous journey," reporters from the Boston *Globe,* the *Journal,* the *Advertiser,* and the Associated Press climbed in. The driver cracked his long whip over the six-mule team and the stagecoach rocked away. Indians lay in ambush, but Cody and his men chased them back to the badlands.

Frank Richmond announced the broncobusters and their murderous mounts. After a fierce struggle Tom Clayton mastered the furious Dynamite and rode him around the ring. Buck Taylor stuck to Suicide, and an Indian got aboard a saddled elk and raced across the arena. While Cody appeared on his famous horse Charlie, a half naked Indian rider, daubed with war paint, galloped over the prairie. They enacted Cody's famous fight with Yellow Hand. Under the flaring lights ten thousand people pictured the Indian and the scout dueling on the Kansas plain. When they had emptied their pistols they leaped to the ground. Buffalo Bill drew a knife, Yellow Hand leveled a spear. They charged, fenced, dodged, maneuvered. At last the knife struck home and Yellow Hand fell. Bending over the prostrate savage, Buffalo Bill took "the first scalp for Custer."

A final act, newly elaborated for the Boston audience, showed a settler's hut on the plains with Indians creeping through the grass. After a brave but futile defense the pioneer woman and her children (old John Nelson's half-breed daughters) were captured. But over the prairie came a drumbeat of hoofs. The cowboys arrived and the Indians were routed. With a final burst of music the show was over.

But the crowds lingered, strolling through the grounds, buying Sitting Bull's photograph, handing out cigars to old John Nelson, admiring Annie Oakley's gun rack, asking Tom Clayton how to ride a fractious horse. His answer was simple: "Doggone it, jest sit in the saddle and don't get skeart."

Boston had an endless curiosity about the Wild West. The *Transcript* described Miss Annie Oakley, "the demure sharpshooter of the western plains" as a "characteristic product of frontier life," and classically referred to Sitting Bull as "Sedentary Taurus." To please the crowds Sitting Bull was kept in public view; after his announced appearance he climbed onto the bandstand and tapped his feet to the music. He received the press at his tepee, greeting each reporter with a solemn "How," and presenting his photograph. The *Transcript* reporter wrote: "They are the faces of thoughtful men that are worn by these Indian chieftains. Their leader, Sitting Bull, has especially strong lines in his countenance which is something of a reminder of the features of Daniel Webster."

On the third day of the engagement Major Burke invited the press to a barbecue. Over a pit of smoldering embers a Texas steer was broiled and basted. While Cody kept the whisky flowing the reporters attacked smoking joints of beef. Then, according to a ceremony arranged by Major Burke and willingly carried out by "Sedentary Taurus," Nate Salsbury was adopted into the Sioux nation. Salsbury, Cody, Frank Butler, Bill Halsey, and a dozen newspapermen entered Sitting Bull's tent. They bared their heads and sat cross-legged in a circle while the chief pressed tobacco into a long-stemmed pipe. He scratched a sulphur match and puffed out three clouds of smoke. Around the circle each man puffed in turn. When the pipe came back to Sitting Bull he blew smoke to the four winds. Then in sonorous Sioux phrases, with Bill Halsey interpreting, he named Nathan Salsbury *Wah-see-sha-e-ton-sha*—Little White Chief. Buffalo Bill, a Pawnee chief by past adoption, solemnly nodded his handsome head.

Grave as a British barrister, Nate Salsbury responded. He was gratified to be a member of the Sioux, and to be Sitting Bull's own son; he pledged eternal friendship to the tribe. Sitting Bull declared that if he were at home on Grand River he would give Salsbury a pony. Now he knocked out the ashes and gave him the pipe, as a souvenir of this ceremony. From his headdress he plucked an eagle feather which he gave to his son as a symbol of rank. After a general handshaking around the circle, they filed outside for more beef and whisky. Salsbury, the Boston papers reported, was the only white man ever adopted by the Sioux, and Sitting Bull's only adopted son.

Nate Salsbury was well known to Boston audiences from years past; "Salsbury's Troubadours" had often played in the Hub City. Now, with the help of Major Burke, the papers gave him a new character, stating that he owned a huge cattle ranch in Montana and observing that he "carried the breath of the Sierras around him." Salsbury wore a cutaway coat, striped trousers, and sometimes a silk top hat;

with his long face and the fine lines around his eyes he looked more like an English man of letters than a rancher. But the reporters made him a plainsman. When he passed Annie Oakley's tent, they declared, he gave her a greeting in sign language. He and Little Sureshot were in the same family; they were son and daughter of Sitting Bull.

CHAPTER 6

The Conquest of Canada

The largest share of applause was bestowed on Annie
Oakley, a young girl whose proficiency with shotgun and
rifle seems almost miraculous.

—London (Ontario) *Free Press*, Sept. 2, 1885.

SHOW life was the unloading in an empty place, it was the packing
up and moving on. It was the all-night clicking of rails, the wail of
the train whistle, the big dark unknown country passing by. It was
the band playing, horses prancing, people lining the streets of a
strange city. It was the hot noon confusion of the grounds, the
sweaty canvasmen lying in the shade of their wagons, steers bawling
from the corral, the cook clanging an iron skillet with an iron spoon.
It was the roar of ten thousand voices when you ran out of the arena
leaving a tang of gun smoke in the air.

Show life was rain drumming on the tent roof while you stood on a
bale of straw to change a costume. It was the teamsters lashing the
draft horses while the wagons sank hub-deep in straw-strewn mud.
It was the cowboys sitting on a wagon tongue in the sunset, picking
their teeth with stems of hay and talking about the outfit back on the
Niobrara River. It was homesickness, the aching mind and heart and
muscles, the desire for a quiet fireside and the circle of lamplight on
a checkered tablecloth. Show life was the tumult of the arena and
the night silence when stars looked down on the tents of the Indians
and the tethered ponies—like a Pawnee camp far out on the Laramie
Plains. Show life was the wild and boundless West, and it was also

Chicago and Indianapolis, Binghamton and Elmira, Springfield and Boston. Sometimes a girl from the back roads of Darke County woke up in the dead of night and wondered if it were real.

They all regretted leaving Boston, but the schedule carried them on. In the parade at Burlington, Vermont, the Indians looked up at every cross street to the lift of the Green Mountains, and in the tumult of making camp at Howard Park, Cody kept gazing off where the shadows of clouds lay on the hills. Then to St. Albans, and across the border to Canada. It was Annie Oakley's first foreign country, though she would see many more. She looked out the train window, curious as a child, all the way to the long bridge over the St. Lawrence and the spread of Montreal under the lift of the Laurentians.

Montreal gave the Wild West a hectic welcome. The parade passed through cheering streets—Wellington, McGill, St. James, Catherine, Windsor—and thousands followed it out to the show grounds at Point St. Charles. The first performance was held in a summer downpour. Annie Oakley did her shooting through a curtain of rain and splashed her horse through standing water. But the crowd cheered wildly and the sky brightened. Before the final rout of Indians from the settler's cabin, sun streamed down and the wet ponies shone like paint.

As guests of the city the Wild West people were taken to La Chine on the St. Lawrence, where once La Salle had dreamed of setting out with a canoe caravan for China. Sitting Bull was presented to a group of Iroquois chiefs, and the whole party, red men and white, boarded the steamer *Filgate* for a swift and swirling trip through the rapids. Back at the dock in Montreal they inspected the spanking new steamers *Sarnia* and *Sardinia*. To meet the Canadian demand for photographs, Annie Oakley, Buffalo Bill, and Sitting Bull posed for new plates at the William Notman studio.

On to Ottawa, Kingston, Toronto, Hamilton, London, with the newspapers running columns on Buffalo Bill "who bears upon his body 137 scars received in encounters with the Indians," the redoubtable Sitting Bull who after the defeat of Custer had sought sanctuary in Canada, and the demure plains heroine Annie Oakley. At Toronto a delegation met them on the grounds at Woodbine Park and took them to the Holman Opera Company for a performance of *Iolanthe*. The next day a reporter stated that "local capitalists have made an offer for the right to take the Wild West Show to Europe." On the train pulling out of Toronto even cautious Nate Salsbury felt expansive. He splashed whisky into a glass and turned to Cody. "We're started now, and we won't stop till we have reached the heights. Cody, I'll land you at the foot of the throne of England." A European tour had been Nate Salsbury's dream from the beginning.

Sitting Bull, who had given the U.S. Army a dramatic and stinging defeat, was a hero in Canada. Well aware of the growth and arrogance of their friendly neighbor nation, the Canadians were glad to remember that the great chief had found refuge across their border when General Terry's "walk-a-heaps" and his "pony-soldiers" pursued him. Clusters of boys hung around his tent and followed him across the grounds, copying his bowlegged, limping gait, when he went to buy them Cracker Jack and candy. Annie Oakley, always careful with a dollar, kept money for some of the Indians who had been poker victims of the cowboys, but she never served as banker for Sitting Bull. Years later she described him as "an open-handed uncle" to all the boys who swarmed over the lot. He couldn't read newspapers and his moccasins wouldn't take a shine, but he passed out coins to the newsboys and bootblacks. "The contents of his pockets were often emptied into the hands of ragged little boys, nor could he understand how so much wealth could go brushing by, unmindful of the poor."

There were other things that puzzled the chief. He was amazed at the extent of the white men's cities and the multitude of their people —greater than blackbirds in the sky or the remembered buffalo on the plains. "The white people are so many that if every Indian in the West killed one every step they took the dead would not be missed among you." He still remembered the strangeness of being taken through a tunnel under the Chicago River—seeing across the water the very buildings he had passed before entering the cave mouth. In his first astonishment at these wonders he had said, "Indian no good"; but he had some second thoughts. Through his interpreter he regretted that the white man was not as honest as he was full of brain power. When reporters asked about Custer's defeat, he stated: "Nobody knows who killed Custer; everybody fired at him. Custer was a brave warrior but he made a mistake. The Indians honored him and did not scalp him. I fought for my people. My people said I was right. I will answer to my people. I will answer for the dead of my people. Let the palefaces do the same on their side."

In the mellow atmosphere of Canada even Cody made generous statements about the Indians. "I never shot an Indian but I regretted it afterward," he told the Toronto press. "In nine cases out of ten when there is trouble between white men and Indians it will be found that the white man is responsible for the dispute through breaking faith with them." He had one simple rule for living in harmony with the tribes: "Don't break your promises. Indians expect a man to keep his word. They can't understand how a man can lie. Most of them would as soon cut off a leg as tell a lie." The Canadians bought thousands of photographs showing Buffalo Bill posed with Sitting Bull—"Enemies in '76, Friends in '85," the chief in a bonnet of two hundred eagle feathers and the goateed plainsman in boots and spurs, cream-colored trousers, and a crimson shirt embroidered with prairie flowers.

Canadian newspapers revived the lore and legends of Sitting Bull. He was credited, in a published volume of The Works of Sitting Bull, 1878, with authorship of French and Latin poems—though his only attainment in letters, accomplished during his exile in Canada, was the writing of his name. Another legend said that the chief was really a half-breed named Charlie Jacobs, born near old Fort Garry and educated at St. John's Anglican College in Winnipeg. Another said that he was a devout Roman Catholic, a convert of the devoted Father de Smet. It was true that in 1868 when de Smet was one white man among three thousand Indians at the great council on Powder River, young Sitting Bull had walked at the priest's side through the smoldering camp and had stood guard over his tepee. Father de Smet gave him a crucifix which the chief wore along with a necklace of bear claws; he liked jewelry of any kind. One writer had declared that Sitting Bull spoke fluent French, was an admirer of Napoleon and a student of his campaigns. A rumor made him a graduate of West Point, another said he had conspired with Louis Riel to form an independent Indian state in Canada. According to report, Sitting Bull once told a missionary named Beede that after the Battle of the Little Big Horn the ghost of Custer informed him that he would die of treachery in fifteen years. That prophecy gave him five more years to live.

In Canada Sitting Bull overshadowed the flamboyant Cody, and though it was good business for the show it was painful to the showman. He had two rivals now—a gray-eyed girl with an uprolled hat showing a silver star, and a massive chief in eagle feathers. When they crossed the Detroit River and played again to American crowds, the jeers that greeted Sitting Bull sounded pleasant to the long-haired *Pahaska*.

From Detroit the show moved to Saginaw, where Buffalo Bill was wined and dined by lumber barons at the Bancroft Hotel. The town was full of lumberjacks on their way to the winter season in the woods. When the riders cried "Yip-ee!" to the milling steers, the loggers in the grandstand yelled "Ye-ouw!" Saginaw, the cowboys said, was a town with the hair on.

Playing in Columbus at the end of September, the Wild West was visited by the officers of the 17th U.S. Infantry, quartered at Columbus barracks. When they approached his tent, Sitting Bull stared at one of the men. "How! How!" He jumped to his feet, his pockmarked face breaking into a smile. While Bill Halsey relayed a greeting, the chief shook hands with grinning Lieutenant McMartin.

"This young man," Sitting Bull said through his interpreter, "rolled cigarettes for me at Fort Randall."

McMartin obligingly rolled another, licked it, touched it with a match, and handed it over. While the chief smoked it down, Lieutenant McMartin explained to reporters that he had been in charge of the army's top prisoner at Fort Randall, a hundred miles below Pierre on the Missouri.

They made their last camp of the season in St. Louis, setting up at Sportsman's Park in a cold October rain. Sitting Bull, always a reader of weather sign, put his head outside his tepee, sniffed the wet wind and studied the leaden sky. The skies stayed heavy but crowds streamed in. The cowboy band struck up and the horses came to life. Inside the gate Major Burke and his assistant Ben Circle passed out a new broadside celebrating the season now reaching its end and declaring that the Wild West had played to a million enthralled spectators in the past five months.

To advertise the show Burke took Sitting Bull in his feathered headdress and dirty jewelry on a tour of St. Louis hotels and restaurants. In a hotel lobby the chief's dark eyes found a rugged, bearded, uniformed man with gold braid on his shoulders. *Hiah!* he muttered —the alert of the plains Indians. It was Three Stars, his old pursuer in the Bad Lands. General Carr, the most famous Indian fighter of his generation, had once said he would rather be a colonel of cavalry than Czar of Russia. Now their eyes met. The general shouldered through the crowd and the two stood face to face. Three Stars greeted him like an old comrade, but the chief stood silent. He was glad to get away from there; he was ready to go home to the empty plains.

On the last day, October 11th, the final performance came to a close and reporters stood in the rain around the tent of Sitting Bull. —What were his plans for the winter? Would he travel with the Wild West another season? What would he tell his people about the places he had seen? Through his interpreter the chief gave his last word to the press: "The wigwam is a better place for the red man. He is sick of the houses and the noises and the multitudes of men."

Then he stalked off to see his daughter *Wan-tan-yeya Ci-sci-la*, in her tent; she was putting away her costumes and her guns. He brought presents—a quiver of his finest arrows, beaded moccasins, a feathered headdress. They stood together for a moment, two who could not understand each other's language but who knew each other's feelings. Annie followed him outside in the thin cold rain, and Sitting Bull looked off at the western sky. Bill Halsey appeared and the chief spoke.

"What did he say?" she asked.

"He sees it will be a cold winter," the interpreter said.

They had early supper in the cook tent, with the band playing *Auld Lang Syne* to mark the season's end. The animals would be wintered in St. Louis, but the company would scatter. Nate Salsbury rarely made a speech, but now he stood on a bench and talked for a minute before they left the tent.— It had been a wonderfully successful season. They had drawn a million people and made a profit of $100,000. A year ago the Wild West was still a venture, now it was an established organization. Next year they would have a bigger show, a longer train, better equipment. Speaking for himself and Mr. Cody, he thanked all the company for their part in the success of the season. He wished them a good winter and looked forward to a happy reunion in the spring. He would write them about the date of opening.

While the band played *Home, Sweet Home*, they said their goodbyes. In cabs they splashed over the muddy grounds and rattled through the wet dusk to the station. They scattered in all directions —Nate Salsbury to New York, Cody to Nebraska, Major Burke to Washington, the cowboys to the Western railroad towns and ranches, the Mexicans to adobe houses in the sun, Sitting Bull to the gaunt gray plains beyond the Missouri, Annie Oakley and her husband to an Ohio farmhouse in Darke County.

CHAPTER 7

South Wind and the Sioux Princess

Because the Sioux believed that the south wind brings
sickness, they think of the South as the land of death.
—STANLEY VESTAL: *Sitting Bull*

SITTING Bull was right: it was a hard winter. Ice gorges filled the
Hudson and huge gray slabs sloshed in the tide of New York harbor.
Storms whooped over the wastes of Dakota, buried the prairie towns
in snow, besieged farmhouses for a thousand miles. The Ohio froze
solid from shore to shore, with steamboats wedged in ice at the
Cincinnati levee. In Greenville sleighs jangled through the snowy
streets and bobsleds pulled up at the Broadway hitching racks. Children skated on Greenville Creek, dragging dead branches to a fire
beside the frozen basin of Tecumseh's spring. The back roads of
Darke County lay white and unbroken, with only the fence tops
showing. In the farmyards people tramped a path to the woodpile
and kept the hearth heaped high.

Winter was a time when life drew inward. The meaning of the
world was the red coals in the stove's grating, the kettle singing on the
fire, lamplight in the purple dusk, logs glowing in the black throat
of the chimney. For Annie Oakley there was a deep contentment
inside the frosted windows.

The farmhouse was more comfortable now, with a newly built living
room, new furniture, new things in the kitchen; Annie had been
sending money home all season. That winter she kept her books in
her sewing basket—a school reader, a big worn geography, a speller,

a history. With the same steady purpose that kept her practicing on the target range, she studied the lessons that her childhood had been denied. She practiced writing, spelling, reading; she traced the boundaries of states and countries; she read about Julius Caesar marching into Gaul, about King John signing the charter on the banks of the Thames at Runnymede, about the Minute Men of Boston and Sutter's discovery of gold in California.

When she took up her sewing her mind kept on with history and geography, relating the maps and stories to the places she had seen. In her hands, as skillful with a needle as with a repeating rifle, a fringed and pleated skirt took shape and embroidered flowers grew over a broadcloth jacket. That winter she made a whole set of new costumes for the new season.

Sometimes Frank Butler sat by the fire, reading, writing letters, or frowning over a page until he had finished a humorous or sentimental poem. Often he was away all day, tramping the white fields with a shotgun on his shoulder. He came in at dusk, stamping his feet and pulling off his baggy jacket. He brought quail, squirrel, rabbits, and soon the pot was bubbling on the stove. At supper he told in his broadest Irish about the Irish woodchopper he found at Indian Creek and how they had swapped stories of their boyhood on the Old Sod while they ate bread and tea beside a brush fire in the snow. All the family listened to Frank's storytelling. Sister Emily couldn't take her eyes from him, and the dim-sighted old stepfather nodded his head gravely. Susan said: "That would be old Paddy O'Shea, who lives alone in the Lost Timber. Tha must have been good for him, Jimmy."

Sometimes the neighbors came in for an evening, pulling up in a bobsled and throwing a blanket over the team. They could not hear enough about the Wild West; they marveled over the feathered headdress and beaded moccasins that had once been Sitting Bull's. They stared at the battered show trunk, studying the pictures and clippings pasted inside the lid. When they drove home over the white roads their minds were full of distant cities, of charging buffalo, of Indian camps on the plains.

Occasionally Annie put on her old hunting clothes and went with Frank through the woods. She could guide him across the frozen swamp to where the grouse nested and quail flew out of the thickets. In the deep timber they heard a sawmill snarling; they found a "deadening" in a grove of girdled oaks and hickories. Hitched to a pyramid of logs a team of horses stood with smoking breath; the snow was stained with sawdust. It was good to leave that stumpland for the snow-hung woods where blue jays shrilled from the treetops and chickadees scolded. They came home through long blue shadows with the game bag full. On the back stoop Jimmy lifted her out of her heavy boots and swung her through the kitchen door.

March brought sunny days, but the wind was sharp as a knife and the pale sky quickly darkened with squalls of sleet and snow. But with the first week of April a soft wind came out of the southwest. Snowbanks shrank in the meadows and running water glinted at the roadside. Each morning the grass showed a richer green and starched white clouds drifted over the Lost Timber. Frank scribbled down a verse:

> How do you do, Miss April?
> I'm mighty glad you're here;
> Never did like old Miss March,
> She acts so very queer.

While meadowlarks sang from the fence rail, Annie set out a row of gooseberry plants on the south slope of the garden; that was the first ground to warm and dry in the April sun. She would not see the vines blossom and bear fruit, but it gave her pleasure to put them in the ground. She looked at the apple trees where the buds were swelling. Now the house was a close, confining place. A wayward wind blew over the swamp, water was a restless voice in all the little creeks, in the April sky, a hawk circled higher and higher. She had fine sight, the sight of a sharpshooter; she could watch a hawk still diminishing in the blue after it had vanished from other eyes. But she could never see the real secret of spring. There was much to see—fuzzy pink buds on the maples, sleek brown buds on the beeches, the new gloss on the wings of blackbirds, the pale green of sycamore trunks and the old feathery seed balls falling, the spreading green of hepatica and Mayflower in the woods. But there was another thing, in the earth itself,

an unseen restlessness and stirring. At night the wind blew cool-warr
out of Lost Timber; it came in the windows, it seemed to pa
through the walls of the room. The house yielded to it, and a gi
lying with her husband in the silent dark, seeing a half-moon sailin
through torn white clouds, felt the whole familiar world dissolv
around her, dissolve and change into a world of strangeness an
promise. The night wind came from distant places. It went on, res
less and seeking, to the world beyond Darke County, as her lif
had done.

When the letter came from St. Louis they were packed and read
to go. She looked once more at the orchard, seeing the first pin
and white on the apple boughs. When the train pulled out of Greer
ville she waved to the dwindling figures on the platform. Then sh
turned to her husband, making the odd little dance step and curts
which finished her act in the show ring. Frank threw an imaginar
gun to his shoulder and crooked his trigger finger.

*   *   *

Camp was already set up at the St. Louis Fair Grounds when the
arrived. It was a bigger show. Twenty-six freshly painted cars on th
railroad siding, a long row of Indian tepees, a corral of restless ponie
buffalo milling in their enclosure. Across the lot strode Cody i
gleaming boots and a white Stetson. He swung Missie off her feei
and before he set her down a stranger appeared, calling her name. I
was a stranger, though not a stranger's voice. For a moment sh
studied the slight man in a frock coat and striped trousers. He carrie
a briar cane; he wore a dark clipped beard. "Nate Salsbury!"

Cody explained with a wink and a smile that his partner envie
his own goatee; this year he wanted to attract the ladies. "Well," h
said, "come along, Missie, and see your new tent. And see how th
outfit grew."

This season the show carried its own seats with a canvas canopy
a lighting system, and a huge wood and canvas background of colore
buttes and mountains. There were 240 in the company—new roust
abouts, canvasmen, teamsters, and new performers in the ring. Im

mediately they began rehearsals. To the program was added the Wild West's first spectacle—a feature that would be retained and varied in every future season. "Custer's Massacre," planned by Burke and Salsbury during the winter, would climax the program with noise, color, and drama straight out of Western history. Nate Salsbury kept them at rehearsals till every Sioux and soldier, every cavalry horse and Indian pony knew his part to perfection.

Annie Oakley's popularity had led the management to add three other women performers. Dell Farrell and Georgie Duffield, cowgirls from Colorado and Wyoming, were to stage a daily pony race. Miss Lillian Smith, "the California huntress," was billed as a shooting star. The program stated that at seven she had tired of dolls and begun playing with a rifle; soon she was hitting mallards on the wing and shooting bobcats out of towering redwood trees. She was a rawboned girl without a trace of grace or magnetism, and she left the show before the season ended. The notorious Doc Middleton, ex-badman of the Black Hills, now slept in the bunk tent beside Con Groner, the Cowboy Sheriff. In place of Sitting Bull, Burke had added two Sioux chiefs, American Horse and Rocky Bear. Among the new cowboys were Jolting Jim Kidd from Nebraska, Big Dick Johnson from Wyoming, Dick Bean of Texas, and Sunday Jim Mitchell the Cowboy Preacher from the Plains. Billy Johnson was a new rider for the Pony Express and Antonio Esquivel the new leader of the Mexican vaqueros. Another feature was the exhibitionist character Sergeant Bates, a Civil War veteran who had marched from coast to coast carrying a large American flag and giving patriotic lectures.

Annie went through the grounds, breathing the old smell of dust and horses, finding old friends among the Indians and cowboys. Johnnie Baker appeared, an inch taller since October, striding in the shadow of Buffalo Bill; his hair was growing over his shirt collar but he couldn't yet start a mustache and goatee. He had been in school all winter, and he thought the spring would never come.

Major Burke had another feature for the season—a figure from prairie history, the half-breed leader Gabriel Dumont. A man of powerful shoulders and the trim hips of a horseman, he had plotted with Louis Riel the Métis Rebellion on the northern plains; at this moment, in 1886, he was a fugitive from Canadian justice. Legend surrounded his name. The program notes told how at the age of ten he had demanded a gun to help defend the half-breed camp. He became the best marksman among his people and the winner of countless horse races. As a young chief of the hunt he led the buffalo chase: he had a mysterious power of "calling" buffalo, and his hunters never came home unladen. On every hunt he made a "free run," donating a dozen buffalo to the needy families in his camp. With Louis Riel he had hoped to establish an independent state for his people. But the rebellion was crushed, Riel was captured and hanged, and Gabriel Dumont raced for the border. He rode six hundred miles, eluding hundreds of Canadian pursuers, and gained safety in Montana. Then Major Burke offered him sanctuary and salary with the Wild West show. This "prince of the prairies . . . now in exile from his home and people" spoke fluent French and seven Indian tongues, but he knew no English. An interpreter came with him to the Wild West.

The season opened with 40,000 crowding the fairgrounds, while General Sherman, General Carr, and Governor Phelps of Missouri occupied a decorated box. Burke had warned that this was the last time the Wild West would play in St. Louis: "Lovers of amusement, the family circle, the scholar, the student should attend this farewell." The public took heed; crowds jammed the arena for each performance. Then on a moonlit night in May the engine whistled, a brakeman swung a lantern down the track, the show train pulled away. They were heading east—two days in Terre Haute, two days in Dayton, two days in Wheeling. There, enacting his duel with Yellow Hand, Cody caught a foot in the Indian pony's bridle. Keeping his mount he wrenched free, but after the performance the doctor bent over a foot swelling like a saddlebag.

"First time I was ever downed by an Indian," said the plainsman, reaching for whisky.

With Cody confined to his parlor car the show moved on to Cumberland, Hagerstown, Frederick City. It unloaded in Washington, at the Ivy City Fair Grounds, at daybreak on Memorial Day.

The cowboy band in new red shirts and ten-gallon hats led the parade down the avenues of Washington to the strains of *Marching Through Georgia*. On a stand in front of the White House sat Postmaster General Vilas, representing President Cleveland, and a row of senators and congressmen. Sergeant Bates, marching behind the band wagon, dipped his flag, and the Indians loosed a quaver of war cries toward the house of the Great White Father. During the parade the western sky began to darken, and at noon, while they were streaming into the cook tent, the sun went under. With a roll of thunder the downpour came. Cody, still limping with his week-old sprain, cursed the weather, the luck, the muddy grounds, the whole show business. Nate Salsbury, always apprehensive, stared at the drowned arena. They needed a success in Washington. It was a kind of symbol—the national spectacle in the national capital. Failure in Washington would cast a long shadow.

In streaming slickers the cowboys got their horses saddled. One of the girl riders, mounting a pony in an instant of lightning, was thrown against a fence. They carried her off, rain pelting her white still face. Nate Salsbury pulled at his little beard and trudged through the mud.

As suddenly as it had begun, the rain stopped. Miraculously the clouds opened, and out of a washed blue sky the sun streamed down. A special train pulled up on the B. & O. siding and a thousand people poured out of the cars; down the track another train was waiting. Cody, with Johnnie Baker splashing at his side, came whistling to the headquarters tent. While Johnnie wiped the great man's boots, Cody began to hum: "Tenting tonight, tenting tonight—"

After a triumphant week in Washington they moved to Philadelphia. On June 6th the parade filed through the narrow canyons of Broad and Chestnut streets. Three days later carpenters were making a din at the Belmont Driving Park, adding tiers of seats to accommodate the crowds. Fleets of stages rumbled to the grounds from Arch and Chestnut, from the Centennial Park, from the Zoological Gardens; the Pennsylvania Railroad ran special trains from Broad Street. In two weeks the Wild West played to 200,000 cheering Philadelphians.

High spirits filled the lot, except in the tent that bore the neat placard ANNIE OAKLEY. For a week the heroine of the plains had been fighting a silent battle. During the final performance in Washington, in the midst of her act, a furious buzzing filled her right ear. She took a hand from her rifle and probed the ear with her finger. The buzzing stopped and a boring began. She finished her act and ran off to the crowd's applause. In her tent Frank warmed some water and swabbed the ear with cotton. The pain pierced deeper and her hands clenched white. When the doctor came he could find only a small insect sting. He left sweet oil and cotton, and a deepening, stabbing pain. That night the show moved to Philadelphia.

To Cody and Salsbury Philadelphia meant twenty thousand dollars' profit. To Annie Oakley it meant an agony of pain. Her head throbbing with every pulse beat, she lay in her darkened tent while Frank wrung out cold towels. At show time, tilting the broad hat over her swollen ear, she ran out to the arena. She galloped her pony after the flying targets; with a furious concentration she steadied her hands and cleared her clouded sight and did her shooting. Like a swimmer floundering under water she finished her act. At the gate Frank was waiting. He helped her to the tent and laved the inflamed ear with warm water and Castile soap.

When she heard his soft exclamation she opened her eyes. "What —Jimmy?"

"Look—" In the basin floated a small black insect.

"That tiny, tiny thing?"

"Now you'll feel better. I'll bring a cup of tea."

But she did not feel better. Her head throbbed brutally and she tossed all night with fever. At show time Frank begged her to go to a hospital, and then helped her with her costume. She was in the arena for the fanfare. When Frank Richmond announced "—the peerless woman sharpshooter, in feats of skill and daring, the lovely girl of the plains," her shoulders braced and her hands were steady.

On Sunday, with no performance at the grounds, the Indians were taken on a tour of Philadelphia. That evening Johnnie Baker came into her tent to tell about it. They had seen the cracked Liberty Bell in Independence Hall and had walked the narrow street where Ben Franklin once lived. They had crossed the Delaware on a ferryboat; they had marveled at strange creatures in the zoo. Most impressive of all, they had stood beneath the huge cyclorama of the Battle of Gettysburg. He described the Indians' excitement at the strewn battleground, the life-size men and horses, the vivid bursts of smoke and flame. Annie's mouth tightened. She felt like a battleground herself.

From Philadelphia the show moved to Staten Island, where it would settle for an all-summer stay. At daylight on June 26th they unloaded and in midmorning they got ready for the great New York parade—Indians in paint and feathers, draft horses brushed and curried, the Mexicans in their brightest serapes, cowboys combing out their mustangs' manes. But in Annie Oakley's tent the doctor closed his satchel and shook his head. She must lie quiet for at least three days.

From the tent she heard them scuffle off toward the ferry landing where a chartered boat was waiting. She stared at her costume, laid out and ready—the fringed skirt and jacket, the upturned hat with a silver star, the horse trappings with her name embossed in gold. Across the grounds the band began to play.

With a dressing gown around her she stepped out in the morning sunlight. A wrangler came from the corral, twirling a halter rope. "Saddle my horse!" she cried. Three minutes later her pony raced out of the grounds. She reached the landing as the Deadwood Stage lumbered aboard. She galloped across before the ramp went up. When her pony was tied to the rail she looked up at anxious Frank Butler and beaming John Burke. She smiled back. The pain had suddenly vanished; she could not miss the New York parade.

It was the only parade of the summer, and the longest they would ever make—across Twenty-third Street to Eighth Avenue, up Eighth Avenue to Forty-second, across Forty-second Street to Fifth Avenue, down Fifth Avenue and Broadway to the Battery. They landed at Twenty-third Street and formed into line on the wide stone concourse outside the ferry station. Already the street was filled with people. The band played, Sergeant Bates unfurled his flag, horses stamped and whinnied. Nate Salsbury shrilled a whistle and they moved away. Past miles of sober brownstone housefronts trooped Indians in war paint and eagle feathers. Cowboys rode like conquerors (according to the New York Herald) between the mansions and hotels of Fifth Avenue. The Deadwood Stage creaked and rumbled, the Pony Express dashed up and down the long line of Indians, cowboys, Mexican vaqueros. The streets were walled with "stock-brokers, street gamins, nurse maids, dudes and other such civilized people."

Sitting sidesaddle, shoulders straight, her body rhythmic with the pony's cow-trot, Annie Oakley waved to massed thousands under the trees of Madison Square and tried to forget the throbbing in her head. By that time a swarm of dogs had joined the parade, and an Italian with a monkey and a hand organ was marching in step with Sergeant Bates. Crowds filled the street behind the lumbering stage-coach and followed all the way to the Battery. While the Wild West boarded the ferry, a troop of boys filled the air with war whoops, a woman fainted, a man cried "Stop thief!" and the police arrested three pickpockets. The ferryboat churned off for Staten Island.

Annie Oakley had ridden for three hours in the hot June sun. Now she reined her pony and slid down from the saddle. When she swayed, Frank's arms kept her from falling. That was the last she knew till she looked up in her dressing tent to see the doctor frowning at a clinical thermometer.

"Blood poisoning," he said. When he lanced her ear she fainted.

All day and all night she tossed on the cot while a June wind rustled the Erastina woods. A warm wind. A warm south wind. To her wandering mind came the weather lore of Sitting Bull: the south wind brings sickness, it blows from the land of death. Now the Sioux princess Wan-tan-yeya Ci-sci-la heard the south wind in the branches. It stole into the darkened tent. It lifted her from the cot and carried her away. She was light as thistledown and the soft wind held her. For three days she drifted southward in a huge and empty sky.

But on the fourth day the fever broke and she slept like a child. She woke with clear eyes. "Jimmy—the pain is gone. I'm hungry." The next afternoon, with her hat hiding the white bandage, she dashed into the arena. In six quick shots she put out six candles on a turning wheel. She had missed four shows—the only performances she would miss in seventeen years and 170,000 miles of travel.

CHAPTER 8

Staten Island: Where the West Begins

THE Wild West was at Staten Island under the aegis of the Staten Island Amusement Company whose backers were the capitalist Erastus Wiman and the B. & O. railroadman Robert Garrett. At the new pleasure resort of Erastina Woods they had set up a fifty-acre show lot around a huge arena illuminated for night performances by new electric arc lights. They had chartered a fleet of ferryboats and built four miles of narrow-gauge railroad from Mariners Harbor to the Erastina gateway. They were ready for the crowds, and the crowds came. To Mariners Harbor boats ran from the Battery, Brooklyn, Jersey City, East Newark, Elizabethport, and points along the Hudson. The ferries were jammed from morning to midnight. Performances were held at 12:30 and 7:00 P.M., but visitors wandered all day through the Indian village and around the corrals of buffalo, steers, and wild horses. They could dine at Arden Inn on the beach to concert music from Major Cappa's Seventh Regimental Band, or they could lunch from refreshment booths in the spacious Erastina grounds.

Twenty thousand people filled the stands, half of them framed in a shady grove on the western side of the lot; other thousands spilled out onto the grass. A succession of notables filled the boxes—Governor David Bennett Hill from Albany, Mayor William Russell Grace of New York, Mark Twain of Hartford, Mr. Henry Irving of the London stage, Prince Dom Augusta of Brazil with the Brazilian ambassador and the captain of the visiting warship *Almirante de Barrosa*. Governor Hill was a bachelor, habitually aloof and silent, but when the Deadwood Stage was ambushed he whooped like an Indian. Phineas

77

T. Barnum forgot professional rivalry and praised the Wild West as a unique and magnificent performance; he walked the grounds on a foot bandaged for gout and told reporters, "When Salsbury takes this show to Europe, it will astonish the Old World."

For New Yorkers that season the fabled West lay just across the bay. It was a fine excursion, through the harbor, past Castle Garden swarming with immigrants in peasant caps and kerchiefs, past Bedloe's Island where a massive pedestal was ready to support the Statue of Liberty, past the bristling guns of Castle William and so to Mariners Harbor on the wooded shore. From there it was a short railroad ride to Erastina where the West began. The Black Hills loomed on a huge backdrop, and under them spread the tepees of the Indians. Ponies, mules, steers, elk, and buffalo grazed in hay-strewn enclosures, cowboys lounged in the shade of covered wagons, sombreroed Mexicans rolled cigarettes in the sun. From the target range came the crack of rifle fire and the smell of powder. Indians strolled over the grounds draped in red blankets and checked tablecloths. The children of squaw man John Nelson clung like monkeys to a rope swing under a maple tree. In the oak grove the braves slung red and green hammocks bought at a Staten Island store on their first pay day. They climbed in happily, tore open a box of Cracker Jack, and swung in the dappled shade.

People came again and again, until they knew the Indians by sight and the bucking horses by name and reputation. They peered into the tents—at Annie Oakley's gun trunk, at the saddle Gabriel Dumont had used in his great ride for freedom, at the shriveled scalp of Yellow Hand tacked to the ridgepole above Buffalo Bill's couch. They nodded to Chief American Horse and his small son—"American Colt" the reporters had named him. The stolid little savage said "How," shook hands gravely, and was reported "ready to wrestle any white boy up to the age of four." They speculated on the paternity of a red-haired papoose slung on the back of an Oglala squaw who wore a purple skirt, glass earrings, and a dozen strings of colored beads.

When the stands began to fill, the cowboys roped their horses, the Indians daubed themselves with grease paint, teamsters hitched up the old stagecoach and the covered wagons, Annie Oakley dressed in her shooting costume while Frank Butler loaded her guns. Frank Richmond, tall, deliberate, handsome in his pseudo-frontier clothing, strode across the arena and mounted a rock-like pedestal under the mimic mountains. His voice carried over fifteen acres. *Ladies and Gentlemen: Buffalo Bill and Nate Salsbury proudly present America's national entertainment, the one and only, genuine and authentic, unique and original Wild West Show.* Onto the track came the grand review with twenty-thousand voices cheering.

A repeated visitor that season was Mark Twain, who had his own memories of the wide plains, the swaying stagecoach, and Indian camps under the colored buttes. After his second visit he wrote a letter:

DEAR MR. CODY:

I have now seen your Wild West Show two days in succession, and have enjoyed it thoroughly. It brought vividly back the breezy wild life of the plains and the Rocky Mountains. Down to its smallest details the Show is genuine—cowboys, vaqueros, Indians, stagecoach, costumes and all; it is wholly free from sham and insincerity and the effects it produced upon me by its spectacles were identical with those wrought upon me a long time ago by the same spectacles on the frontier. Your pony express-man was as tremendous an interest to me yesterday as he was twenty-three years ago when he used to come whizzing by from over the desert with his war news; and your bucking horses were even painfully real to me as I rode one of those outrages once for nearly a quarter of a minute. It is often said on the other side of the water that none of the exhibitions which we send to England are purely and distinctively American. If you will take the Wild West Show over there you can remove that reproach.

Yours truly,

MARK TWAIN

Another repeater was Nym Crinkle, a feature writer for the New York *World*. Tall, shambling, profane, he became as plains-struck as any twelve-year-old. He smoked with the Indians, played poker with the cowboys, took a shooting lesson from Annie Oakley, lunched at the beach club with the owners, and began to let his hair grow down to his shoulders. He discovered the West on Staten Island. Even in Nate Salsbury, with clipped dark beard and striped trousers, he saw a hero of the plains. "Nate Salsbury has the color of a golden dusk among the piñon trees and gulches. There are scars on his face and a bunch on his sinewy brown neck where a bullet passed through. He is not a large man, but every motion conveys the idea of solidity and elasticity evenly compounded. So the Sioux, who made him a chief, call him Little Big Man." Buffalo Bill left the reporter almost wordless; he did not attempt a word picture of the hero, but he marveled at his horsemanship. "He fits a saddle as the diamond he wears at his throat fits its setting. He could ride with a cup of water on his head and not spill a drop."

After the evening show Nym Crinkle borrowed a blanket from the cowboys and stretched out on the ground. Vaguely across the arena lifted the cardboard mountains; the smoke of Indian fires sifted toward the stars. He told the readers of the World how it felt: "A bivouac within half an hour of the City Hall, with Buck Taylor, who can stand in the path of any Mexican steer and turn it over by the horns, and listen to Con Groner, the Sheriff of North Platte, who took Jesse James and his gang off a train, and find Bronco Bill, full of bullets, on one side of you, and notorious Doc Middleton on the other, is quite an experience. I could almost hear the chimes of Trinity when I went to bed on the ground under a tepee . . . and caught the whinnying and stamping of Indian ponies in the grove. . . . You can't help fancying that the toot of the absurd Staten Island railroad is the yelping of coyotes."

There was no show on Sunday, but the seventeen ferryboats shuttled across the harbor crowded to the rails. G.A.R. men came to see Sergeant Bates; his tent was a meeting place for veterans endlessly reliving the battle of Shiloh Churchyard and the fight for Missionary Ridge. Lodges of the Benevolent and Protective Order of Elks sent delegations to see the first twin elk calves ever born in captivity. School children trooped through the grounds to see Chief American Horse, the half-breed hero Gabriel Dumont, the one-time desperado Doc Middleton, and the great Buffalo Bill. When the Staten Island church bells sounded through the woods, Sunday Jim Mitchell rounded up a congregation and delivered a sermon under the trees. On one July Sunday his discourse was interrrupted when the buffalo herd broke out of their corral. Sunday Jim leaped onto a pony and headed them back. He finished the sermon on horseback.

All summer newspapermen from New York, Boston, Philadelphia, and Albany were treated by Major Burke to "Indian roasts" and special Western exhibitions. Two chiefs introduced as Red Quilt and Spotted Blanket communicated in sign language while Bronco Bill interpreted. Buffalo Bill gave a demonstration with a twenty-foot bull whip, and a cowboy neatly dropped a lariat over an editor forty feet away. The newsmen went back to their press rooms full of barbecued beef and Western extravagance. "The Wild West," one of them wrote, "has come to New York like a cyclone to a Kansas town. Samson carried off the gates of Gaza, but Buffalo Bill brought the great West to New York."

Major Burke kept the papers supplied with stories—of the dramatic ride of Gabriel Dumont, of shooting records made by Annie Oakley, of the twin elks newly born on the show lot, of how the Wild West Indians ate in one afternoon a wagonload of watermelons, of the visit of an Armenian scholar seeking to prove that American Indians were descended from the Lost Tribes of Israel, of how the Sioux camp bought a Staten Island mongrel for thirty cents and held their annual dog feast under the trees, of a prairie fire now sweeping the grasslands of Buffalo Bill's ranch in Nebraska. He described stampedes of the camp-pent steers and buffalo, furious struggles to saddle the wild horse Dynamite, a midnight scalp dance of Sioux warriors dispersed by Buffalo Bill himself. In another story he told of the warriors attending the Mariners Harbor Baptist Church, joining in the hymns and listening intently to the Reverend Webster R. Maul's sermon.

In mid-July the Canadian government pardoned rebellious Gabriel Dumont. At the news, Arizona John reported, joy went through the Wild West camp like a wind over the prairie. In the exile's tent "tears coursed down Dumont's rough cheeks. When he had somewhat recovered, Messrs. Cody and Salsbury offered to release him from his engagement."

Perhaps Staten Island looked better to Dumont than the plains of Winnipeg. He made a swift renunciation. "No," he declared through his translator, "when I was in exile, without home or shelter, and with but few friends and they unfortunate as myself, you nobly offered me an asylum in your camp, treated me as a brother with kindness, courtesy, and love; and so long as my poor services can be of any use to you, just so long will I remain."

Unfortunately Dumont's pardon diminished the value of his services. Despite the best efforts of a master press agent the public soon lost interest in him. He was paid off, without publicity, and his tent was taken by more newsworthy occupants.

A show-struck Jersey City girl of nineteen haunted the Pawnee village day after day until a brave named Push-a-luck began swinging her in his hammock. When they disappeared together on August 15th, Arizona John had a story. There was a still better story three days later when they returned. They had eloped to Philadelphia, where they were "regularly married by a clergyman." Now, as Mr. and Mrs. John Push-a-luck, they took up residence in the tent vacated by Gabriel Dumont. As though to prove the aptness of their unlikely name, the story concluded: "The bride has some $7,000 in her own right and is respectably connected. She seems happy with her choice."

*   *   *

That summer, while thousands thronged the grounds at Staten Island, a morose and battered little man sat wheezing in an invalid chair in the shadow of the Catskills, a hundred miles away. Soon after Dumont's pardon another news dispatch reached the Wild West camp. Ned Buntline was dead.

That night flamboyant Will Cody sat silent in his tent. Ned Buntline was dead. Without Ned Buntline, Buffalo Bill would have been an unknown name and Will Cody would be in some dusty Kansas town running a livery stable or driving a team of dray horses. When Cody was a tall young plainsman, ignorant of all the world beyond the Indian camps and army stations, Ned Buntline had found him napping under a wagon.

Buntline's real name was Edward Zane Carroll Judson—Colonel Judson, he called himself—but he had used his salty pseudonym as a writer of sea stories based on a brief and inglorious career in the

U.S. Navy. He fought for a season in the Seminole War and again in the Civil War, being discharged with a record "thoroughly discreditable" in 1864. By that time the West was the drama of America. Covered wagons rocked over the California and Colorado trails, the pony express raced from Sacramento to Omaha, cowboys were driving Texas cattle to the northern ranges. Capitalists from New York and London invested in the cattle business, railroad and telegraph lines were reaching across the plains, thousands of homestead families pounded corner stakes into the buffalo sod. So, versatile Ned Buntline turned to writing Western stories, dime novels of the badmen and heroes of the plains.

In 1869 he rode the Union Pacific to Nebraska for fresh material. He got off the train at North Platte, wearing twenty medals of lodges and secret societies he had formed, and boarded the stage for Fort McPherson, eighteen miles away. As he wandered around the post some soldiers thought he was drunk, though he was merely limping with injuries from his hair-breadth past. He soon found material; he found Will Cody asleep under a supply wagon, and when the young giant got up, long-haired, handsome, nonchalant, the novelist recognized a prince of the plains. When he saw him ride a wild horse and learned that he had been a buffalo hunter for the railroad camps, his mind began racing with unwritten stories. A prodigious legend was in the making.

Back in New York Ned Buntline poured out tales of the prowess and valor of Buffalo Bill, while Cody lounged around Fort McPherson waiting for some assignment that would net him a dollar a day. The railroad was built, the buffalo were vanishing, the Indians were quiet on their reservations; he thought of going to Kansas City or St. Louis, where he might become a coachman or the driver of a fire engine. But in Ned Buntline's thrillers Buffalo Bill was back in the years of glory and danger—leading the wagon train past an ambush, fighting the wily Sioux, strewing the ground with shaggy buffalo.

When Buntline wrote a drama, *Buffalo Bill: King of the Border Men*, he urged Cody to come to New York. At his appearance in the Bowery Theater the house shook with applause. Next season Ned

Buntline presented Buffalo Bill himself in *The Scouts of the Plains*, and crowds were turned away. The showman's career was started.

On a summer afternoon while Buffalo Bill galloped past the packed stands at Staten Island, Ned Buntline sat in a wheel chair writing his final serial. "It will be a grand story, full of mystery, the best I have ever written." He was ill, his old wounds were aching, he was in debt. It never took him long to do a novel (he once wrote 610 pages in 62 hours) but he did not live to finish this one. While Buffalo Bill rode to the rescue of the settler's wife and children, the sun was dropping over the high ridge of the Catskills a hundred miles away. As the shadow crept across his window Ned Buntline's pen dropped from his hand.

*   *   *

When Annie Oakley, driving on a Sunday afternoon through Staten Island, saw a swarm of children behind the iron fence of an orphanage, she stopped and left a message; she had not forgotten the drab life of the Darke County Home. Next day she reined her pony at the far end of the stands and waved her hat to fifty special guests. For a moment the orphans' shrill voices drowned out the cowboy band. That was good copy for the press, and Major Burke quickly sent free tickets to the orphans for miles around. "Annie Oakley Day" was a combined Fourth of July and Christmas; the orphans went home with their stomachs full and their heads swimming.

Toward the end of summer Nym Crinkle brought a friend to the Wild West, introducing him to everyone in sight. It was Steele Mac-Kaye, playwright and theatrical producer. MacKaye, who had a professional eye for drama of any kind, was fascinated by the skill, verve, and audacity of the Wild West performance. After the show he told Nate Salsbury there was nothing like it in the world.

Over glasses of whisky around a barbecue pit, he talked with Cody. They were a striking pair, dark slight intense Steele MacKaye, like a later Edgar Allan Poe, and showman Cody in his Western splendor. They quickly found common ground. They agreed on the quality of the whisky, on the historical significance of the Wild West exhibition, and on the American manner of riding horseback—both scorned the English "rise in the saddle." In riding, Cody declared, a man should be a horseman, not a man-on-a-horse. Nym Crinkle scribbled that in his notebook while MacKaye declared that there were endless new possibilities in the enactment of Western history. "What a spectacle it would be!" His dark eyes flashed and his nervous hands kept working as he described its effect on a vast stage where it could play all winter. He could see it in Madison Square Garden—the Drama of Civilization!

His rhapsody was interrupted by the call to supper, but throughout the meal Nate Salsbury was at his side, asking about indoor staging, lighting, seating capacity, and quarters for men and animals. After the feast Chiefs Red Shirt and American Horse talked in sign language which MacKaye found beautiful, graceful, poetic, and thoroughly intelligible. He left the grounds reluctantly, promising to see the show again.

Before the end of the season newspapers were reporting details of the Wild West as though it were a vital and eventful province of America. A widely circulated political cartoon showed "The Democratic Stage Coach Chased" by Indians and attacking newspapers. It was the hectic time of Grover Cleveland's first administration, after his defeat of James G. Blaine. On July 28th *Judge* ran a famous double-page cartoon in color—"Our Political Wild East," showing the race of the stagecoach, the scalping, the burning at the stake, and long-haired horsemen pounding down the presidential trail. The Wild West had become an American institution.

CHAPTER 9

Custer's Last Stand—In Madison Square Garden

> A visit to the Madison Square Garden will speedily
> convince everyone that . . . there is as wide a gulf
> between the "Wild West" and the Circus as there is be-
> tween a historic poem and the advertisement of a quack
> medicine.   —STEELE MACKAYE

IN September, 1886, Steele MacKaye, dramatist and producer, was in
St. Louis preparing an "oration" to accompany the exhibition of Matt
Morgan's War Pictures. That was a tame assignment, despite the
size of the Morgan panorama; there were twelve paintings, each 45
feet long and 27 feet high, showing in dramatic detail the crucial
battles of the Civil War. After a stint of writing in his room at the
Southern Hotel, MacKaye walked restlessly down to the riverfront
where Matt Morgan, at the top of a ladder in a warehouse smelling
of tobacco, tar, and turpentine, was putting some final touches on
the Shiloh churchyard.

Steele MacKaye liked St. Louis, the big, bustling river city with its
air of distant commerce. In the terminals and on the landings were
men just in from New Orleans, from Denver, from Fort Worth,
Cincinnati, and St. Paul. The palatial *Cape Girardeau* and the *J. M.
White*, with brasswork bright and chimneys smoking, towered above
lesser craft on the levee. The M.K.T. flyer stood panting in the

Wild West parade, Broadway and Union Square, New York City, 1884. Cody on white horse, Nate Salsbury in top hat at right.

En route to England. The Wild West on shipboard, 1887. Buck Taylor and Cody front row center, Annie Oakley and Frank Butler third row right.

Annie Oakley—Little Sure Shot—
as she appeared in her first season with the Wild West.

smoky canopy of the station. Past the city rolled the Old Big Deep Strong River, the timeless Mississippi that began in the dark northern woods of Minnesota, and the Big Muddy swung in from the west, from the distant country of the Little Big Horn and the Yellowstone. St. Louis was a crossroads and a meeting of rivers. Once, clumsy dugouts filled with honey and bear grease and pirogues piled with baled beaver skins had steered to the river landing; bull whips had cracked from the seat of the great Santa Fe wagons. Now log rafts, big as a baseball field, came down from Wisconsin; long trains of grain and cattle cars pulled in from the Western plains. St. Louis had big rivers, huge energies, a feel of distance.

Even its art was prodigious. Forty years before, in a St. Louis warehouse John Banvard had painted a Mississippi panorama advertised as three miles long. His huge reels of canvas showed the varied shores of the great river—Indian villages and squatters' cabins, bold wooded bluffs and prairie grasslands, trading posts and river cities. He took that panorama on a triumphant tour, unrolling it before exclaiming audiences in New York, London, Paris. Banvard's success was followed by other mammoth paintings of the wonders of the West. And now an Englishman, Matthew Somerville Morgan, who had come to America five years after the meeting of Grant and Lee at Appomattox (he painted them eighteen feet tall), was perched on a ladder touching up "Shiloh—Second Day," where the wounded lay in mounds of dead leaves under a shell-blasted poplar tree. Steele MacKaye would soon have his orotund explication ready ("Nelson's Division on right of Picture—at the rear of Grant—who sits in solitude—Sphinx-like—deserted by all") and they could begin their travels. MacKaye had agreed to a tour of thirty-five weeks at $150 weekly.

But something better happened. Back at the hotel MacKaye found a letter from Nate Salsbury, business manager of Buffalo Bill's Wild West which MacKaye and Morgan had visited at Staten Island during the recent summer. Salsbury and Cody wanted MacKaye to stage the Wild West at Madison Square Garden for the winter season. This was a real assignment—not a commentary to read in front of a roll of canvas, but the shaping of the Wild West's color, vitality, and power into a dramatic spectacle. MacKaye hurried back to the riverfront. He quickly persuaded Matt Morgan, already a little bored with Missionary Ridge and Shiloh Churchyard, to paint a Badlands panorama for the Wild West. So they left the Battles of the Civil War and took the train to New York.

*   *   *

On the north side of Madison Square, facing Twenty-sixth Street between Fourth and Madison avenues, there stood in 1870 the depot of the old Harlem and New Haven Railroad. When the tracks were moved the depot was converted into an amusement hall called Gilmore's Concert Garden. It featured band concerts on summer evenings for patrons seated at tables amid the greenery of tubbed ferns and potted palms. In 1880 a spacious stage was built on the Fourth Avenue side to accommodate large ballets and dramatic spectacles; it then became Madison Square Garden. The building still looked like a railroad station. A square tower at the corner dominated an acre of flat roof; round windows like a liner's portholes were spaced along the sides. Inside, a U-shaped gallery enclosed a riding ring and a huge arena.

Madison Square itself was a central point in the city, surrounded by theaters, hotels, and clubs. In the wooded park an elaborate bird house, upheld by four pillars and resembling a small Burmese temple, housed a noisy flock of English sparrows recently brought to New York to combat the caterpillar moth. In 1876 the right arm of Bartholdi's Goddess of Liberty was unloaded from a French steamer and set up on the Fifth Avenue side of the Square; the huge stone hand rose higher than the shade trees, holding aloft the symbolic torch. With the cheerful sounds of traffic around them people strolled through the little park, admiring the fountain with its rhythm of falling waters, marveling at the massive fragment of Liberty, throwing bread to the pigeons that fluttered along the paths. Two towers rose on opposite sides of the square—the tapered spire of Dr. Parkhurst's church and the square white tower of the Madison Square Garden. Nearby, on West Twenty-third Street, was the Eden Musée, then featuring Ajeeb the automatic Chess Player and Prince Lichtenstein's Hungarian Gypsy Band along with some new wax figures of the Chicago anarchists. Fashionable shops lined Broadway below Twenty-third Street. Across from Madison Square Garden stood the famous old Fifth Avenue Hotel, preserving its long tradition. Just north of it rose the marble fronts of the Albemarle Hotel and the Hoffman House. The Brunswick, at Fifth Avenue and Twenty-sixth Street, was famous for its bird and game dinners and its matchless wine list. Across the avenue stood Delmonico's magnificent new restaurant.

While the Wild West took to the road for an autumn season in Chicago and the river towns of Iowa and Illinois, Steele MacKaye and Matt Morgan checked in at the Union Square Hotel and went to work at the Garden. They worked at night because Adam Forepaugh was holding a horse show at the Garden; he would not vacate till mid-November.

Adam Forepaugh, notable circus man, had gone west from Philadelphia at twenty. In Cincinnati he began dealing in horses; during the next twenty years he supplied teams for the horsecar lines in New York and for many of the two hundred circuses then roving the country. When he furnished horses to the Johnny O'Brien Circus he took half-interest in the show in payment. So he became a circus man himself, featuring the famous clown Dan Rice, the trick horse Excelsior, and a herd of trained Burmese cattle. On tour Adam Forepaugh, huge, red-faced, with flying side whiskers, sat in his open pavilion before the big tent booming a welcome at visitors and friends. He had a menagerie in New York, and Steele MacKaye arranged to borrow some antelope, elk, and a couple of trained bears to animate the opening scene in his Wild West spectacle.

While the horse show was on, MacKaye and Morgan worked in the roomy loft above the huge arena. They bought wagon loads of canvas, tons of paint, huge coils of rope and wire. Morgan painted a backdrop that would dwarf his Civil War Battles—he covered 15,000 square yards of canvas with a sweep of sagebrush plain breaking into colored buttes and badlands. Two years before, MacKaye had lighted the Lyceum Theater by electricity, to the wonder of all New York; now he bossed a crew of workmen installing light towers, spot and flood lights, and moving screens of light. He hired an ingenious mechanic, Nelse Waldron, to build a cyclone machine in the old Stevens car shops across Twenty-seventh Street, leading the wind tunnel underground to the Garden.

MacKaye was restless, exhilarated, never tiring. He worked all night at the Garden and then hurried back to the hotel to write long letters to Nate Salsbury and to elaborate his scenario of the Wild West's "Drama of Civilization." Salsbury doubted that MacKaye could produce a convincing cyclone. MacKaye was so confident that he sent wagons to the Westchester woods to bring in tons of leaves, brush, and branches for his underground wind to scatter.

Meanwhile the torch of Liberty had been removed from Madison Square. On October 26, 1886, in an all-day downpour of autumn rain President Cleveland, with M. Bartholdi and his Cabinet ministers beside him, stood at Madison Square reviewing a procession five miles long. When that sodden parade had passed down Broadway to the Battery a fleet of three hundred vessels made another procession in the North River. President Cleveland and his party crossed the rain-blurred lower harbor to Bedloe's Island. There the Statue of Liberty —a gift of the people of France on the hundredth anniversary of American independence—was dedicated, and its torch shone out in the rainy autumn dusk. The scheduled display of fireworks was postponed until the first clear evening.

It was an eventful autumn in New York. In November Henry M. Stanley arrived with trunks full of souvenirs from Central Africa. After speeches by Chauncey Depew, Lieutenant Adolphus Greely, explorer of the Arctic, and Whitelaw Reid, Stanley told the members of the Lotus Club how he had found Dr. Livingstone in the heart of the Dark Continent and had made treaty rights with four hundred native chiefs in the forests of the Congo. At the Metropolitan Opera House, Albert Niemann and Lilli Lehmann were rehearsing the title roles for the first American performance of Tristan and Isolde. Theodore Roosevelt had just been defeated in a hectic campaign for the New York mayor's office. Everywhere, from the hotels on Fifth Avenue to waterfront taverns on West Street, men were talking about the

"Arcade"—a projected underground railroad which promised to transport people from the Battery to Harlem River at forty miles an hour.

*   *   *

In that vibrant season Cody and Salsbury arrived in town with their Indians and cowboys, their stagecoach and covered wagons, their steers and buffalo and broncos. The November days were crisp and short. In the chilly dusk horses pounded the pavement, wagons rumbled past, cabs and carriages pulled up at the hotels, people streamed down Fifth Avenue and Broadway to the warm lights of restaurants and cafés. And Annie Oakley, walking through Madison Square with all the tiers of windows lighted and the murmur of the avenue filling the autumn dark, knew that no city in the world held such exhilaration.

The Wild West Indians made their camp at Erastina Woods on Staten Island; they would be commuters during the winter season. Cody, Salsbury, and press agent Burke occupied hotel suites; the cowboys and Mexicans bunked in a side-street rooming house. Annie Oakley and her husband took an apartment in a brownstone front on Murray Hill. After months of tent life on the show grounds, that was like going home. They had their own friendly living room with a fire of cannel coal, their own deep-silled windows looking on the restless city. They could make their own breakfast coffee in their own kitchen and have their friends for tea or sherry while the gaslights brightened in the dusky street.

Night and day the Show was in preparation. After Adam Forepaugh removed his horses, Steele MacKaye took possession of the Garden. Even on Sundays his workmen filled the amphitheater with the clatter of hammers and the rumble of drays. High up under the roof he had his men installing rigging lofts and panorama grooves. On the huge floor Waldron and his carpenters assembled the set pieces. Perched on extension ladders Matt Morgan and his crew painted mimic mountains on semicircular screens forty feet high and half a block long. Over the whole arena strode disheveled Steele MacKaye with frock-coated Nate Salsbury beside him.

Every afternoon MacKaye turned from the construction crews and became a stage director. He drilled the Indians and cowboys in a sequence of episodes. He placed the actors on the enormous stage and led them through their parts. While paint was drying on the sets and the huge scenery was being hung, he put the whole Show through its last rehearsal. On Wednesday night, November 27th, the eve of Thanksgiving, came the grand opening.

Through the November weeks press agent Burke had been busy with his own preparation. Despite the Statue of Liberty, the political campaign, and Stanley of Africa, he kept the papers filled with news of the Wild West. "At the Madison Square Garden Mr. Matt Morgan is painting a picture half a mile long and fifty feet high. Mr. Morgan puts in mountains whole, and the chief criticism made by finical art critics is that his valleys are larger than the original. The artist swung in a chair-scaffold, yesterday, away up in the roof of the Garden. At this dizzy height he was painting the top of a California redwood tree. He limned a crow on one of the topmost boughs at such an airy pinnacle that the bird took fright, and almost fell into the middle distance." He described MacKaye's rehearsal of the Sioux, the Pawnees, the Comanches, and the Crows; he told of smoldering hostility between the tribesmen, held in check only by the power and authority of the imposing Buffalo Bill. He recounted the unfading devotion of Chief Sitting Bull, recently with the Wild West, for Annie Oakley and recalled that when the chief had been angry only the soft-spoken girl could quiet his storms of violence; then Annie Oakley, fearless horsewoman and matchless rifle shot, went back to the reading of her New Testament. Major Burke even wrote a sketch of himself as a Western desperado who had killed fifteen men. He reported festive dinners given to Buffalo Bill by New York capitalists whom he had guided on a Dakota buffalo hunt ten years before; the guests included Colonel Bob Ingersoll, Admiral Harbaran of the French Navy, Roscoe Conkling, the Honorable Amos Cummings, Leonard Jerome, owner of the great racehorse Kentucky, and the Marquis de Mores who had waged a cattle war with Teddy Roosevelt in the Dakota badlands. He wrote that Nate Salsbury, hater of circuses, was determined to make the Wild West the most educational and uplifting entertainment ever offered to the American people.

*   *   *

On opening night nine thousand spectators streamed into the Garden, crowding the huge galleries to the roof. In the boxes sat Henry Ward Beecher, General William Tecumseh Sherman, Erastus Wiman, Pierre Lorillard, August Belmont, General Philip H. Sheridan, and the widow of General Custer. The overhead beams were draped with flags and bunting, the arena floor was covered with fresh tanbark. From a side stage the cowboy band, in big hats, chaps, and spurs, played a medley of popular tunes. The music faded, the lights went dim. A ghostly clatter of hoofs filled the vast hall and from the looming mountains came the rich voice of Buffalo Bill: LADIES AND GENTLEMEN: THE WILD WEST PRESENTS THE UNIQUE AND UNPARALLELED SPECTACLE OF WESTERN LIFE AND HISTORY—THE DRAMA OF CIVILIZATION!

Swinging spotlights, dramatic as a prairie sunset, picked out a group of riders in the scenic entrance. They loped across the plain and pulled up under a purple butte. One spotlight held them there while another swung back to a file of cowboys on half-wild mustangs, then to a band of Mexican vaqueros, and at last to a party of painted Sioux on shaggy ponies. Each raced around the arena and pulled up at the far end. LADIES AND GENTLEMEN: THE WILD WEST PRESENTS THE LOVELY LASS OF THE WESTERN PLAINS, LITTLE SURESHOT, THE ONE AND ONLY ANNIE OAKLEY. The spotlight found her, tiny, graceful, alive, eye-catching and breath-catching on a calico pony under the colored mountains; it raced with her across the tanbark plain. Now came the voice of Frank Richmond, master of ceremonies—LADIES AND GENTLEMEN: THE WILD WEST PRESENTS THE GREAT PLAINSMAN, THE GREAT HUNTER, THE GREAT INDIAN FIGHTER, THE GREATEST SCOUT OF THE OLD WEST—BUFFALO BILL! Amid fanfare the majestic plainsman galloped across the arena and halted his white horse on hind legs, forefeet in the air. The spotlight glittered on silver bridle, spurs, and silver-mounted saddle. The horse, famed Charlie of the buffalo chase, bowed on one knee while Cody swept his Stetson from his flowing hair.

Now the MacKaye "scenario" began. Silence and shadow held the empty plain; then the lights came up like sunrise, showing a "Primeval Forest" with bear, antelope, and elk grazing at its edge. Into the scene trotted two bands of Indians. They joined in a friendly dance, which ended abruptly with the attack of a hostile tribe. In silence the savages fought with bows and arrows, stone hatchets and stone-tipped spears. The lights dimmed on a battleground strewn with dead and dying redmen.

Then came the first interlude, and the first gunfire. Around the ring on an Indian pony raced Annie Oakley, in her fringed skirt and flowered deerskin jacket, shattering targets thrown in the air by a companion rider. She leapt to the ground, seized a rifle from her gun stand, and broke five glass balls thrown simultaneously into the air. She vaulted over the stand, swung a new gun to her shoulder, and shot the flames off a revolving wheel of candles. She was all swiftness, grace, and magic, on horseback and afoot. When she made her quick little curtsy and ran from the ring on twinkling feet, the roof shook with applause. And the Wild West's first indoor audience had been reassuringly introduced to the sound of firearms. The rest of the Show would blaze and crackle.

Scene two opened with the coming of settlers—an emigrant train plodding across the prairie, the wagons pulling into a circle for the night camp. It was a peaceful scene till the Indians came whooping. The whirr of arrows was answered by the rattle of rifles. The Indians fell back, but another peril followed. As sunset faded over the plain a lurid light began. The wagonmaster cried the alarm—*Prairie fire!* Up in MacKaye's light towers the crews worked swiftly, and on the mimic plain the fire came racing. Frantically the teams were caught, the camp dismantled. The prairie schooners rocked away, followed by antelope, elk, and buffalo. The whole prairie was on fire behind them.

After an interlude—cowboys and cowgirls in a Virginia reel on horseback—the floodlights showed a cattle ranch with cowboys roping, riding, skylarking around the dusty corral. Into that careless scene crept the painted Indians. The attack was stealthy; they caught the owboys off guard and helpless. But while they bound their captives heir victorious war whoops drowned a drumming of hoofbeats. With a blaze of gunfire Buffalo Bill and his scouts raced in. A dozen avages lay sprawled in the dust and the rest ran back to the Badlands.

In the next interlude young Johnnie Baker, in an oversized cow-oy hat, did some acrobatic shooting, and a Mexican worked magic vith a lariat. Then the band swung into *Garry Owen*, the marching ong of the Seventh Cavalry—Custer's regiment. A screen of light howed the rolling grasslands of the Little Big Horn, with Custer's nen fighting off a ring of howling Sioux. They tightened their circle and the Sioux crept closer. Firing from behind dead horses, rushing n with drawn blades when their guns were empty, the Indians cut lown the doomed regiment. At the end one man was left standing, George Armstrong Custer, played by the long-haired King of the Cowboys, Buck Taylor. He fell under a rain of bullets and the furious battleground was still. The Indians moved from one grotesque form to another, taking their last grim trophies. When they were gone the strewn field was as silent as in all the aeons of the geologic past. But a muffled hoofbeat sounded and a lone rider halted a foam-flecked horse. The spotlight held him on the littered field while on the back-drop mountains a light screen spelled the words Too LATE. The greatest scout of the Old West bared his head among the fallen, and the scene went dark. Custer had made his last stand.

After a group of Indians had performed the grass dance, the rain dance, the antelope dance, the scenario's final scene showed a mining camp in the Rocky Mountains. To the relay station raced the Pony Express, a dusty rider on a frothing horse. The mailbags were slung onto a new mount; with a staccato of hoofs the rider raced away, toward St. Joe or Sacramento. Then a teamster's voice rang out and wagon wheels sounded; up the rocky road rumbled the storied old Deadwood stage. Bandits lay in ambush. With a volley of pistol fire they halted the six-mule team and cut them loose from the traces. They shot the passengers and carried off the treasure. But at that moment the sky darkened. A howling wind began and a frantic voice cried "Cyclone!" Tumbleweed fled by and a storm of leaves and brush swept the arena. Tents tore loose from their guy ropes and fluttered in the air. As the wind moved on to the painted hills a desolate night fell over the lifeless plain.

When, according to MacKaye's light cue, the lights came up again, the whole Wild West company, soldiers and cowboys, Indians and Mexicans, were assembled, with tiny Annie Oakley smiling beside long-haired Buffalo Bill. An ovation shook the rafters where the light crew mopped their streaming faces. The winter season had begun with triumph.

*   *   *

The next day was Thanksgiving. In the family party in the private box of Steele MacKaye one of the matinee spectators was eleven-year-old Percy MacKaye. He forgot the recent excitement of a turkey dinner at the long table in the household on Lexington Avenue. For two hours he lived in the far-off Badlands, amid Indians, scouts, and cowboys, and at the end, still staring at the colored buttes, he asked, "When can I come again?"

That winter Percy MacKaye, who would write his own dramas in years to come, lived a double life—part New York schoolboy and part plainsman. After school he haunted the Badlands of Madison Square, hearing the cowboys' stories, learning the names of the bucking horses, gravely saying "How" to the Indians and "Amigo" to the Mexicans. Annie Oakley showed him how to point a pistol without sighting, and Buffalo Bill gave him a battered cowboy hat. At home in the back parlor on Lexington Avenue, with his seven-year-old brother Benton, he produced a Wild West of his own, where Steele MacKaye paid twenty-five cents for a front-row chair. Years later he wrote, "During that autumn and winter the compelling life of the Wild West totally filled my imagination."

Another frequent visitor to the Madison Square Badlands was Denman Thompson, whose new stage hit The Old Homestead would delight the public for the next twenty-five years. After the show he waited with Frank Butler, and when Annie came up from the dressing room he led them off to dinner, stopping to buy her a bunch of violets from the maudlin old German woman on the corner. Over the lamp-

it table, eating breast of quail and wild rice, he could not ask enough
about Annie Oakley's life: Had she truly shot game for Cincinnati
hotels and paid the mortgage on her mother's homestead before she
was fourteen? He had grown up on a New Hampshire farm, and he
traded memories of Cheshire County and Monadnock Mountain for
the Ohio girl's memories of North Star township and the deep
timber of Darke County. At sixteen he had left the New England
fields to travel with a circus; they had tales of tent life to exchange.
Denman Thompson looked like his rustic character "Josh Whitcomb"—ruddy, stout, slow-moving, with bald head softened by a
fringe of snowy hair, long ears, fine gray eyes under frosty brows, a
deep slow voice. He was a set and settled man, kindly but with a
strain of skepticism and a tinge of melancholy. He was vastly unlike
the stolid Sitting Bull, but in his way he too adopted the soft-spoken
girl with wide gray eyes and a sudden, suffusing smile. He became
Annie's lifelong friend.

Playing under a roof made a difference in the Wild West company. They were closer to the audience, and closer to applause.
There was more individual performance. And so began rivalries—a
new thing in the Show. Buck Taylor rode after the Indians, but
also after the applause of nine thousand spectators, and when he
stole a scene or lingered in the spotlight Cody began to grumble.
Annie Oakley felt the electric tension of the crowd. To those enchanted thousands she was the Western girl—the maid swaying on
the wagon seat framed in the canvas canopy, the young wife watching
with hand-shaded eyes from the door of a sod house on the prairie,
the new school ma'am coming West in the stagecoach, the rancher's
daughter commanding chivalry from uncouth men. Fearless yet
feminine, she was the girl of the plains. Annie Moses of Darke
County, Ohio, had become Annie Oakley of the sunset, of the great
plains and the shining mountains, of the prairie campfires and the
square dances in the mining towns. She was the girl singing in the
rough choir stall of the new frame church, the girl with the ribboned
box supper at the schoolhouse social, the girl of the golden West.
In that realization she rode with grace and daring; her gun was magic

in her small firm hands. And when she ran off with a tumult o
applause she saw the petulance in Cody's handsome face.

For the first time they were rivals. On the road the outfit had lived
together; now they were scattered. Outside the arena they had thei
own life and their own friends, and in the drama of the Wild Wes
they bowed to individual applause. When Custer's widow asked
Annie Oakley to join her in her box, when Denman Thompso
waited outside her dressing room, the Greatest Scout of the Old
West sulked like a schoolboy. After the Show he mended his vanit
with admiration and rye whisky in the glittering Hoffman Hous
bar. If the Wild West was immortal drama, as Major Burke adve
tised, it was made up of mortal actors.

*   *   *

While Custer fought his daily desperate battle in the Garden
Elizabeth Bacon Custer lived just a mile down Fifth Avenue, in a
Greenwich Village flat near Washington Square. She had consulted
with MacKaye during rehearsals; she sat in the owners' box on the
opening night and at many other performances. Backstage she be
came a familiar figure in her short tailored jacket and feathered hat
moving among the Indians and hunters as she had done at For
Lincoln on the wild Missouri. Two women in the masculine back
stage setting drew together, and Annie Oakley instinctively under
stood a widow's poignant feeling at the daily drama of her husband's
death. Elizabeth Custer was living intensely in the West, though he
summers were spent at Delaware Water Gap and her winters in a
narrow street off Fifth Avenue. Just a year before, she had published
Boots and Saddles; or Life With General Custer in Dakota; thi
winter she was writing another book, *Tenting on the Plains.* Now
Annie Oakley, adopted daughter of Sitting Bull whose triumph was
the Seventh Cavalry's disaster, sat with the woman whom the Sioux
chief had made a widow. The buffalo plains, which she had never
seen, had become the country of her kinships and emotions.

In a brownstone house, over Annie Oakley's tea table, or in the
candle-lit flat in Greenwich Village, the two women had much to

hare. George Armstrong Custer had been an Ohio youth, and Elizabeth Bacon had grown up a hundred miles from Darke County, just
over the Ohio border in Michigan. She had married the gallant
"Autie," already at twenty-five a brigadier general in command of
he Michigan Volunteer Cavalry, between fierce battles in 1864; all
her married life had been shadowed and exalted by hazardous
campaigns.

She had gone with Custer to the Indian frontier, first to Kansas
in 1866 and then to Dakota when gold was discovered in the sacred
Black Hills of the Sioux. She had lived with him in wagon, tent, and
barracks. She had ridden at his side on antelope hunts, her horse
matching strides with his powerful Phil. She had watched him ride
away at the head of his column while the band played *The Girl I Left
Behind Me*, and she had waited at Fort Abraham Lincoln for his
return from the Little Big Horn. The band always played *Garry Owen*
on his arrival from the field. But that July day in 1876 there was no
music; and she had not heard *Garry Owen* again until the Wild West
came to Madison Square. At Gettysburg and in the Virginia campaign his men had talked of "Custer's luck." It failed him on the
Little Big Horn when the troops rode off toward Sitting Bull's warriors. Now, in the New York winter two thousand miles from the
buffalo plains, it rushed over her like a wind on those prairies. For
Annie Oakley, sharing that valor and sorrow while snow sifted down
in the city twilight, the Last Stand of Custer became almost as
personal as a memory.

Elizabeth Custer had seen Annie Oakley's dressing room with the
little touches that made it pleasant and personal. That recalled her
own tent life on the plains and the succession of garrison quarters
where she had made a home for her husband. As Mrs. Custer talked,
Annie could see the tall lean soldier, blue eyes set in his wind-burned
face that never toughened, his long mustache and flowing hair. He
was the dashing cavalry commander who loved action and danger,
but there was another nature in him. In lonely posts on the plains
he unpacked his trunk of books and trimmed the wick of his study
lamp. His mind could range over ideas and reflections as well as
over the strategy of war. In the iron winter, when snow swirled over

the frozen country, he turned to his books. On gray afternoons Libby
filled the teapot and the firelight brightened as dusk came on. They
read aloud *The Life of Daniel Webster* and *The Campaigns of
Napoleon* while the wind brought a quavering of wolves.

On the reservations the army quartermasters had built log houses
for the Indians, but the Sioux would not move from their tepees; they
had observed that people began coughing when they lived in a
house. Custer respected their choice and left them crouching around
their fires. When spring came he made a tour of the scattered camps
concerned where there was hunger or sickness. From these trips he
often brought home a pet to add to his collection at the commandant's
cottage at Fort Lincoln. He had a badger, a porcupine, a raccoon,
a prairie dog, a wild turkey with a broken wing. There was even a
field mouse that nested in an empty inkwell on his desk; it ran up
his arms and perched on his shoulders while he did his paper work.
Once, on a blowing April day when all the doors of the sky were
open and the grass rippled like water to the horizon, he carried the
mouse in his pocket and set it free on the prairie. The next day it
was back in the cottage, curled up in the general's inkwell.

In those outposts, while the seasons changed on the great prairie,
they talked of life back in "the States"—of friends in Michigan and
Ohio, of the home they would have after the wars were past. There
would be a room with books and lamplight at the top of the house;
it would have no staircase but only a ladder that could be drawn
up after them. They talked about growing old in an old and quiet
town where trees would arch the street, where the wind would
rustle autumn leaves and lamplight would warm the windows. But
"Autie" never had those years to spend.

That winter in New York, Custer made his last stand to the
applause of a million people, and each time he fell among the dead
it was more than a spectacle to Annie Oakley. She had come to
know him.

*   *   *

It was a season of friendship, festivity, discovery. To Annie's
dressing room came baskets of flowers and letters of invitation. There

were suppers with Denman Thompson, Mark Twain, A. C. Wheeler ("Nym Crinkle" of the New York World), James Gordon Bennett, Alexander Graham Bell. And always there was the city—soft snow blurring the gray buildings, the violet dusk coming on and the gas-lights gleaming, hansom cabs *clop-clop-clopping* through the streets, past the Battery, the wide gray sea-mouth opening, and the big ships sheathed in ice after a stormy crossing, church bells ringing, the sudden thunder of trains on the iron lattice of the Elevated, the cries of newsboys, the policeman's whistle, the lifted voices of the street singers.

One snowy morning with the city newly white and sleigh bells jingling, while Frank was recalling his Ireland boyhood, Annie jumped up from the breakfast table. "Let's take a sleigh ride, Jimmy!"

Over to the Garden they went. In the stalls the horses whickered and stamped and watched with pointed ears. But Annie passed on to the stall of Jerry, the tall tame moose. She stood on tiptoe and stroked his powerful neck; he lowered his hairy muzzle and sniffed at her hand. When she opened the gate he followed her like an enormous puppy. Frank threw the harness over him. The bells rang as he lumbered out where the snow was falling. When the sleigh was ready Frank lifted her up and then settled in beside her, under the buffalo robe. Annie's eyes were spilling light and two spots of color glowed in her cheeks. She took the reins. "Come on, Jerry."

Off they moved to a jangle of bells. Jerry lifted his head with its branched enormous antlers. He smelled the chilly air. Snow lay deep in the little park, and around the Square gray buildings lifted like fading hills into the snowy sky. Jerry threw back his head and trumpeted, a long wild bellowing cry that halted people on the sidewalks and stopped the traffic on Fifth Avenue. Then he broke into a headlong run. The bells jangled, jangled, and the sleigh raced through the snowy streets. Cab drivers pulled their horses to the curb. From the upper deck of an omnibus sleigh people waved and shouted.

They turned into Twenty-first Street and the bells rang back from the shop fronts. At Sixth Avenue Jerry halted beside a pedler's push-cart decorated with sprays of mistletoe and laurel. With one sweep of his huge muzzle he denuded the cart and chewed up the greenery. Two minutes later he swallowed the last of the vendor's apples.

Frank managed to find his wallet. "Here's five dollars," he said. "Take it before—" Jerry threw back his head and trumpeted.

They were off again, past amazed shoppers and whooping children, past wondering teamsters and startled drivers of horsecars. When they pulled up at Madison Square, Annie's eyes were shining.

"Isn't it fun, Jimmy! Isn't New York wonderful! Isn't Jerry a darling!"

"Jerry," said Frank, "is snow-crazy."

They rocked with laughter in the falling snow.

*   *   *

The winter passed quickly—the gala, triumphant season. In the streets, in hotels, in restaurants, people pointed out the Wild West actors—"There's Buck Taylor, King of the Cowboys, the tall dark man with long hair. There's Buffalo Bill, the big handsome man with the goatee. See the diamond in his cravat. That's Annie Oakley, the tiny girl in the trim fur hat. That's her husband with her, Frank Butler, the big smiling ruddy man."

Even the Indians carried glamour and excitement with them. From their camp on Staten Island they ferried daily up the Hudson to the Twenty-third Street station. They rode the cross-town horsecars to Madison Square, hunched in their bright blankets, staring out at the busy streets. When they filed across Fifth Avenue traffic stopped and the shrill newsboys fell silent. The policeman on the corner exchanged grave greetings with the chiefs from Standing Rock. "How," he said. "How," they answered.

While crowds thronged the Madison Square arena other plans were in the air. Nate Salsbury was in daily conference with shipping men, the English consular office, the American State Department. His mind was already in London where the Wild West would open in May, along with the American Industrial Exhibition. Backstage at the Garden the Indians were being told about a long journey in a ship as big as a chief's town, across wide waters to another country.

On February 22nd Custer made his last stand at the Garden. There was the excitement of packing up, of moving out, of taking down the cardboard mountains and moving the whole spread to the docks on the North River. For Annie Oakley and her husband there was a ten-day leave—time for a brief visit to Ohio, a few days tramping in the fields of Darke County and a few evenings in the family circle talking about the past and the future. Then in blustery March weather they were on their way back to New York to board the steamer for London. "America's National Entertainment" was going international.

CHAPTER 10

The Outfit at Earl's Court

We can easily imagine Wall Street for ourselves, we
need to be shown the cow-boys of Colorado.
—*The* (London) *Times*, Nov. 1, 1887.

ON the last day of March, 1887, at the foot of Leroy Street on the
North River just below the Christopher Street ferry, the big new
steamship *State of Nebraska* loaded an unfamiliar cargo. Horses, mules,
and steers clattered up a cleated runway, rolling their eyeballs white.
Cowboys, swinging the knotted ends of lariats, kept them moving
down the dim 'tween-decks to their stalls. Steers went forward, mules
and horses aft; bellowing and neighing filled the straw-strewn aisles.
On the dock a herd of buffalo lowered their shaggy heads and sniffed
the planking. They would not drive aboard, at the prodding of pitch-
forks they tossed their heads and bellowed. Finally steam winches
rattled on the ship's deck and big mesh cargo slings swung down.
Stevedores spread the nets, cowboys whooped and jabbed. The
winches labored and the nets came up with dangling buffalo. They
were lowered like cargo into the hatches. Big Jerry the moose
trumpeted at a steamer in the river and trotted up the gangway.

With a press agent's shrewdness Major Burke had chosen the
State of Nebraska to transport the outfit to England. The Wild West
would arrive in London like a wind off the Platte River prairie, and
at its head would ride a familiar figure with a new title. Buffalo Bill
had become Colonel Cody. For years Burke had written of the
Honorable William F. Cody; the plainsman had once been elected

by his North Platte neighbors to the Nebraska legislature, though
he promptly went on a scouting errand and never sat among the
lawmakers. With a foreign tour in prospect Burke had persuaded
Governor John M. Thayer of Nebraska to appoint Cody to his staff
as an honorary colonel; Arizona John went further—from thirteen
generals, brigadier generals, major generals, and colonels he got
statements commending Cody's services as guide, scout, dispatch
rider, and chief of scouts, and attesting to his vital part in the winning
of the West. With these titles and testimonials Burke, already in
England as advance agent, managed to give the Wild West an air of
official U.S. sponsorship. The show grounds in London would rival
an embassy.

When animals and scenery, wagons, harness, saddles, and the
battered Deadwood stage were loaded, a line of abject Indians filed
aboard. Red Shirt, Little Bull, Cut Meat, Poor Dog led the procession, shuffling up the gangway with their blanket bundles. Despite
all of Buffalo Bill's assurances, they were followed aboard ship by
a superstition. Legend said that any Indian who crossed the big
water would waste away and die.

The first Indian who had crossed the big water was Pocahontas,
and it was a good thing for Red Shirt and Poor Dog that they did
not know her story. She went to England as Mrs. John Rolfe, the
wife of a Virginia gentleman, but she was received like a chief's
daughter. The Bishop of London drank tea with her, chatting about
the climate in America and the fragrance of Virginia tobacco; the
King and Queen received her in the palace drawing room. She saw
the great houses of London, the plumed horsemen at the palace
gates, the gray cathedral tower soaring over the city, great boats and
barges on the Thames; and at the end of that visit full of wonders
she fell suddenly, mysteriously, ill. The tall ship sailed down the river
mouth and back to Virginia, and Pocahontas died three thousand
miles from home. She died at Gravesend—where the State of Nebraska
was bound. If the Sioux had known of Pocahontas ("Playful One")
they would have dropped their bundles and run.

The tide was turning, the gangway swung aboard, deep in the ship
the engines came to life. Captain Braes called through a megaphone

from the bridge wing, and the hawsers were cast off. The whistle roared, and a great crowd waved from the dock. From the cargo rail Indians watched the water widen, on the promenade the cowboy band played The Girl I Left Behind Me, and Cody waved his Stetson. Nate Salsbury jammed his derby on his head and went down to the paper work in his stateroom. Halfway along the deck Frank Butler stood with a hand hooked in the arm of his girlish wife. Annie wore a bunch of violets, a rosy scarf blew from her shoulder.

"Isn't it exciting, Jimmy!"

Frank gazed ahead, past the harbor islands to the open sea. She gave his arm a tug. "Isn't it exciting?"

He looked down at her. "I hope you never get seasick, Missie."

The sky grew overcast and the wind freshened while they swept past Castle Garden and the new Goddess of Liberty. Beyond the Narrows the wind came stronger, the ship began to lift and roll. Frank pointed across the broken water. "There's Coney Island and Gravesend Bay. I wish it were the other Gravesend—the one we're going to."

"Why, Jimmy, you used to be a sailor."

"That was a long time ago."

Though the wind was chill his forehead glistened. He dabbed it with a handkerchief. A long roll sent them staggering across the deck. At the passageway he said: "You had enough up here? Want to go to the cabin?"

"Oh, no! Look, there's a boat coming. All those sails in the wind. Look, Jimmy, how it rolls!"

He mopped his face again.

"Why, Jimmy, you're gray as ashes."

"A little dizzy. I'll go and lie down."

She toured the deck alone. On the far side a tall figure, holding a broad-brimmed hat, his long hair blowing, leaned over the rail. "Fine weather, Colonel!" He looked up with a wrathful glare and bent over the rail again. The next time she came around the deck was empty. She watched the lofty ship swing past, its great sails weaving on the slate-gray sky. When it was gone there was the empty ocean, a few crying gulls, the wet bow heaving. She breathed the sea-keen air and felt the salt spray on her face. It was like tramping the frozen marshes of Darke County in a stinging snow. But it was more than that—it was the wild enormous ocean and the ship surging through.

When Captain Braes came down the steep accommodation ladder, his weathered face broke open. "I saw the Indians close their hatches and the cowboys go below. Then the Colonel disappeared. I thought the whole Wild West was battened down. But you look pleased, Miss Oakley."

"It's my first time out of sight of land!"

"You'll get wet in this weather. I'll have the steward bring you a set of oilskins."

For two days she ate alone in the big dining room and tramped alone on the deck. Under the after hatches the Indians huddled together. In the long dim 'tween-decks the horses and cattle swayed, heedless of the hay that languid cowboys forked along the aisles. The third day was Sunday, and the wind went down. The ship grew steady, the throb of the engines was a steady pulse beat through the decks and bulkheads. A pale Buffalo Bill appeared, and Nate Salsbury herded the Indians into the dining room for a reluctant meal. After dinner the sun streamed through a breaking sky. Salsbury called the whole outfit into the saloon—ninety-seven Indians, a hundred teamsters, scouts, and cowboys, a score of others. They overflowed the chairs and sofas and sat cross-legged on the floor.

From now on, Nate Salsbury announced, there would be a daily gathering of the company; in the long week ahead of them they would entertain each other and keep their spirits up. Colonel Cody added a few hopeful words, and Chief Red Shirt (*Ogil-sa*) said something cheerful in the Sioux tongue.

For their shipboard shows Frank Richmond, wearing his outsize hat and a flowing neckerchief, acted as master of ceremonies and Nate Salsbury led off with a comedian routine from Salsbury's Troubadours. Frank Butler did a juggling act he had learned in his youth in vaudeville. Old John Nelson and Chief Rocky Bear conversed about the voyage in sign language. Sergeant Bates did an elaborate manual of arms ending in a salute to his flag while the band played Marching Through Georgia. Big Jim Kidd gave an exhibition of fancy knot tying. Mustang Jack, who could leap over a standing horse, now jumped nimbly over a piano and back again, like a bouncing ball. The Mexicans sang a song about the señoritas in old Sonora. Buck Taylor stood Tom Clayton against a screen and outlined him with six thrown hunting knives. Johnnie Baker and little Ben Irving romped through an acrobatic routine. Annie Oakley did rope tricks the cowboys had taught her; at the end she swung the loop around her head and neatly lassoed two ship's officers standing in the ornate doorway. The band played again and the show was over.

On the seventh morning the sky was hung with dirty rags of cloud and the sea surged colorless and cold to the horizon. In the nearly empty dining room a ship's officer grinned at Annie Oakley. "Where's all the show people?"

"I guess they're like my husband. He said he wasn't hungry."

"I'd like to see those cowboys on deck today. There's going to be some bucking—the barometer's way down."

After breakfast, sheathed in oilskins on the pitching deck, Annie braced herself against the wind. Seas broke gray-green over the bow and ran off white in the scuppers. Overhead the tattered clouds were moving and changing. The ship reeled and swung, rose and fell, then buried the foredeck in solid water. She didn't hear the booted step behind her, but she looked up at the gleaming face of Captain Braes under his oilskin hat.

"Come up to the bridge," he shouted.

She followed him up the steep ladder and across the bridge wing into the shelter of the glass-walled pilothouse. A seaman stood at the wheel, easing the spokes around, his eyes on the lighted compass bowl, and the mate peered through the wet glass at the breaking seas. Captain Braes opened a door to the snug little chart room. "You're just in time for coffee."

While she drank black coffee he showed the ship's position on the big Atlantic chart.

The mate came in. "The chief is on the speaking tube, sir. There's trouble in the engine room."

When the engines stopped, the ship rolled in the trough of the sea. A crash of dishes came up from the galley skylight. The mate made a round of inspection and came back with dripping oilskins. The Indians, he said, were saying prayers to the Great Spirit and the cowboys had taken to their bunks. He had sent sailors down into Number Three hold to double-lash the paintings that would be hung in the American Exhibition Hall adjoining the Wild West grounds in London. The cattle and horses were still on their feet.

All day Annie stayed on the bridge, eating sandwiches brought by the captain's steward, watching huge seas crash over the foredeck. Years afterward she recalled that scene like a hearty sailor—and a wide-eyed schoolgirl: "I learned the power of the mighty waves. It was a glorious sight, our boat being dashed from side to side; I felt that one foot farther and we would be turned bottom-side up." At last word came from the engine room. A throb of life went through the deck, the wheelsman found his course, and the ship heaved on toward England.

Next day the wind was quiet and sunlight glinted on the sea. The Wild West came out of their quarters, the Indians creeping up from the after hatches and the cowboys gathering on the wet foredeck. All the animals had survived except one draft horse. Sailors were rigging a boom to lower him over the side.

Eleven days out from New York they kept searching for land, but night closed down on a horizon of water. Next morning, with sunlight streaming in and the ship riding smoothly, Annie looked out the porthole. Land—quiet green shores rising out of gray water. A cluster of cottages above the beach, white houses perched on a green hillside. "Jimmy!" she cried. "Get up, Jimmy!"

That morning the Wild West crowded the port rail, watching the shores of England pass. They had made the crossing. They had found land beyond the endless water. They pointed things out to each other—the houses, the spire of a church, a road climbing a wooded hill. In the Thames mouth the commerce of London streamed past—grimy little coasting boats, red-sailed fishing craft, lofty East Indiamen with sails catching the April wind, liners bound to Italy and Egypt and South Africa. Ahead, under a low and heavy sky, lay the vast dark spread of London, the greatest city of the world.

To Annie Oakley the world had never seemed so vast and strange. Her thoughts went back to Darke County, to the old familiar places, a meadow lark singing across the pasture slough and a wagon creaking on the Greenville road. Her hand tightened on Frank's arm. "It's a long way from home, Jimmy."

He had recovered his Irish grin. "But the ship's not rolling."

As they neared Gravesend a tugboat churned out with its whistle blaring. They expected Major Burke, who had been in London for a month, but when the boat came alongside there was no wide-brimmed hat among the derbied figures at the rail. Up the rope ladder came customs and quarantine officials to check the Wild West passports and inspect the animals. Half an hour later the State of Nebraska swung in toward the Gravesend dock. Over the many-chimneyed roofs rose the spire of old St. George's Church, where Pocahontas lay buried under the chancel. Buffalo Bill's Indians looked hungrily at the land.

A burst of music came from the river. Another tugboat boiled alongside with a red-coated band playing The Star-Spangled Banner. Sergeant Bates rushed below decks and reappeared with his flag, standing at salute on the quarterdeck. A familiar voice boomed up. They saw the ruddy, mustached face, the burly shoulders, the long hair blowing when he waved his hat. It was Arizona John, big as life and beaming.

He was the first man up the gangway. Behind him came Lord Gower, the directors of the American Industrial Exhibition, and a swarm of London pressmen. The reporters wandered over the ship, staring at the sombreroed Mexicans and the blanketed Indians, watching the cowboys herd stiff-legged steers and buffalo down the cleated runway. The ship was alive with clank and clatter, roaring and shouting, bawling and neighing. But the London newsmen were most impressed by the Indians. A writer for the Daily News, remembering The Last of the Mohicans, scribbled excited notes about "moccasins, feathers, beads, war paint, ugly faces made uglier by rude art; dignified countenances which retain a stamp of high breeding through ochre and vermilion, free-springing strides even when the journey was from the hatchway to the scuppers. Not a glance was wasted on a stranger. All that came to the Indians was taken for granted; an archbishop in all his finery would have fallen short of their mark." Another writer admired "the sound white teeth of the Indian women, the grave papoose slung on a squaw's shoulder, and dusky youngsters playing with tackle blocks in the necessary absence of prairie dogs and rattlesnakes." The correspondent for *Sporting Life*, shown around the ship by Buck Taylor himself, wrote the most complete story. He had the pleasure of conversation with Miss Annie Oakley, the marvelous markswoman who looked more like a schoolgirl than like a heroine of the plains, he shook hands with the squaw man John Nelson—*Cha-sha-sha-na-po-ge-o*—and exchanged greetings in sign language with Little Bull and Poor Dog. When he left the ship he looked back and saw "a cluster of braves on the hurricane deck gazing wistfully over the mighty forest of masts into the dim and distant twilight of the west where lay the spacious silent prairies of their people." The Wild West had come to the Old World.

*   *   *

While the Indians made camp at the Earl's Court Exhibition Grounds in the west end of London and the cowboys moved into a bunk tent beside the animal corrals, the principals of the Wild West were settled in the Metropole Hotel on Northumberland Avenue near Charing Cross. Above the clatter of hoofs and the voices of street singers, Annie Oakley unpacked her trunks and hung up her costumes. Out at Earl's Court an army of carpenters made a din in the big arena. Meanwhile Major Burke scheduled a round of tours, dinners, plays, concerts for the Wild West stars. In a doeskin skirt and beaded jacket Annie Oakley stepped into a hansom cab. The driver tipped his top hat, "Evening, Miss Oakley," and drove through twisting streets, past the glow of gaslights in the misty English dark. At the restaurant, the theater, the concert hall, eyes followed her and people told each other, "It's Miss Oakley, of the Wild West show." . . . "Would you think an American could be so small and so graceful?" . . . "She doesn't look like a rider and a shootist." . . . "See the silver star on her hat."

Major Burke had not been idle. Wild West posters in every borough of the city had made London familiar with the names and faces of Buffalo Bill and Annie Oakley, Little Bull and Red Shirt and Buck Taylor. A Globe reporter commented in rhyme on the ubiquitous placards showing the long-haired plainsman:

> I may walk it, or bus it, or hansom it; still
> I am faced by the features of Buffalo Bill;
> Every hoarding is plastered, from East-end to West
> With his hat, coat and countenance, lovelocks and vest.

Now Burke kept his headliners in public view. They visited Westminster Abbey and the Tower of London. They rode an excursion boat up the Thames to Hampton Court. They saw The Beggar's Opera at Toole's Theater, an English comedy at the Haymarket, a variety show at the Palladian Music Hall. On the invitation of Henry Irving who had visited the Wild West at Staten Island, Nate Salsbury assembled half the company for a performance of Faust at the Lyceum. A pied delegation of Indians sat in the front rows, eating sugarplums and staring at the stage, while Cody and his colleagues occupied boxes. After the performance Mr. Henry Irving (a few years later he would be "Sir Henry") brought them onto the stage—Colonel Cody and Nate Salsbury, Annie Oakley and Frank Butler, Buck Taylor in his chaps and cowboy boots, Red Shirt in his eagle feathers. Red Shirt, asked about his impression of the performance, aptly said through his interpreter it was "like a great dream." When they left the theater Burleigh Street was blocked by the crowd watching their departure. Faust was forgotten while people talked about the opening of the American spectacle at Earl's Court. The magic of Mephistopheles was less potent than the magic of the Wild West.

At Earl's Court the show grounds were being readied. After their ocean voyage the animals were fattening in stables and corrals. The big cook tent was spread beyond the arena, the "A" tents rose under budding chestnut trees, stray London dogs came sniffing around the Indian camp. By the light of bonfires workmen finished the arena, seating thirty thousand in roofed seats around an oval a third of a mile in extent. At the end of the horseshoe rose a lofty panorama of plains and rugged mountains. On a bright May morning Sergeant Bates marched through the gate with his faded flag; he had walked the length of England, carrying the Stars and Stripes from Land's End to Gretna Green, whistling *Yankee Doodle* on the English roads. He was ready to lead the Wild West parade.

From the show grounds an arched bridge passed over the Midland Railway, leading to the Industrial Exhibition. In twenty acres of malls, courtyards, and gardens stood the Exhibition Hall, ornamented with huge medallions of Washington, Lincoln, and Cleveland, and embellished with scrolls and eagles. Here the industrial products of America were on display—farm machinery, steam engines, firearms, machine tools, electric generators. Smaller halls held cultural exhibits—an art gallery, a historical museum, a diorama of New York harbor designed by M. Bartholdi on his recent visit to America. Around gardens showing the flora of North America stood restaurants, pavilions, bandstands, and an "Uncle Tom's Cabin" of Carolina pine logs. This was the business part of the Exposition, and it did not excite Londoners, who had their own vast Crystal Palace Exhibition still on display a few miles across the Thames. But the Wild West camp, the Indians and buffalo, the huge arena with its mimic Rocky Mountains—that was something different. For days before the opening performance visitors thronged the grounds. On April 28th Mr. and Mrs. Gladstone called at the headquarters tent. After a tour of the Indian village they lunched in the cook tent to music from the cowboy band. While Mrs. Gladstone chatted with Annie Oakley in her dressing tent, the Prime Minister smoked a cigar with Cody, Salsbury, and Chief Red Shirt. Before the gates had opened, the Wild West was the talk of London.

One of the impatient visitors was Edward, Prince of Wales, who would be King of England in a few more years. On the sunny afternoon of May 6th a line of gleaming carriages drove into the grand entrance on the Lillie Road and drew up at the Exhibition Hall.

Word crossed the bridge—it was His Royal Highness, with the Princess, their wide-eyed children, and a retinue of lords and ladies. The Wild West went into action. While Cody showed the visitors around the camp, Salsbury and Burke got the arena cleared and ready. They assembled the band and alerted the performers; a show would be staged for the royal party.

Cody and Edward were old friends by the time the Prince of the Plains led the Crown Prince of England to a royal box draped with the colors of Britain and America. Then Buffalo Bill leaped astride his horse and led the grand entry. It was an impromptu performance, the first show after weeks of waiting, but they all felt its importance. Even the horses arched their necks and pointed their ears when Frank Richmond announced "—the Wild West in its spectacle of history and drama."

For a moment the huge arena was empty as a Wyoming valley, the red buttes lifting over a lifeless plain. Then Annie Oakley galloped in. She leaned from the saddle, snatched a pistol from the ground and shattered a series of flying targets. With her final shot a herd of buffalo appeared and a hundred savage figures burst out from the badlands. With cries and gunfire they swept after the plunging bison. From the far end a herd of long-horned steers came charging. Cowboys thundered behind them, waving hats and whirling lariats, racing the stampede past the royal stand.

That electric opening brought Prince Edward to his feet. An hour and a half later, when the red buttes were darkening with shadows and the Deadwood Stage rocked off in a last rattle of gunfire, the arena fell quiet again. The Prince asked his new friend Cody to present the actors. Frank Richmond, bowing like a chamberlain, made the presentations. "Your Royal Highness—Chief Little Bull . . . Buck Taylor . . . Mustang Jack. Your Royal Highness—Miss Annie Oakley." Slim and straight as a willow, she flashed her wide smile. She made a quick bow and held out a hand to the Princess. It was a gesture as Western as the buffalo hunt, and the royal visitors returned her infectious smile. As she recalled years later, both Edward and Alexandra gave her a warm handclasp and congratulated her on her shooting. Still fascinated by the Wild West the Prince made another round of the camp and the corrals. Before he left he emptied his cigarette case into the hands of Chief Red Shirt.

Next day every newspaper in England told of the royal visit to the American exhibition and the command performance staged by Indians and cowboys. Major Burke himself could not have written a better press release. On official opening day, May 9th, special trains brought thousands to the West Brompton station, and a stream of busses, cabs, and carriages filled Brompton Road and Lillie Road. Even the lackluster Industrial Exhibition was overrun with curious Londoners. They listened to speeches extolling the commercial ties that linked England and America, then they streamed across the bunting-draped bridge to the Wild West. In the U-shaped stands, looking across a wide prairie to the mimic mountains, they were in London no longer; they had come to the far country of the Big Horns and the Yellowstone. At the opening performance the boxes held an impressive gathering—Lord Dalhousie, Lady Devonshire, Sir Henry de Bothe, Henry Irving, Ellen Terry, Leopold Rothschild, Cardinal Manning, John Lawrence Toole, the Princess Victoria of Teck, and His Excellency the Turkish Ambassador. When the homestead wife was rescued from Indian captors by Buffalo Bill and his men, the noted guests cheered as loudly as the children from Hammersmith and Walham Green.

Three days later a liveried messenger brought a sealed message to Nate Salsbury, and soon an electric word went through the camp. Queen Victoria, whose jubilee was being celebrated after fifty years of glorious reign, requested a performance for herself and her jubilee guests. On the appointed morning the Queen arrived in the regal carriage flanked by a file of outriders. Other carriages brought the King of Denmark, the King and Queen of Belgium, the King of Saxony, the King of Greece, the Crown Prince of Austria, the Crown Prince and Princess of Germany, Grand Duke Michael of Russia, Prince Louis of Baden, and, as Annie Oakley added in her notebook, "dukes, duchesses, lords and ladies." Prince Edward was there, waving to his Wild West friends, impatient to see the show again.

During a medley of English and American songs by the cowboy band, Sergeant Bates with an extension on his flagpole carried the

Stars and Stripes past the Queen's box. The grand entry was followed by Annie Oakley's shooting. Then the show was fast and furious—the dusty rush and thunder of the steers, cowboys leaping from their horses amid the hoofs and horns, a bronco bursting across the ring while a rider fanned the laid-back ears with a crumpled hat. In a quiet interlude a medicine man beat a drumhead with the legbone of a turkey while Frank Richmond translated the death chant: *From La-no-wa the windswept tumbling land of the Sioux the young buck rides away. He makes his campfire in the western sky.* Then the Pony Express raced around the ring and Custer's men fought their doomed battled above the Little Big Horn.

Prince Edward, along with four kings from other lands, asked to ride in the Deadwood stage. Cody ushered them in and closed the door. A crack of the long whip, and the six mules raced away. Above the noise of hoofs and wheels Utah Frank roared out the old driver's song:

> "Pound 'em on the back
> Let the leaders go;
> Never mind the weather
> So the wind don't blow."

But the wind did blow. The cyclone scene began as the stage went swaying up the mountain. After the storm a horse thief was hanged, and Indians tortured a white man (slouching old John Nelson) at the stake. Buffalo Bill rode to the rescue of the homestead family, and the show was over.

Again there was a presentation, the Wild West performers lining up before the black-bonneted Queen. She smiled down at Annie Oakley in her fringed skirt and jacket. "You are a very clever little girl."

May gave way to June, June to July, and the crowds kept coming. They couldn't see enough of Buck Taylor, Jim Kidd, and the bronco-busters; they speculated about the past crimes of the ex-bandit Doc Middleton and the exploits of seamy-faced Sheriff Con Groner; they crowded around the tent of leathery, long-haired, hooded-eyed John

Nelson who had guided the Mormons to Utah, married the daughter of the Oglala chief Lone Wolf and had six children "whom he supports, between show seasons, by hunting and trapping on the plains." They were fascinated by the Indian village, the varicolored Indian ponies, the wide-horned Texas steers and the shaggy buffalo. Even tedious Sergeant Bates had a knot of admirers who heard his eulogy of the Stars and Stripes and paid tuppence for his photograph. For Englishmen the Wild West was inexhaustible. One London gentleman, the program boasted in later years, attended eighty-six consecutive performances.

Annie Oakley's tent was filled with gifts and flowers, and every mail brought letters of admiration. Distinguished visitors signed her autograph book while reporters waited for interviews. She met them all simply and naturally, with her quick smile and girlish charm. Always she had learned quickly; she had learned to wear tailored clothes, to pose for photographs with unconscious ease, to talk with polished people. Now, far from Darke County, she was serenely at home. To thousands of admirers she showed her trunk of guns and pistols, her badges and medals, her gifts from Sitting Bull. While her English maid gave them refreshment, the reporters scribbled in their notebooks. "After the exciting performance we sought the peaceful seclusion of Miss Annie Oakley's tent, where she charmingly served us various American juices of choice and agreeable flavor." The "marvelous shootist," they wrote, was twenty years old (she was now twenty-seven, but she would remain twenty to the public for another fourteen years) and already she had won a trunkful of medals and prizes.

One summer morning a messenger brought a note for Colonel Cody from his friend the Prince of Wales: Would Miss Annie Oakley shoot a friendly match with the Grand Duke Michael of Russia? Royalty thronged London that summer of the Queen's jubilee, but the Grand Duke had a special reason to be there: he was a suitor of the Princess Victoria, a prospect not popular in England. He fancied himself as a sportsman as well as a suitor. Annie Oakley promptly agreed to a shooting contest.

Two days later four carriages drew up at the entrance to the arena. Out stepped a dozen princes and princesses, dukes and duchesses. While they were taken to the royal box, Annie Oakley led the uniformed, bemedaled Grand Duke into the ring. It was not much of a contest. Annie was at her careless, uncanny best, swinging with the target, high or low, full or quartering; she could not miss. The Grand Duke fidgeted, shuffled his feet for a better stance, scowled at his gun when a target sailed on toward the painted mountains. Annie slacked off toward the end. They shot fifty birds, with a score of 47 to 36. When Prince Edward pinned a medal on her jacket, he looked as pleased as though it were his victory.

All over England newspapers reported the defeat of the Russian Grand Duke by the girl from the American prairies. Recalling those stories years afterward, Annie wrote, "It was the most amazing and unexpected publicity I ever experienced." Soon Michael went back to Russia, rejected by the English princess, and English people read that "Annie Oakley of the magic gun" had won two matches from the Grand Duke. Everything came Annie's way in London.

Reporters talked with quiet, middle-aged Frank Butler who managed Annie's engagements and looked after her ammunition. If they knew he was her husband, that did not make newspaper copy; she was always the demure maiden from the Western plains who had become the darling of London. Inevitably she had suitors of her own. A French count bowed, kissed her hand, and proposed marriage. An English sportsman wanted her to become mistress of his estate. A Welshman who had repeatedly seen the show sent a solemn-faced photograph with his solemn proposal. Annie set the photograph on a corral post, walked off thirty steps, and put six bullets between the earnest eyes. When Frank brought in the photograph she wrote "respectfully declined" and mailed it back to Wales.

Of all her London letters from sportsmen, journalists, actors, fashion designers, and anonymous admirers, she saved just one. Years later it lay faded and yellowed among the programs, press clippings, and souvenirs from many countries—a letter from an English youth whom Annie had never seen though he had seen her, day after day for seven weeks. It was a gentle, chivalrous, touching letter, telling how he had watched the opening performance at Earl's Court and

Before the Show. Sioux Indians playing poker, Staten Island, 1886.

After the Show.
Pawnees about to attack a watermelon, Staten Island, 1886.

Part of the company in Rome, 1890.
Buffalo Bill at left, Johnnie Baker left center, Annie Oakley
right center, Frank Butler standing extreme right.

When the Wild West visited Venice, 1890.

once seeing Annie Oakley was unable to forget her. He had attended every performance since, and though he had watched thousands visiting her tent he did not trust himself to keep his feelings hidden; he had adored her from a distance. It was not her skill that kept him lying sleepless, but "your grace, your gentle bearing, and your sweet face with your expressive eyes that look out from under that broad-brimmed hat so becomingly worn." He had bought her photograph and kept it on his desk dreaming that he might meet her. Then he learned that she was married. —"I feel that you will understand my stupidity when I tell you that I lost my father when I was a very small boy and my mother, who is of gentle birth, brought me up very close to her. So you see my worldly experiences have been limited. I have explained everything to my mother. Should I remain in London I fear I could not trust myself to keep entirely away from your presence, though I shall never become known to you. I am leaving on the morning boat for South Africa. Suffice it, if this epistle, the outpouring of a broken heart, will be touched by your gentle hand while I put distance between us."

He was George Widows, a youth of twenty-one, and he did go to darkest Africa. After his departure his mother and sister called on Annie at Earl's Court. George Widows, as he had foretold, remembered her all his life. Twenty-five years later he visited the Butlers at their home on Chesapeake Bay, bringing a collection of horns from Kenya Colony.

During the summer Annie gave teas for mothers and children on the small lawn before her reception tent. Sometimes she added Indian children to the party—Little Eagle, Little Money, Seven Up, Little Emma. In their buckskin clothes they stared at the starched and ruffled visitors, and the English children stared back till Annie's maid put them all at ease by serving lemonade and biscuits. For these receptions Annie wore her most feminine clothing—a white muslin redingote lined with pale blue silk, a blue linen blouse with a white lace waterfall, or a white spencer blouse with rose collar and cuffs. An hour earlier she had been in the arena shooting flying targets from a galloping horse, now she was hostess at a lawn party. That transformation made her more magnetic than ever. London police kept crowds moving past the tiny lawn, and when the party was over the Bobbies finished the lemonade.

London seemed more interested in Annie Oakley than in Buffalo Bill himself. Reporters wrote about her skill, her modesty, her charm. "Miss Oakley, whose feats with glass balls and clay pigeons are phenomenal, bade us welcome to her canvas dwelling with as perfect an absence of hauteur as if she could not have hit a ten-cent-piece held between our thumb and forefinger at a distance of thirty feet." Every post brought invitations to receptions, garden parties, cricket and tennis matches, shooting exhibitions. Her tent filled with gifts of books, handkerchiefs, gloves, fans, silk and satin scarves. At the London Gun Club she was given a handsome rifle with a tiny gold figure of herself set in the stock above the trigger guard. There was not time for all the parties and receptions, but she visited Lord's and Wimbledon, and she had a week-end's shooting with the Prince of Wales on his favorite hunting grounds at Sandringham.

Meanwhile Buffalo Bill was living lavishly, keeping a suite in a hotel on Piccadilly, giving elaborate dinners, being entertained in Park Lane and Grosvener Square. He stood at the head of banquet tables, a diamond flashing from his knotted scarf, and made florid speeches. "The march of American civilization started on the Atlantic coast and moved ever westward, over the mountains, across the majestic Mississippi and onto the vast buffalo pastures of the Great Plains." He was handsome, dramatic, theatrical. He was an actor, playing a part that he relished, and while he devoured adulation in Mayfair and Piccadilly he must have remembered his homeless Kansas boyhood and the great gaunt country of his youth. From Dismal River to the Thames, from the Badlands to Earl's Court—it was like a story. Sometimes, his head still swimming with champagne and brandy, a longing for that other life came over him. At midnight he took a cab to the show grounds; he walked through the sleeping Indian camp, heard the horses stamping in the corral, and breathed a dust as sharp as gunpowder in the soft English air. He was at home, pacing under the crags and ledges of the cardboard mountains. Next day he was a showman, ordering his valet to bring more drinks for his visitors, referring to his friend the Prince of Wales, driving off with an English actress, Katherine Clemmons, who would be seen with him in the cities of Europe and America in years to come.

By the end of the summer two and a half million people had visited the outfit at Earl's Court. Will Cody, who had once traded a horse at Fort McPherson to pay his wife's grocery bill, was rich and famous. He was also vain, touchy, petulant. Success had changed him, and it had changed the spirit of the Wild West company. Over the show grounds hung rivalries, jealousies, disagreements. Annie Oakley drew the longest applause in the arena and the most frequent mention in the papers. The women riders of the Wild West resented her favored place on the program and her featured place in the show bills. Even Cody resented her popularity with press and public, and when she was invited to Germany to shoot before the Kaiser he sulked in his tent over a bottle of Scotch whisky. Salsbury and Burke shook their heads. There was nothing a business manager or a press agent could do about it.

In October the Wild West gates were closed. Down came the cardboard mountains. Horses, steers, and buffalo were loaded into stock cars. The show people packed their trunks. After a last dinner for Colonel Cody the outfit would move on to the Midlands, setting up in a huge hall in Manchester for the winter season. As a valedictory the London *Times*, the organ voice of England, made the Wild West the subject of an editorial which concluded, "Colonel Cody has done his part in bringing America and England nearer together." But the season had separated Buffalo Bill and Annie Oakley. When the show train pulled out of West Brompton station, Missie was not aboard.

CHAPTER 11

Shooting for Pawnee Bill

AMONG the frequent visitors to the Earl's Court show grounds had been Mr. R. Edward Clark, a country gentleman from the west of England who talked with the Butlers about wing and trap shooting and spoke of his shooting grounds on the Severn. He invited them to Shrewsbury for a fortnight's hunting after the London season. That was in midsummer, and they were surprised, ten weeks later, when the letter came.

In the hotel room with London traffic beating at the windows, Frank took the letter from the pile of greetings, invitations, press clippings. He read again, "—partridge, pheasant, black cock in the uplands, snipe in the marshes . . . the best season in Shropshire . . . our lodge ready for guests . . . meet you at Shrewsbury station."

Annie stood beside him, looking down at the swarming life of the Strand. They were both thinking of dark hills under a windy sky, of dogs and horses, of birds flying up from the undercover. On the table were requests for shooting lessons at the London Gun Club and exhibitions that would bring £50 for an afternoon. But here were two railway tickets for the Shropshire hills.

They were both shrewd about money, but now they hesitated. Impulsively Annie said: "Let's go, Jimmy. Let's go hunting!"

He swung her off the floor. "You pack some clothes. I'll get the guns ready."

Three hours later London was behind them. It was a day of changing skies, with the green fields fading into autumn brown. The countryside was friendly—solid stone houses always in a cluster of trees, winding roads lined with neat-clipped hedgerows, sheep in the meadows, cattle around the hooded haystacks. They passed through the rolling Cotswolds and over level fields to Worcester with its massive cathedral tower against the sky. In another hour they were at Shrewsbury, and their host was waiting on the station platform—a lean tall man with ruddy cheeks and a shaggy mustache, dressed in riding boots and a Norfolk hunting jacket.

Welcome to "Shrowsbury," he bade them, giving the broad local sound to the name. —Had they brought their gun trunk? Right enough. Never better shooting than this time of year. Do well, he'd venture. Train was a bit late, but they could make it to the country in time for tea.

While his man took their things, he led them to an open high-wheeled carriage in the station court. He might have known the Americans were curious and a little lost; he began to point things out as soon as the driver mounted and the carriage rumbled off. Up on the hill stood the castle, the home of the two young princes who were put to death in the Tower of London. Looking up at the grim old fortress Annie caught her breath; she had seen the room in the Tower of London where the little princes died. Again the Englishman was pointing—the old Market Hall with the statue of Richard of York in the midst of two-wheeled carts drawn by shaggy Welsh ponies. Between the timbered houses of Dogpole Street they had glimpses of the old Shrewsbury School where Sir Philip Sidney learned his first Latin and Charles Darwin studied a schoolboy's science. The road curved upward and the town gave way to fields, bordered in stone walls green with moss and creepers, with gray-green hills beyond. On high ground their host pointed out the battlefield of Shrewsbury Plain, where Harry Hotspur fought—long before America was a name.

"And Falstaff with him," Frank Butler said.

The Englishman began quoting: " 'Turk Gregory never did such deeds in arms as I have done this day. . . . we rose both at an instant and fought a long hour by Shrewsbury clock.' " He pointed back to the spire of St. Mary's Church; there was the clock that marked the hour of that battle long ago. He turned to his guests. —They liked the fat prince, Falstaff? And Owen Glendower, the fiery Welshman? Again he pointed; there in the west rose the dark mountains of Wales.

Annie looked over the tumbled landscape and her mind was crowded with discoveries. The Wars of the Roses . . . Ludlow Castle . . . the house where Mary Tudor lived in childhood . . . the ancient Roman city of Uriconium. . . . It was like being dropped into history.

They turned into a parkland with a many-gabled house at the end of the lane. While the driver took their trunks to the guest lodge, their host led them into a long living room with a fire glowing in the broad black chimney mouth. Leaded windows looked across the uplands to a line of darkening hills. In a moment a handsome, vigorous woman was welcoming them, settling them by the fire, explaining that the old sheep dog that went straight to Annie was allowed the house because he had grown lame and could not hold his own in the kennel.

A maid brought in a tea tray and reappeared with bread and butter, honey, jelly, jam, and plates of cakes and muffins. Mrs. Clark was an easy hostess. She knew about the Wild West, though summer house guests had kept her from London. She turned to Annie, "And you are really the celebrated shootist the newspapers tell about. I expected—"

"A ruddy squaw," her husband said. "Tomorrow we take the horses and go for partridge."

One day it was partridge, the next day pheasant, then black cock, then to the marshes for snipe. On the estate were uplands and lowlands, woods and meadows and moors. It was a hunter's dream—up early and out in the dales before the mist had risen, over the hills, across bare sheeplands, down through the poplar-bordered marshes. Game was plentiful, the dogs were trained to perfection. After all day in the field they came back to tea in the big house. Then a hot bath in their guest lodge, a dinner of Severn salmon or saddle of Shropshire mutton, or of pheasant or partridge, and coffee and brandy by the fire. They talked about the Wild West, about England and America, about the Indian treaty in Greenville, Ohio, and the site of the Roman city in the Severn Valley.

At dusk on Sunday the Englishman pointed to a twinkling on the far dark line of the Clee hills, explaining that beacon fires were burned in all the shires of England, signaling fifty years of Victoria's reign. Across the valley they saw an answering blaze on Wenlock Edge. He took a newspaper from the tea table and read:

> From Clee to heaven the beacon burns,
>   The shires have seen it plain;
> From north and south the sign returns
>   And beacons burn again.

Frank Butler, always alert to poetry, asked him to repeat it. He read all the stanzas of a poem entitled simply "1887," printed in the weekly paper at Shrewsbury, and signed "A Shropshire Lad."

On the last day of their visit the Clarks had other guests for luncheon. They could not believe this soft-spoken American girl was the shooting star of the Wild West; finally they asked for a demonstration. When Frank had brought a rifle, Annie took thirty steps across the terrace, turned, threw the gun to her shoulder, and punctured a playing card, dead center, in her husband's hand. —How was it done? the guests demanded.

—You *feel* the target, she explained. Brain, eyes, hands, and trigger finger all work on a single impulse. In the field and at the London Gun Club she had learned that English birds were fast; they were blue streaks leading up and away, you had to shoot without a conscious, calculated aim. It was the same in the saddle. From a galloping horse you couldn't hold your sights on a target. You had to *feel* it, and if you felt it truly you would not miss.

The guests thought it most likely they could miss. They dared say it was a gift only an American could have.

On the way to the station their host talked about another visit to "Shrowsbury" and some hunting in the wild Welsh mountains. As the train crossed the leaf-strewn Severn they looked back at the church spire in the soft gray sky and the old Norman castle crouching on the hill. Soon Shropshire was gone, but they kept in their minds the far sweep of the moorsides, dogs flushing up game birds from the tangled marsh, dusk gathering on the Clee Hills, and the red fog darkening over Ludlow, Longmynd and Wenlock Edge with beacons burning on their crest.

*   *   *

London was a gray city under the November skies. A chill mist hung in the air, slow gray smoke sifted from the chimneys, every street ended in gloom. It was a somber city, and yet it became more intimate and friendly than the London of midsummer. Candles flickered in the tea shops, the public coaches were strewn with straw to warm the travelers' feet, wet pavements glimmered beneath the gas jets, chestnut vendors stood on the street corners, their steam ovens whistling a little song. They were reluctant to leave the gloomy, homelike city, but a renewed invitation came from Germany. Crown Prince Wilhelm wanted Annie Oakley to shoot for the Emperor at Charlottenburg. Again they packed the guns and costumes. From the train window they saw the green fields of Kent and the rolling downs of Sussex. England was falling behind. It seemed longer than eight months since they had come ashore at Gravesend.

At Newhaven the sky was lifting, and beyond the river mouth the channel flashed silver in the sun. Frank had some qualms about the crossing, but the broad-beamed steamer rode steadily, with a web of gulls around it. Annie took off her snug beret and let her hair blow in the wind. They stood at the rail watching the great chalk face of Beachy Head settle into the sea. When England was gone, France grew up above the water; soon they were in the harbor of Dieppe with its stuccoed housefronts facing seaward under the cliff-walled coast.

On the pierhead a sign read something that Annie could not understand. The men waiting to catch the mooring lines called up in another language. It was strange to be looking at France, the country that Frenchy La Motte thought about, smoking his clay pipe beside the stove in Greenville. While Frank stood over the open gun trunk, having a hectic two-language discussion with a knot of excited customs men, she found a picture postcard to send to Frenchy La Motte. "Tomorrow we will see a Paris manager about an engagement for the winter season. Then we go to Berlin to shoot for the Emperor. Some days I get very homesick, but there isn't time now."

There was no time to be homesick in the streets of Paris, in the Grand Café with an American booking agent and a voluble French manager, on the train crossing the Rhine with the twin cathedral towers soaring above Cologne, in the ringing streets of Berlin. Or a cloudy Sunday morning a courier led them to a carriage with the Hohenzollern eagles on its doors. While they drove down Unter den Linden, beneath the massive Brandenburg Gate, and through the wooded Tiergarten with its statues and fountains, the courier sat rigid, staring at his passengers with steely eyes. Annie was nervous and vaguely irritated when they arrived at Charlottenburg on the curving Spree.

The central gallery of the Charlottenburg Race Course held formidable rows of royalty and rigid Prussian officers with side arms and iron crosses. As the Americans stepped out of the carriage a helmeted man in a blue bemedaled tunic clicked heels together and addressed the courier in German; he turned to the Americans and spoke in heavily accented English. —The Emperor was indisposed and unable to be present.

Perhaps that weighed upon the gallery. They stared in silence as a tiny figure in a Western costume ran across the infield to the shooting stand. For a moment Annie felt like a lost child. She was far from home, in a foreign land, amid strange people and strange ways. She had come from a backwoods cabin to stand before these lords and ladies, field marshals and generals, who were at home in castles and palaces. She stood there alone—no fanfare, no feathered Indians, no riders racing through a hail of arrows, no storied backdrop of colored buttes and mountains. The arena was huge, cold, immaculate, and empty—except for a white-faced girl in an absurd fringed skirt and beaded jacket. Clouds streaked the November sky, the light kept changing. She stood there in the chill wind and the Prussian silence, curtsying beside the gun stand, wishing she were home in Darke County.

When Frank came out to throw her targets he answered her pleading look with an all but imperceptible shrug and a quickly gone smile. He bent down to her. "They're just people, Missie, and crazy about shooting. Like those Germans at *Schuetzenbuckel*, in Cincinnati."

Her face changed. Shooter's Hill—so long ago—the strange crowd watching, the November wind tugging at a girl in country clothing, the target sailing up, the referee crying "Dead!" She gave him back a fleeting smile. *Thanks, Jimmy. Thanks.*

A minute later her voice rang over the empty field. "Pull!" As the bird flew out, she swung her gun and fired; the disk shattered at the crest of flight. "Pull!" It banked off sharply, and at the crack of the gun it scattered in the air. She forgot the cold and silent gallery, the chill wind and the changing light. All she thought of was the flying target and the familiar gun in her hands.

She ran out the clay birds without missing. Then came a run of live pigeons. They were fast; they flew up and away, never twice at the same angle. But she was poised, relaxed, and ready. She grassed them all. When she bowed there was a patter of handclaps, brittle as breaking glass and as quickly over. Frank tossed up pairs of colored balls and she pulverized them. Then she went to the target line. She threw six balls into the air, ran to her table, seized a shotgun and fired. Without an instant's fumbling she raised a second gun, and then a third. Six targets were shattered before they touched the ground. When the last ball vanished she stood with the gun smoking and her breath coming fast. The gallery broke into spontaneous applause.

Frank grinned at her. "You got 'em, Missie."

The rest of the exhibition was punctuated by bursts of approval. When, at the end of the show, she shot a coin from her husband's fingers, cries filled the big arena. The gallery went silent as Prince Wilhelm strode down and across the grass. While Annie curtsied, he examined her rifle, cradling it on his withered arm with the stiff gloved hand. He spoke of a trick he had seen her do in London, asking her to repeat it. He lighted a cigarette, held it in his mouth and stood erect while Annie paced away. She turned, raised the gun and fired; the cigarette stopped smoking.

"*Wunderbar!*" the voices cried. "*Ganz wunderbar!*"

That night in the hotel room she felt tired, more tired than she had ever been. The next day she stayed in bed, though Prince Wilhelm sent his carriage to take them on a drive through Berlin. When Frank bent over her she said, "Just tired, Jimmy. Tired. You go, and tell them I'm sorry." He returned with a young American doctor who frowned over her as he took pulse, temperature, blood

ressure. When he spoke his voice was strict as a schoolmaster's.
—She must have rest, complete rest. Annie began to shake her head.
—Could she fill a five-week contract in Paris? He was definite.—No.
Not even five days. She had been going on nerve and her nerves were
exhausted. She needed rest and she needed it now.

On the train to the channel port she leaned against the window,
and Frank covered her with a steamer rug. In the chilly dusk she saw a
family burning brush beside a hedgerow—a woman with a wooden
rake heaping brambles on the blaze, firelight touching the metal
buttons on a farmer's blouse, a child reaching hands to the fire. The
next minute they were gone, but for weeks that picture stayed in her
mind. The leaping firelight and the work-worn faces. What was it in
that glimpse of people whose words she could not have understood
that filled her eyes with tears? She was tired, deeply tired, and far
from home.

The voyage was a tonic: long nights of sleep and days in a steamer
chair wrapped in a rug with the seawind on her face. On a gray
December day they stood at the rail and watched Sandy Hook grow
out of gray water. Then the harbor, the lifted torch of Liberty, the
familiar shore of Staten Island, the lights of New York trembling in
the winter dark.

*   *   *

They settled in a small hotel near Madison Square. After two
months of quiet she opened the battered trunk and tried a gun in
her hands. Frank was making the rounds of theaters and press rooms,
sitting at restaurant tables with agents and managers. The team of
Butler and Oakley needed an income, but show people are quickly forgotten. The New York papers carried stories of the Wild West's
success in England and the plans of Cody and Salsbury to bring the
show to Staten Island for the coming season, but there was no
publicity for a girl who had left the outfit and come back tired,
homesick, and alone. Until her name was in the papers no stage door
would be open. Frank was not a press agent, but he was a veteran of
the shooting range. He scheduled matches which might bring a

modest sum of prize money and some publicity without the benefit of Major Burke.

Her first match, against the holder of the "championship of England," was an ordeal and a disappointment. In a January sleet storm at a New Jersey race track she stood at the traps, her tiny figure muffled in woolens and braced against the wind. Eight of her birds were blown out of bounds—her 20-gauge with its light charge of powder was not equal to the winter gale—and seven others fell unbroken. The English marksman lost five birds out of bounds and won a miserable match, 36 to 33.

That night the team of Butler and Oakley sat silent on the train, Frank tugging at his mustache and Annie staring at darkness. The future looked as bleak as the cold New Jersey flats. At Hoboken they boarded the ferry. It was nearly empty, the big dim cabin bare as a barn, and their breath smoked in the raw air. Halfway across the river they went outside in the wind. At the rail Frank put an arm around her.

"Tired, Missie? We could go back to Ohio. You could rest all winter."

Her head came up from the fur collar, the thin snow misting her face. "When we go back to Ohio"—a muscle flickered in her cheek— "we'll go back winners."

They stood in the cold harbor-smelling air. Below them the water curled white in the darkness and winter's sadness and excitement were in the glimmering city lights.

His big hand closed on hers. "Not too tired?"

"When is the next match, Jimmy?"

"Next week."

"You'll see."

At that match, at Easton, Pennsylvania, shooting in gusty weather against a veteran of the skeet clubs, she missed a single bird and won by a margin of five. She had been confident before the contest and she was serene afterward. Frank stopped pulling his mustache. They were on the way. On Washington's Birthday, before a noisy gallery at Trenton she won the toss and took her stand while the crowd hooted; her opponent was a local champion. Years afterward she remembered that contest. It meant $200, and headlines in the papers; it seemed to mean the future. Her crafty rival quibbled and delayed and the crowd was hostile. But she stood as carefree as a country girl waiting for a squirrel to show in the fork of a walnut tree. "Pull!" she cried, when the traps at last were ready. Her gun swung up with the wind-blown target. It shattered on the rise. She won the match, 47 to 45.

Now there were footlights for her. With a new row of medals on her shooting jacket she appeared at Tony Pastor's Opera House, the top variety show of New York. On the showboard in Fourteenth Street hers was the featured name; on the stage she appeared with Little Tick, the Armstrongs, Beane and Gilday, Renane and Athos— ventriloquists, magicians, vocalists, and tumblers. It was not Madison Square Garden, but when she made her bobbing little curtsy and ran to the wings the house shook with applause. She was in business again.

*　　*　　*

In the spring of 1888, while Buffalo Bill was still abroad, two rival companies went after the American trade. A frontier show was organized by a Philadelphia businessman; he hoped to exploit the fame of the original Wild West and he had a featured place for Annie Oakley. When he offered $300 a week, Frank Butler signed; the next day they reported at the show lot on the Philadelphia Exposition Grounds. It was a sorry outfit—a string of half-wild Texas ponies, a camp of sullen Comanche Indians, and a set of pseudo-cowboys who had never held a branding iron or clung to a pitching bronco. Now Frank chewed on his mustache. It looked like a bad thing to be tied to.

At the same time an honest Western road show, organized by Gordon W. Lillie, Pawnee Bill, had opened the season in western Pennsylvania. Pawnee Bill was a genuine plainsman who had traveled with the Wild West as an Indian interpreter in its early seasons. Now he had his own "Frontier Exhibition," but he was in debt to the railroads. When Frank Butler read that Lillie's show was stranded in Pittsburgh, he persuaded the Philadelphia showman to make a merger with Pawnee Bill. The combined show would have adequate capital and it would have professional and experienced personnel.

In the newly organized company Annie Oakley was the star. She led the parade and the grand entry. She did trick riding and trick shooting. She gave press interviews, displayed her cups and medals, held public receptions. She kept the show on the road even after the return of Cody and Salsbury.

Buffalo Bill's Wild West came home in triumph after a year of resounding success in England. At the end of the first week of May, 1888, the steamer *Persian Monarch*, dressed in all her flags and pennants, brought the outfit into New York harbor, docking at Bechtel's Wharf on Staten Island. Major Burke's old magic was still working. Said the New York *World*: "The harbor probably never witnessed a more picturesque scene. . . . Buffalo Bill stood on the captain's bridge, his tall and striking figure clearly outlined and his long hair waving in the wind; the gaily painted and blanketed Indians leaned over the ship's rail; flags of all nations fluttered from the masts and connecting cables. The cowboy band played *Yankee Doodle* with vim and enthusiasm which faintly indicated the joy felt by everybody connected with the Wild West over the sight of home."

They set up in the old Staten Island location, at Erastina Woods, and on Memorial Day began a summer season before a crowd of thirty thousand. Steele MacKaye was there—delighted to see his former colleagues and bubbling with his own new success, a drama of the French Revolution which made a pointed parallel with the recent Haymarket riots in Chicago. *Paul Kauvar* was playing to packed houses—every newspaper account of the Chicago anarchists was an advertisement for MacKaye's drama. But there is no such thing as too much publicity, and when Major Burke suggested bringing the Wild West company to a performance MacKaye enthusiastically agreed. Cowboys and Mexicans clumped into the Standard Theater to watch the mob storming the streets of Paris. Huddled in blankets on the front rows the Indians stared uncomprehending, though they liked the music; the overture and interludes, composed by young

Edgar Stillman-Kelley, took hold of them like a beating of drums. The weird minor measures of confusion and unrest, the soaring theme of aspiration, the explosion of anarchy—the brooding Sioux knew all those feelings. At midnight they went back to their Staten Island camp still swaying with remembered music. And for both the Wild West and *Paul Kauvar* the newspapers had new copy.

That summer Buffalo Bill rode a dizzy crest of popularity and indulgence. Always ready to "drink a cup o' greeting" with old friends and new, he was followed by reveling admirers of both sexes. The Wild West played to New York crowds until the end of August; then it toured south to Philadelphia, Washington, Baltimore, and Richmond, while Annie Oakley finished the season on the road with Pawnee Bill.

In October the Butlers were back in New York, freelancing again. During the summer Tony Pastor's Opera House had been refurnished and enlarged. For its grand opening on October 22nd, Tony billed a sequence of top acts; his show opened with Annie Oakley, "the prime shot," and went on with King Kalkaska, the Japanese contortionist and tumbler; Bibb and Bobb, the versatile St. Petersburg musical artists; and Millie Hylton, the English impersonator. After that engagement came shooting matches before sporting crowds in New York, Philadelphia, Trenton. Her clippings read: "Annie Oakley defeats John Lavett at Exposition Park, 23 to 21 birds at 30 yards." . . . "In a match for $50 to shoot at 25 pairs of clay birds, Annie Oakley broke the 50 birds straight, beating all records." . . . "Annie Oakley defeated Miles Johnson, champion of New Jersey, in a match of 50 live pigeons. Traps had to be moved three times on account of the overflow crowd." From Annie Oakley's notes: "I shot a match with Fred Kell on a guarantee basis, but when my husband learned that it was taking about all that Mr. Kell's backer had, he dropped the guarantee back on the table."

There was an interlude of two weeks' quail hunting in the Shenandoah Valley and then the starring role in a Western drama in a Fourteenth Street theater. "Through all the strife," a reporter wrote, "the beautiful character of Sunbeam, taken by Annie Oakley, was a poem hewn in rocks." It was a poor, creaking play, but it held on through the winter.

In March, when even in Union Square the wind brought hints of a new season, came a note from Nate Salsbury. He wanted Annie Oakley back in the Wild West for its imminent tour of Europe. Colonel Cody wanted her, so did Major Burke and everybody in the outfit. He offered a new contract, and they signed. Arizona John went to work with the newsmen. Buffalo Bill had gone to Washington to ride in the inaugural parade for President Benjamin Harrison, but the New York papers featured another name. After less than a year at home the Wild West was sailing again for foreign shores; it would play at the great Paris Exposition, with famed Annie Oakley as its shooting star.

There was time for a quick trip to Ohio, some walks in the Darke County woods, hours getting acquainted with small nephews and nieces, evenings sewing costumes for the new season. Then back to New York in the first week of April.

It was pouring rain when they boarded the ship. Horses stood streaming on the dock, buffalo hung their matted heads. The cowboys looked morosely at the sky, and Indians huddled under blankets on the half-deck. Beside Number Four hatch the old Deadwood Stage stood leaking like a crate. But when Annie came up the gangway in a dripping slicker the band burst into *The Girl I Left Behind Me*. Cody enveloped her in his arms. "Missie! Little Missie!" Arizona John beamed and Nate Salsbury gave her a welcoming kiss. They made the rounds of all their friends—cowboys and Mexicans, Indians and outlaws. They even went down to the dim 'tween-decks to see big Jerry the moose. Back on deck the band was playing. From the fuming stack the ship's whistle roared in the rain. They were on the way to a long season in Paris and a tour of seven countries, but they were home again.

CHAPTER 12

Under the Eiffel Tower

For the West is the most American part of America,
that is to say, the part where those features which dis-
tinguish America from Europe come out in strongest
relief.   —BRYCE: *The American Commonwealth*

EXPOSITIONS were a familiar sight in Paris. Every eleven years the
French Government held an industrial and cultural exhibit, but the
Exposition Universel of 1889, celebrating the centennial of the
French Republic, dwarfed all its predecessors. The exhibition grounds
spread over two hundred acres along the Seine in the heart of Paris,
including the Champs de Mars, the Trocadéro Garden, and the
Esplanade des Invalides. Above halls and palaces rose the lofty
latticework of the Eiffel Tower, the architectural feature of the
Fair and a wonder of the world in that centennial year.

To attract the exposition crowds the Wild West management had
secured a location in sight of the stately grounds. At the edge of the
Bois de Bologne in the Parc du Neuilly, just a little way beyond
the Place de l'Étoile and the Arc de Triomphe, the Indians had
their camp. At the end of the arena the mountains of Montana
rose above the forks of the Yellowstone. Steers, buffalo, and wild
horses were corralled within sound of coaches and carriages on the
Avenue de la Grande Armée. Thirty acres of fashionable Paris had
become the American frontier.

On opening day, May 18th, twenty thousand people filled the

U-shaped stands while Bill Sweeney led his cowboy band in a medley of American songs. In color-draped boxes sat President Carnot, the members of his cabinet, the new American ambassador Whitelaw Reid, the genre artists Meissonier, Detaille, and Rosa Bonheur, along with bemedaled army officers and international sportsmen. During the grand entry the spectators sat silent; while the Wild West rounded the arena they seemed miles away. Nate Salsbury paced at the entrance, studying the crowd that watched in silence while the Deadwood Stage rumbled off the track. When Annie Oakley appeared, he met her with a heavy face. —The French, he said, knew nothing about the American frontier. They did not understand Indians or cowboys, or a stagecoach from the Black Hills. But they did understand shooting. Up there were thousands of army officers, veteran soldiers, sportsmen. And they understood skill, grace, and charm. He put a hand on her shoulder and nudged her through the gate. Perhaps she could bring the crowd to life.

Two riders went ahead, leaping off their ponies to hold her targets. She ran in on twinkling feet and bowed to the silent stands. She turned to her gun table and shattered glass balls with pistol and rifle. In a staccato cadence she shot the flame off a revolving wheel of candles. There was a rustle in the stands—was it restlessness or interest?—a girl in the huge arena, under the wild vista of the Yellowstone, could not be sure. But she could shoot as no one in Paris had ever done before. She called for twin targets and seized a shotgun from the table. They broke almost together. She called for four. A double report, a lightning exchange, another double report and the targets were gone. Again four disks. She broke two, seized a new gun, spun twice around, and shattered the second pair. Then she ran to the target line. She threw twin balls into the air and raced back to her station. She jumped the table, seized a gun, and whirled while the balls were falling. As the barrel swung up the targets vanished.

When she bowed, flushed and breathless, the crowd found its voice. *Vive! Vive! Vive Annie Oakley!*

The noise swelled as she ran off the field, and at the gate Nate Salsbury sent her back for her riding act. A cowboy loped in, leading a spotted pony. She leaped astride. She dropped her hat and picked it up at a gallop. She slid head-down from the saddle and tied her neckerchief around the flying pastern joint of her pony. She snatched a pistol from the grass and shattered six glass balls over the rider's head. Twenty thousand Frenchmen could not see her heart pounding and her breath coming short and hard, but they saw youth, ardor, and daring in the huge prairie under the painted mountains. They began to understand the Wild West.

When she galloped off, the show was launched. As cowboys went yipping after a stampede of steers their cries were lost in the shouting stands.

Before the performance was over reporters were at her tent. They looked, talked, pointed, asked questions of her French maid, and scribbled in their notebooks. She could not comprehend a syllable of their talk, but she understood their admiration, and they understood her wide smile and the light spilling from her eyes. After the show Major Burke with an interpreter brought a line of dignitaries: smiling President Carnot, who within five years would be assassinated at a public banquet in Lyons; snowy-haired Jean Louis Ernest Meissonier famous for his paintings of French sports; bowing, bearded Jean Baptiste Edouard Detaille, hearty painter of military life; and a courtly man with white hair and a white goatee who bent over Annie's hand and astonished her with the friendly greeting of one Ohioan to another—Welcome to Paris. Afterward she kept repeating to her husband—that was Mr. Whitelaw Reid, from Xenia, Ohio, just two counties away from Greenville.

French reporters found endless copy at the Wild West. This season the show included a team of Eskimo dogs driven by a sweating Indian in a mothy parka. There was no snow in the Parc du Neuilly, but under the crack of his rawhide whip the huskies raced over the green enclosure toward the white peaks of Montana. More appropriate to a French audience was the newly added Red River cart driven by a French halfbreed in a sky-blue jacket and a jaunty beaded cap. Thousands of those two-wheeled carts had carried the commerce of the prairies—buffalo hides and pemmican, skillets, knives, and whiskey—across the Red River plains from Winnipeg to St. Paul.

In the Parc du Neuilly the wooden wheels turned on wooden axles, and even a Paris reporter could imagine the ear-shattering screech that filled the summer prairies when the Red River brigades were on the trail. The Deadwood Stage had a bizarre history for readers of *Les Temps*. The reputations of Buck Taylor, Con Groner, Duke Graham, Tom Clayton, the skill of the Mexican vaqueros, the fame of Chief Rocky Bear beyond the Missouri, the hunting of buffalo and the herding of cattle—all the lore of the Wild West was new and strange. But the best copy was the matchless markswoman, the daring horsewoman, the demure girl heroine of the plains. As Buffalo Bill seemed the natural man, she seemed the natural woman. She moved like a pony running. She was artless, spontaneous, free as the long-stemmed grass under the prairie wind. The French knew little about bronco-busting, but they felt Annie Oakley's magnetism.

By midsummer the Wild West was a fashion and a frenzy. Paris shopkeepers and concessionaires could not keep up with the demand for Indian blankets, bows and arrows, moccasins, buffalo robes, bearskins, lariats, and high-horned Western saddles. Colonel Cody was fêted at breakfasts, luncheons, dinners. Annie Oakley was presented at receptions and garden parties, where she was made an honorary member of gun clubs and riding clubs. The President of France, waiving all precedent, gave her an honorary commission in the French army.

International visitors to the Exposition were taken to the Wild West as though it were a traditional part of Paris. The Sultan of Turkey, the Shah of Persia, and the King of Senegal admired the daring of the cowboys and marveled at Annie Oakley's skill. The Senegalese ruler, thinking of man-eating tigers that preyed upon the jungle villages of his land, wanted to buy little Missie; he offered Colonel Cody a hundred thousand francs. Cody led the swishing monarch to Annie's tent and let him make his offer directly. He took her refusal with courtly regret. As she remembered it years later: "When I told him I did not wish to go, he went down on one knee with a sweeping grace that would have done credit to ye knights of old England, and lifting my hand raised my fingertips to his lips. He departed with the air of a soldier."

During the long gala summer Rosa Bonheur virtually lived at the camp. She was nearly seventy, gray and weathered like an Indian, but she strode over the lot in an artist's smock and faded beret, stabbing the ground with a rough walking stick. She set up her easel in the corrals, on the shooting range, in the arena. She sketched Indians crouching over their fires, cowboys climbing into the saddle, Annie Oakley on the spotted pony Billy that Cody had brought her from Nebraska, the Red River cart and its driver in his coarse blue coat crossed with a scarlet sash; while she worked she tried her French with his half-Sioux patois from the northern plains. She sketched horses—the wiry Indian ponies, the painted bronchos, the lifey mustangs, the big white-eyed outlaws pitching riders off their backs. She made a life-size painting of Buffalo Bill on his favorite dappled gray Charlie; after reproduction in a new set of show posters it was shipped to Scout's Rest on the Platte.

Another frequent visitor was Prince Roland Bonaparte, a leader among the French anthropologists. He haunted the Indian village, asking about the mythology and superstitions of the Sioux and Cheyenne people. He made notes on the texture of their skin and the color of their eyes, and went away with samples of Indian hair which the braves had obligingly pulled out for him.

It was a festive season, with music, cosmopolitan crowds, fireworks arching over the Exposition grounds, and the lofty web of the Eiffel Tower strung with colored lights. Dressed in Paris clothes, looking as though they had never been west of the Bay of Biscay, Annie Oakley and her husband strolled through the Tuileries Gardens and lunched on the sidewalk under the chestnut trees. They wandered through the Bois and sat in the open-air café beside the curving Seine. They sauntered through the Exposition grounds, the brilliant gardens, the Industrial Palace and the twin Palaces of Art. From the top of the lacework tower they saw the huge spread of Paris around the silver sickle of the Seine. For the Bastille celebration in mid-July all of Paris became a fairground. Bridges and monuments were strung with lights, booths and tents lined the sidewalks, there was music at every public square and dancing in the streets. In soft summer twilight two American show people walked above the river and thought they would never want to leave.

* * *

The Bois was leafless and the skies were low when the Wild West broke camp. Annie Oakley had more things to pack—new clothes, medals, gifts, and a silver loving cup which had been presented by the people of France. At Marseilles they found blue skies and a hectic welcome. There was time for a side trip to Lyons where she collected cash prizes and medallions in a series of target matches. In December the outfit moved on to Barcelona, hoping the Spanish would discover the Wild West with the same excitement that a Spanish navigator had discovered America. But misfortune waited there. For the rest of her life Annie Oakley could not think of Spain without remembering sickness and sorrow.

From the first day their Barcelona camp was overrun with visitors. But it was not curiosity and excitement that brought them; it was hunger. Ragged men, wretched shuffling women, barefoot children furtive as coyotes, swarmed over the lot. They crowded around the mess tent, clamoring for food, fighting for scraps and refuse in the garbage cans. Through that swarm Annie Oakley walked to her tent. When she heard voices outside she parted the canvas on a pair of ragged children. She threw out some coins; in an instant a dozen grimy figures were scrambling in the dirt. She let the canvas down and sat in darkness. They had been poor in Darke County, so poor that even now she could not spend a careless dollar. But she was not prepared for the poverty of Spain. It was her first realization of the devouring hunger in the world.

The beggars brought something grimmer than poverty. One after another the Wild West performers took to their beds with chills and fever. The show was crippled, audiences were small. After the first week Nate Salsbury lowered the admission to half-price, and still the stands stood empty. By then the doctor was the busiest man on the grounds. He carried his black bag into the cowboy's bunk tent, the quarters of the Mexicans, the Indian tepees, the big chilly sleeping tent of the roustabouts. Half the company had Spanish influenza, and smallpox had broken out among the workmen. On a raw gray day Nate Salsbury came back from the city hall with word that Barcelona was under quarantine.

As Christmas drew near the camp was desolate. Three roustabouts were dead of smallpox; ten Indians, far from the plains of home, had died of influenza. In the wigwams huddled figures chanted the death song of the prairie tribes. Beyond the corral a reluctant smoke went up from piles of contaminated clothing. The horses turned their rumps to the raw December wind. Two days before Christmas Frank Richmond, the magnetic ringmaster, lay in a chilly tent with a raging fever. The next day he died, and on Christmas Eve his friends stood bareheaded in a cold Barcelona cemetery while his body went into Spanish ground.

After another wretched month Salsbury got a clearance from quarantine and chartered a grimy Mediterranean steamer. When the show was loaded—the horses, mules, steers, and buffalo, the moody Indians and the silent cowboys, the mountains of baggage and equipment—the rusty ship was so overburdened that the captain refused to take it past the harbor entrance where a January gale was lashing the water white. When the wind diminished and Salsbury offered him more money, he got the ship under way. With engines pounding they steamed into the heaving sea.

Two days and two nights the vessel creaked and groaned, laboring on her way to Italy. On the third day the sky cleared and the sea subsided. They steamed through quiet water between the sunny heights of Corsica and Elba. Next morning they entered the Bay of Naples with Vesuvius smoking against a cloudless sky.

Naples had swarms of barterers and beggars, but the streets were full of laughter and singing and the sky stayed blue. The Wild West played to noisy crowds, with Vesuvius rising above the mimic mountains of the Yellowstone. Between performances Chief Rocky Bear and his braves climbed the smoking mountain and stared into the fearful crater. When Annie Oakley admired the volcano, a Neapolitan artist presented her with two paintings, showing the great cone in eruption and in serenity. At Pompeii she stood in a silent street and looked up at the feather of smoke. On the frescoed wall of a ruined house they saw a figure crouched in marshland where a covey of birds was rising from a thicket. A hunter had lived here in the far-off past, before the rain of fiery ashes, and now two Americans looked down the long corridor of the past.

From Rome on the 4th of March a reporter cabled to the New York Herald: "All Rome was today astir over an attempt of 'Buffalo Bill's' cowboys with wild horses which were provided for the occasion by the Prince of Sermoneta. Several days past the Roman authorities have been busy with the erection of especially cut barriers for the purpose of keeping back the wild horses from the crowds. The animals are from the celebrated stud of the Prince of Sermoneta and the Prince himself declared that no cowboy in the world could ride these horses. . . . Anxiety and enthusiasm were great. Over 2,000 carriages were ranged round the field, and more than 20,000 people lined the spacious barriers. . . . Two of the wild horses were driven without saddle or bridle into the arena. 'Buffalo Bill' gave out that they would be tamed. The brutes made springs into the air, darted hither and thither in all directions, and bent themselves into all sorts of shapes, but all in vain. In five minutes the cowboys had caught the wild horses, saddled, subdued, and bestrode them. Then the cowboys rode them around the arena, whilst the dense crowds of people applauded with delight."

Years later Annie Oakley remembered the play of water in sunny squares and shadowed courtyards—the fountains of Rome. There were dinners and receptions, tours of the tombs and the palaces, and a visit to the Coliseum, where the Indians spread their wigwams on the floor and mustangs clattered over the ancient stones. Amid the memories of chariot races, gladiators, and lions feeding on the Christian martyrs, the Wild West was photographed for the American papers. Finally came an audience in the Vatican. On February 20th, the anniversary of the coronation of Pope Leo XIII, the feathered Indians and the weathered cowboys lined the corridor to the Papal throne. Major Burke, sometimes a devoted churchman, had prepared the Indians. They stifled their instinctive ceremonial cries, standing in silence under the raised hand of the Great Medicine.

The show train puffed away from Rome on the 12th of March. The schedule took them to Florence, where the American colony turned out for every performance; to Pisa, Bologna, and Milan. On the shooting grounds of Milan, once a tournament ground for throwers of spears and lances, Annie Oakley shot against Italian marksmen. The targets were live birds, swift and wild, from the high mountains of Lombardy. She shot unerringly in the strong clear light, putting new medals in her trunk and sending prize money to her New York bank. At Verona, the home of Shakespeare's star-crossed lovers, she thought of sad Juliet looking down from her balcony, and moved by poetry and the past she wrote a thoughtful sentence in her diary: "Fancy sometimes helps us out in this big round world." The old stone circus, built by Diocletian three hundred years before the birth of Christ, echoed with the whoops of Indians and the bang of rifle fire. From Verona the company made a tourist's excursion to Venice, and Major Burke showed them the sights—the great bridge arching the Grand Canal, palaces and piazzas stepping down to the water, the tall campanile of St. Mark's with pigeons fluttering in the courtyard. Here was an opportunity that Arizona John could not miss. A photographer posed Buffalo Bill and four feathered chiefs in a gondola before the piazza of St. Mark's; that picture appeared in Wild West programs for years afterward. There was a week of rest and quiet in the grandeur of Switzerland. After strenuous months on the road Annie Oakley was less interested in the towering Bernese-Oberland than in the "quaint little grottoes where the tired wayfarer may rest."

At the end of April they were in Munich, playing to hearty Bavarian crowds and haunted by American students who drank gallons of coffee in the cook tent. Annie Oakley's most ardent admirer was the visiting Count of Monaco; she and Frank dined with him after the show and sat in his box at the Munich opera. Then three weeks in Vienna, with small audiences which she explained by noting that there was "free music in the parks." They had time for drives in the outlying woodlands, dinners in the cafés, an excursion down the Danube. Annie Oakley and Colonel Cody were luncheon guests at the American embassy, where Frederick Dent

Grant, son of U. S. Grant, was minister. This was a Western luncheon, with talk of the Platte, the Missouri, and the Laramie Plains, for Frederick Grant had once served under General Sherman in the Indian Wars and had surveyed for the Union Pacific. Two other guests, Lady Paget and the Duchess of Cumberland, found it hard to picture Annie Oakley, as crisp and tailored as themselves, on the buffalo plains, though Cody assured them it was old country to her.

The summer schedule began in Berlin, with Prince Wilhelm at the opening performance. In Dresden the Butlers were entertained by "a ducal family," and they returned the favor with a Western breakfast on the show lot. Then came Magdeburg, Braunschweig, Leipzig—where Annie could not resist a set of handsome table linen —Hannover, Hamburg, Bremen, Stuttgart. The military Germans marveled at an American girl's marksmanship, and Prussian officers studied every detail of the Wild West's organization—the setting up of camp, the packing of equipment, the transportation. "Every rope and bundle and kit," wrote Annie Oakley, "was inspected and mapped." The Prussians were especially curious about the movable kitchens that supplied the Wild West with hot food at all hours in all weather; a few years later the German army had the finest field kitchens in Europe.

In early autumn the Wild West toured the historic cities on the Rhine—Duisburg, Düsseldorf, Cologne, Frankfurt—and in the chill of November moved on to the Alsatian capital of Strasbourg. Always aware of domestic matters, Annie Oakley found that storied city "a place where the washfraus gathered along the clear river to beat their clothes and dip them in the soft water till they were beautiful. What a gabbling goes on over the washing!" In Strasbourg the season ended and the show shook down for the winter.

It was a gloomy camp. After eighteen months in foreign lands among strange people, the Indians wanted to go home. Ten of the tribesmen had died in Barcelona, another had died of Roman fever in Italy, the rest were tired of show life and longing for their windswept plains. Their discontent was fanned by news from Dakota. A "Messiah craze" had swept the Western tribes; drums were throbbing on the reservations and day and night naked warriors were stamping around the Ghost Pole. From a missionary in Utah the Utes had learned of a Messiah who would set right the wrongs of the redman, from the Utes the Sioux heard this prophecy. The word went like a wind through the reservations: a miraculous leader would restore to the tribes their game and hunting grounds; the white men would be driven out and the tribes victorious. To hasten the Messiah's coming, medicine men painted themselves and performed the Ghost Dance while the people chanted:

> Over the whole earth they are coming,
> The buffalo are coming,
> The buffalo are coming. . . .

At Wounded Knee Creek, on White Clay Creek, on the Porcupine and Medicine Root rivers, thousands of naked Sioux leaped and shuddered, groaned and cried, rolled on the ground, and cut flesh from their bodies as offerings to the sacred pole. Five thousand miles away, in the dark cities of Germany, Rocky Bear and his braves heard rumors of this agitation. They wanted to go home.

Another trouble shadowed the Wild West camp. From the Bureau of Indian Affairs in Washington came repeated inquiries about the treatment of Buffalo Bill's Indians. The Wild West's European triumph had been reported in American newspapers. Success brings envy and criticism, and now Cody and Salsbury were suspect. In 1889 the Reverend Daniel Dorchester, a descendant of Elder Brewster of Duxbury, Massachusetts, had been appointed by President Harrison superintendent of Indian schools. In four years he traveled 96,000 miles and visited 105 reservations, and he had energy left to fill the newspapers, avid for news of the Wild West, with charges of Cody's mistreatment of his Indians during their foreign tour. Indian Commissioner Thomas Jefferson Morgan took up the cause, insisting that the Indians' place was on the agency lands and not on a circus tour of Europe. In German cities unsmiling U.S. consuls paid official visits to the camp, asking to be shown the Indian quarters, questioning the tribesmen about their food, their pay, their treatment. Though the consuls found no cause for complaint in the well fed, comfortable Wild West camp, the charges continued. It was true the Indians wanted to go home, but not for the reasons given to the press. Finally Cody and Salsbury decided to disband the camp, to take the Indians to Washington where they could be seen and heard for themselves.

There was still another dissatisfaction on the show grounds. Buck Taylor, King of the Cowboys, had grown restless. Ever since the first dusty show on the Omaha Fair Grounds in 1883, he had been riding plunging broncos and roping lunging steers for the glory and profit of Buffalo Bill. Now he was ready to pull out. He had seen the appeal of a Western show and he thought he knew how a company was managed. He decided to go home to America and start a show of his own. Cody was a small man in many ways, and a large man in some others; he was both weak and strong. He liked to be consulted, he loved giving help, advice, encouragement. He also liked deference and subordination. With genuine sadness he gripped Buck Taylor's hand—once he had hired him as a raw-boned young cowboy—and wished him well. At a time like this, with all the years and all the changes, a man had a sense of growing old.

For winter quarters the outfit moved to the old Alsatian village of Benfield, a few miles south of Strasbourg. The animals were fenced in roomy pastures and the properties were stacked in a big storage tent. In the winter lot a homesick company watched Cody and the Indians preparing for their journey home. Annie Oakley and her husband tried to forget their restlessness by wandering the narrow streets of Strasbourg. They came back to camp, hearing church bells over the steep roofs in the chilly dusk, and saw the baggage wagon loading. Tomorrow the home-goers would be on the way. In Annie's tent they found Colonel Cody—he had come to say goodbye.

When he was gone she saw that her autograph book lay open. On a fresh page was a fresh inscription in Cody's loose, impatient hand:

To the loveliest and truest little woman, both in heart and aim in all the world. Sworn to by and before myself.

W. F. CODY, BUFFALO BILL, Strasbourg, 1890.

The next day Cody, Burke, and the Indians were gone. Nate Salsbury was away on an advance trip through the Low Countries, booking engagements for the spring season. It was a forlorn company that settled down for the winter at Benfield, the Mexicans talking about sunny Sonora and the cowboys picking their teeth under the vista backdrop of the forks of the Yellowstone. When an invitation came from England, to give a series of shooting exhibitions at the London gun clubs, Frank packed the gun trunk and Annie folded her costumes. Going to England seemed a little like going home.

CHAPTER 13

Christmas Card from Scotland

One should no longer ride the deserts of Texas or the rugged uplands of Wyoming to see the Indians and the pioneers, but should go to London.

—FREDERIC REMINGTON, *Harper's Weekly*, Sept. 2, 1892.

A YEAR later, in November 1891, Annie Oakley sat in a Glasgow hotel room with the thin cold Scottish rain outside her window. The winter dusk came early, and a little fire of sea coal glowed in the darkening room. While she looked over gray rooftops to the Clyde, the rain changed to snow, heavy gray flakes that melted as they fell. But it was enough to recall the winter streets of New York with the lights all burning through the settling snow, and the white drifted fields of Darke County. She was homesick.

Wherever she went, Frank said, she made a place seem like home —a dressing tent, a railroad compartment, a ship's cabin, a hotel room. Now she took a kettle from the fireside and made tea. In the half-light the room looked friendly. It was full of personal things— an embroidery basket, a silver teapot, little flowered boxes, a tray of wineglasses, table runners, a vase of flowers, tintypes and photographs. But the first snow was in the air, Christmas was coming, and she was in a strange country. This was the third winter of the Wild West's European tour. She had been a long time away from home.

Two dark Christmases lay behind her. It was still painful to remember Barcelona, the Indians burning with fever in their tepees and Frank Richmond buried in a Spanish graveyard. There could be no Christmas in a city under quarantine. When church bells rang at midnight over the empty Spanish streets, they had a frantic sound. A year later in the winter camp near Strasbourg the company felt like exiles, their thoughts following Cody and Burke and the Indians across the Atlantic. They were going home. But it had not been a happy homecoming, and now, as she poured another cup of tea, Annie Oakley's thoughts were gray as the Glasgow gloom.

* * *

From New York Cody and Burke had taken the party to Washington for investigation by the Indian Bureau. Rocky Bear and Red Dog spoke for the tribesmen, telling of their treatment and their travels. After the commissioners had dismissed charges of mistreatment, the Indians were taken to the Union Station and put aboard the train for home. When they arrived at Bismarck, fifty of them, attracted by a blue uniform, dry quarters, and three sure meals a day, enlisted in the Indian police. The rest, including old John Nelson and his Oglala wife, scattered to the winter camps on the reservations.

It was a tragic winter for the Sioux. Reports from the agency at Standing Rock told of a sullen gathering of the clans, of frenzied Ghost Dances that went on night and day, and of Sitting Bull's prophecy that the tribes would banish all intruders and reclaim their ancient hunting lands. In this crisis Colonel Cody could not fail to respond. The press had made him the supreme subduer of Indians; he was an undisputed friend of Sitting Bull; he felt called to action. Major Burke was at his side to help make history and publicity. So in late November, 1890, Cody and Burke set out for the West and the wars.

In Chicago they called on General Nelson A. Miles, commander of the Department of the Missouri. He had attended the Wild West in New York and St. Louis, and had written a testimonial for Cody: "Your services on the frontier were exceedingly valuable." On that November day Burke must have been his most persuasive and Cody his most impressive: before the meeting was over General Miles wrote Cody an order for Sitting Bull's arrest. With that commission they hurried on to Dakota. Two days later they got off the train at Bismarck and were met by Cody's old friend Pony Bob Haslam. Buffalo Bill looked around at the great bare plains; he had not been in Indian country since 1876 when, as the Wild West program read, "business engagements compelled him to return to the Eastern States."

At Fort Yates he asked for a team and wagon. With a few bushels of candy and a pile of blankets he prepared to go to Grand River; he was confident that he could bring back Sitting Bull as his prisoner. But the army officers, provoked by this fantastic interference, planned to delay the intruder at the fort while Agent McLaughlin wired Washington for an order rescinding Cody's authority. The delay took the form of an all-night drinking party, the officers thinking that by morning Cody would forget his military errand. But he was a redoubtable drinker, and whisky increased his zeal for the mission. In a bleak wind on the morning of November 27th or 28th, dressed in a fur-collared greatcoat and a curled-brim Stetson, he was on the road with a team of mules and a wagonload of presents for the Sioux. When orders arrived at Fort Yates from Washington, horsemen pounded out of the stockade. In a few hours they overtook Cody and turned him back.

A few days later a band of forty Indian police were ordered to Grand River, on the belief that Indians could take custody of Sitting Bull without violence. Before daylight on December 15th a police detail found *Tatanka Iyotake* asleep in his cabin. He submitted to arrest, asking that his favorite horse—a gift from Buffalo Bill during his summer with the Wild West—be saddled for him. When the blue-uniformed police stepped outside, they faced a circle of angry Sioux, their bodies still painted for the Ghost Dance. A dog snarled and a pack of dogs came yapping. Men ran out of their tepees with guns in hand. In the cabin Sitting Bull's two wives began a wailing, and his deaf-mute son made a blubbering outcry. The police tried to prod their prisoner forward, but angry tribesmen blocked the way. Suddenly, in the chill winter dawn, Sitting Bull gave a cry of resistance and threw off the hands of his captors. Guns roared as Indians and police shot one another down. The first to fall was *Tatanka Iyotake*, with two bullets near his heart. According to legend Sitting Bull had once told a missionary that after the Battle of the Little Big Horn the ghost of Custer had informed him he would die of trickery in fifteen years. That was in 1876. Now, ten days before Christmas in 1890, he lay dead.

In the burst of gunfire Sitting Bull's horse began a strange ritual of bowing, kneeling, tossing his head. The rattle of rifles had recalled his old training in the Wild West. With men falling around him, he went on through his tricks, and when the camp fell silent he was still untouched. Later, Buffalo Bill bought the horse and put him back in the Wild West show.*

A band of Sitting Bull's followers fled south and west to join old Chief Big Foot. When he learned of Sitting Bull's death and his reincarnation in the body of his horse, Big Foot headed his four hundred Ghost Dancers for the Badlands where Kicking Bear and Short Bull were camped with three thousand fanatical tribesmen. Troops were sent to surround them, and at Wounded Knee Creek the Indians were overtaken by the Seventh Cavalry. Though Big Foot met them under a white flag, the troopers established themselves on high ground above the creek and trained four Hotchkiss cannon on the Indian tepees. It was a bitter night, three days after Christmas, with ice on the creek and a thin snow flying. The next morning, December 29th, while soldiers went through the camp searching for weapons, a medicine man, shuddering in the Ghost Dance, kept shouting to his people in their own tongue that their sacred ghost shirts would turn away the white man's bullets. Suddenly he stopped dancing. He scooped up a handful of dirt and threw it in the air. *Hoka Hey!* A rifle banged and battle began. The Hotchkiss guns poured two-pound explosive shells, fifty a minute, into Big Foot's camp. Within a few minutes two hundred Indians and sixty cavalrymen lay sprawled on the ground. Before the day was over a howling snowstorm swept across the plains.

---

* This horse, ridden by an American flag-bearer, led the U.S. Cavalry in the Congress of Rough Riders at the Chicago World's Fair.

After the blizzard a detail from the Pine Ridge Agency hacked out a huge pit and buried the Indians together. The dream of the Indian Messiah, the final fantasy of a dispossessed people, had led to the massacre of Wounded Knee. It was the last resistance of the tribes, and it came at the end of 1890, when the U.S. census showed that for the first time in its history America no longer had a frontier.

While the beaten Sioux returned to their bleak reservation camps, Buffalo Bill went home to North Platte. He arrived on January 19th, looked through his mail, and immediately wrote a letter to Annie Oakley across the Atlantic—a braggadocio letter indicating his important role in the Indian war, with a thousand troops in his command. Old John Nelson, he said, had turned up for the campaign but went home to his wife's people before the battle. Burke was still riding with a cavalry troop, herding Indians back to the agencies.

In the spring, with a hundred new Indians, including Chiefs Short Bull and Kicking Bear, recently leaders of the Ghost Dance, Cody arrived at Philadelphia. Major Burke joined him there, bringing an orphan Indian boy, little Johnny Burke No Neck, whom he had found on the battlefield of Wounded Knee. They sailed on the S.S. *Switzerland* and rejoined the show at Strasbourg, where Nate Salsbury was waiting with the new season's schedule that would take them from Brussels to St. Petersburg.

Now, a year after Sitting Bull lay dead on the frozen ground at Grand River, Annie Oakley in a Glasgow hotel room wore the beaded moccasins the great chief had given her. The south wind, said the Sioux, came from the land of death. There was tenderness in that belief. *Tatanka Iyotake* had gone to the warm and luring land, to the country of deep grasses and kind skies and the soft wind blowing.

*   *   *

In Glasgow the Wild West was wintering in a huge and drafty hall. Annie Oakley could picture that indoor camp—Utah Frank whittling on a tent stake, Con Groner playing a listless game of checkers with Johnnie Baker, Mustang Jack wetting a pencil on his lips and laboriously writing a Christmas letter home, a circle of

Indians staring at the forks of the Yellowstone while Poor Dog pounded the legbone of a turkey on a horsehide drum.

From the Clydeside came a long-drawn whistle. Out there lay the waterfront—the heave and slosh of tide around the pilings, sea gulls dipping over the harbor, the long dim tunnel of the piershed and the steep pitch of the gangway, the clatter of winches and the hiss of steam, a big ship straining its hawsers. Annie Oakley could not go home for Christmas, but she had a Christmas greeting ready. On her table were signed photographs of the Prince of Wales, the Emperor of Austria, the Duke of Monaco. But she was thinking of neighbors in Greenville, Ohio, of friends in New York and New Jersey, of actors at Tony Pastor's Opera House, of some Indians at Standing Rock. She slipped a folder into an envelope and opened her address book.

That was the first personal Christmas card ever printed. She had planned it herself, made a sketch of it, written out the lines, and taken it to a Glasgow printer. Now it was ready to send. It was a folder with her picture on the cover—a trim figure wearing her Western hat with the single star and her medals of marksmanship. Inside were two drawings like miniature Currier and Ives prints: "Christmas in the West," a log cabin against the snowy woods with a slender girl waving to a sled load of visitors, and "Christmas in the East," a well fed man in a city mansion turning away the hungry. The back cover bore an AO monogram and Annie Oakley's Christmas greeting:

> I've built me a bridge of the kindest thoughts
>> Over the ocean so wide;
> And all good wishes keep rushing across
>> From this to the other side.

In the margin a string of gulls were winging over water. That folder found its way to hotels in New York, to farmhouses in Ohio, to wigwams on the Dakota plains.*

* * *

* At least two persons saved this Christmas card. It appears in the Norcross collection in New York and in the Darke County Museum in Ohio.

In the green English April, 1892, the Wild West took to the road. After a few weeks in the provinces they were back in London at Earl's Court, as an adjunct to the International Horticultural Exhibition. The flora of Africa and Iceland, of New Zealand and Ceylon, did not keep any but the most ardent English gardeners away from the neighboring rodeo. Again London was under the spell of the frontier, and daily crowds crammed the arena. Frederic Remington wrote that every visitor in London went first to the Wild West, and cab drivers headed automatically for Earl's Court when they picked up a fare. "The Tower, the Parliament, and Westminster are older institutions in London than Buffalo Bill's show, but when the New Zealander sits on the London Bridge and looks over his ancient manuscripts of Murray's Guide-book he is going to turn first to the Wild West. At present everyone knows where it is, from the gentleman on Piccadilly to the dirtiest coster in the remotest slum of Whitechapel. The cabman may have to scratch his head to recall places where the traveler desires to go, but when the Wild West is asked for he gathers his reins and uncoils his whip without ceremony."

For the new season Burke and Salsbury had engaged new features. Around the arena with their tattered Union Jack marched the survivors of the Light Brigade. The Sioux stared at these remnants of a British regiment that Alfred, Lord Tennyson, had made immortal: *Theirs not to reason why, Theirs but to do and die.* Another feature was the international hurdle race, matching a Sioux on an Indian pony, a Mexican on a pinto, an English sportsman on an English hunter, a German on a cavalry horse, and an American cowboy on a mustang. Every day the race was run, while the Indians whooped from the forks of the Yellowstone and the British cheered their man. To the delight of the stands the English rider always won, but in the dressing tent he pulled off his red jacket, hunting cap, and polished boots, and donned cowboy clothes for the roping contest; he was Harry Stanton from the plains of Kansas.

The biggest addition was a band of Zulu riders freshly recruited from South Africa, a group of gauchos from South America, and a squad of Russian Cossacks. With these horsemen added to the

Mexicans and the cowboys Major Burke coined a memorable phrase; he announced feats of skill and daring by the "Rough Riders of the World." The gauchos used bolas, iron balls on rawhide thongs, throwing them with accuracy that rivaled the lariat-throwing of the cowboys. The Cossacks, dressed in belted coats, high round hats, top boots and silver spurs, armed with dagger, pistol, and long Caucasian rifle, raced their horses through varying formations and maneuvers. They were led by Prince Ivan Rostamov Macheradse, whom the program described as a descendant of the storied Mazeppa, Prince of the Ukraine. Matching one group of riders against another, the Wild West kept up a sequence of dramatic action. Galloping cowboys snatched pistols off the ground, gauchos hurled bolas after plunging steers, Cossacks and Zulus jumped their horses over barricades. For the new season Annie Oakley tried a new costume, appearing in a plaid shooting suit and feathered Tam o' Shanter, given her in Glasgow. But she belonged in buckskin, and she soon went back to her familiar Western dress.

In May the Wild West had an American visitor who drank Buffalo Bill's whisky, roamed the grounds with Burke and Salsbury, yarned with Annie Oakley in her tent, and sat on a wagon tongue talking Sioux with Rocky Bear. Then he set up an easel and began sketching. He was Frederic Remington, a burly weather-burned young man with restless roving eyes. Often he sat in a box with Major Burke—who never tired of the Wild West performance. The Cossacks rode standing on their heads in the saddle; in a few swift pencil strokes on a sketching pad Remington caught the flying horse and the inverted rider. Burke told of fining the cowboys for riding at a headstand—that was supposed to be a Cossack specialty. There was nothing any man could do on a horse, Arizona John declared, that an American cowboy could not equal or surpass. Remington nodded, turned his pad over and scribbled himself a note. He was writing an article for *Harper's Weekly* to accompany his sketches of the Wild West in London.

At his easel Remington worked swiftly, whistling to himself, singing, smoking, occasionally pulling at the bottle in his pocket. When a sketch went wrong he damned it with quiet and furious profanity, tore it off the easel and began again. In quick sure lines he put life on the paper—the angle of a horse's head, the slouch of a rider in the saddle, the drape of a blanket on a crouching squaw. Frederic Remington, just the age of Annie Oakley (he was thirty-two), had traveled the trails of the West. He had followed the long cattle drives, worked with the wagon trains, ridden with cavalry all the way from Mexico to Montana. He had made his own camp in the sand hills and in stunted trees at timber line. For ten years he had roamed the huge harsh Western country with a painter's kit in his saddle-bags. In 1890 he had seen the Sioux uprising in the Badlands, the last resistance of the defiant tribe. With that experience he made a journalistic scoop, articles, drawings, paintings, but he knew it was the end of the old West. Now in 1892 he wryly observed that one might see the Wild West in London better than in America.

When Queen Victoria asked for an exhibition of riding at Windsor Castle, Nate Salsbury moved half the show to the green fields beside the upper Thames. He marked out a ring on lawn-tennis grounds inside the castle walls, enclosing it in sheepfold fences. On massive battlements that had seen five hundred years of history the Queen and her party sat in a carpeted, canvas-covered pavilion while riders raced in dramatic files and formations, ropers and bola throwers pounded after half-wild cattle, and Annie Oakley shot showers of targets out of the air. After the show there was luncheon for the company in the rooms of the Queen's equerry, and the little woman in a widow's black bonnet presented jeweled medallions to the performers.

At the end of summer, after three and a half years abroad, the Wild West sailed for home. Following an exuberant welcome in New York the show disbanded for the winter. Equipment and animals were sent to winter quarters in Bridgeport; the company scattered. Mr. and Mrs. Frank Butler moved their trunks into a New York hotel and began reading long columns of "Houses for Sale" in the papers. After years of homelessness they wanted a place of their own.

CHAPTER 14

Neighbors at Nutley

Nutley: A small town on the Erie road, about twelve miles from New York. Fine scenery. Delightful surroundings. —*A New Jersey Guidebook*

There isn't much that is prettier than this end of New Jersey. It is all upland, tumbling into shallow valleys and bright sunny reaches along the Passaic River, and hill fields white as snow with the daisies, and everywhere trees, in little clumps or in long lines by the roadside.

—H. C. BUNNER

IN 1892 Nutley was a country town surrounded by woods and waters. The Passaic River bordered it on the east; Basking Creek and the Yantacaw, or Third, River, strung with millponds, wound through leafy ravines in the heart of town. It was an old settlement, with memories of Dutch colonial families—the Rutgers, Van Dyks, Rikers, and Speers—and of British raiders stealing up the Passaic during the Revolution. Its central street bore the name of William Franklin, the last royal governor of New Jersey. Scattered through the town were old stone mills—gristmills, cotton mills, woolen mills—and old houses, built from the nearby Belleville quarries, of red and brown sandstone. In the Enclosure, a residential park along Third River, a score of writers and artists had built homes after the Civil War. Half the houses there had glass-walled studios facing the northern light. The town was named from Old Nutley Manor, whose first proprietor

had found nut trees everywhere—walnut, beech, hazel, hickor
(shagbark and smoothbark), oak, and chestnut.

In wooded grounds on Kingsland Road at the north end of Nutle
jovial Eaton Stone had winter quarters for his trained-horse circu
His roomy barn held an indoor riding ring, and behind the barn
larger ring encircled a grove of oak and walnut trees. During th
winter, sportsmen came out from New York to see his horses. Actor
newspaper men, show people were entertained in his rambling hous

When they got off the train at the old Stitt's Station, Anni
Oakley and her husband found Nutley more like a forest than like
town. The low Watchung hills sloped down to the Passaic. Tre
arched the streets, leaf-strewn streams gleamed through the branche
vine-covered mills drowsed beside the ponds. It was just an hour from
Madison Square Garden, but it was as tranquil as Darke Count
They both were thinking the same thing—here was a homelik
place. They forgot Eaton Stone and his horses.

The agent showed them a wooded corner on Grant Avenue, an
the deed was signed before the train took them over the brow
Jersey meadows to New York. In their minds was a picture of th
leafy street leading down to the curving Passaic.

While the house was being built Frank traveled to New York an
New Jersey gun clubs, representing arms and ammunition firms, an
Annie came to stay in the Leidy household in Nutley. John J. Leid
was editor of a Newark newspaper, his wife was an ardent hors
woman, their daughters could not hear enough of Annie Oakley'
travels with the Indians and cowboys. On autumn days they gallope
out the River Road, past the old Belleville quarries, and Annie gav
her hostess shooting lessons on the Passaic meadows. Meanwhil
at 300 Grant Avenue the house took form—a roomy frame hous
with a wide front porch, a railed balcony, and a five-sided alcove su
mounted by a conical tower. It was built without closets—a matte
of intense interest to the neighbors—because Annie had lived from
trunks for fifteen years. She would have to pack up every spring, an
it would be simpler if she used trunks and wardrobes through th
winter.

When the last dray rumbled up Grant Avenue, after furnitur

vas arranged and curtains were hung, the battered show trunks were
carried in. Out came guns, pistols, knives, lariats, bridles, spurs,
moccasins. From the costume trunks rose a faint tang of tanbark.
The noise of the arena haunted the room, like sea-sound in a shell,
while she hung up fringed skirts and beaded shooting jackets. Out
came photographs of kings, princes, and cowhands, scores of scarves
and neckerchiefs, hundreds of lace handkerchiefs, endless pairs of
gloves and leggings. And dress clothes. Annie Oakley loved clothes
with a hunger stored up from a backwoods childhood. While the
neighbor children played with spurs and lariats, she laid out gowns of
ivory and écru, silk and satin blouses, high button shoes, dress slippers, bicycle boots, carriage boots of kid and patent leather, a French
parasol of shot moiré with a Dresden-china handle.

Then they were ready to entertain the neighbors, who had already
invited them to congenial studios and living rooms. In the 1890's
Nutley had its most extensive artists' and writers' colony. Arthur
Hoeber painted the New Jersey countryside with its streams winding
through marshland under a sunset sky. After years of wandering,
E. L. Field lived quietly on Walnut Street, painting and etching in
his cluttered studio. In the wooded Enclosure were the studios of
George Waldo, portrait painter; Ralph Goddard, sculptor; Frederick
Dana March, landscape artist; Frederick Dorr Steele and Albert
Sterner, illustrators; Harry Chase, painter of sea and sky; English-
born Charles Kendrick, illustrator of children's books.

The foremost Nutley writer was Henry Cuyler Bunner, poet, novelist, short-story writer, and editor of Puck, who lived on Whitford
Avenue in the "House of Spare Bedrooms"; he always had room for
Nutley neighbors and for guests from New York, Boston, Philadelphia, London. In a house in the Enclosure Frank Stockton had
written his famous Rudder Grange; now he lived in the country but
he frequently visited Nutley. Once he brought a manuscript, "The
Lady or the Tiger?" which he had written for an evening party. The
guests heard the tale and made their guesses—when the youth in
the arena opened the door indicated by the princess, which came
out, the lady or the tiger?—and Frank Stockton went off to bed,
leaving them still speculating. In his Nutley study English-born

Richard Kendall Munkittrick wrote *New Jersey Arabian Nights* and
volumes of humorous verse. Other Nutley writers were L. Frank
Tooker, an editor of *Century* magazine; James L. Ford, author of
The Brazen Calf; and Henry Gallup Paine who after a term as
Bunner's associate on *Puck* had become managing editor of *Harper's
Weekly*. In a playful column the New York *Evening Sun* had called
Nutley the "Athens of America." Certainly there was fine, far
ranging talk around the Nutley firesides on winter nights.

Years of savings went into the Butlers' new house, and now there
was no weekly pay check from the Wild West treasurer. Between
days of hunting along the Passaic, Frank called at New York gun
shops as an agent for Remington arms. Annie gave occasional exhibitions in drill halls and gun clubs. In February she appeared again
at Tony Pastor's Opera House, climaxing a bill that included Samson
the Strongest Man on Earth; the Ossified Man whose torso gave back
a stony sound when struck with a hammer; the Elastic Skin Lady
contortionist extraordinary; a one-armed juggler, and a troop of
musical artists. After that lackluster offering the curtain parted on a
backdrop of prairie and foothills, the stage bare except for a low table
with a row of guns on a green velvet cloth lettered ANNIE OAKLEY
in gold. To fanfare a girlish figure crossed the stage in a series of hand
springs, landing on her feet beside the table. She shot ten guns
wheeling and whirling, breaking targets in all directions. After each
shot she gave a little backward kick with her left foot, a comic gesture that delighted every audience, and when the final gun was
empty she ran to the wings. For the third curtain call she turned a
cartwheel, whipped off her Western hat, spread her arms wide and
stood, breathing fast, with the footlights in her eyes. She was almost
sorry that the Wild West opening in Chicago was six weeks away.

But at Nutley life was full—costume parties, theatricals, shooting
exhibitions, archery contests, readings, teas, dancing parties. As
spring came on, the town revealed another mood, the hillsides turning green, the rivers and the millponds brimming. Frank tramped
the meadows with a gun on his shoulder while Annie sat in her
five-windowed bedroom sewing costumes for the coming season. Beside an open trunk sat the neighbor children, gingerly touching

Sitting Bull's war bonnet, at last growing bold enough to put it on. In moccasins and headdress they marched around the room, a train of eagle feathers sweeping the floor. From a chest of drawers they took out Missie's trophies—a miniature rifle of German silver, a tiny sharpshooter etched on gold, the names London, Paris, Rome, Milan, Munich, Brussels engraved on medallions and badges. Sixty years later one of those children, Minnie Leidy, still had vivid memories of that many-windowed room, of polishing a silver loving cup and cutting fringe for a new skirt that Annie Oakley would wear at the Chicago Fair. When Frank Butler came in with a hamper of pigeons, they all had a pot-pie supper.

When H. C. Bunner brought New York friends to the country, he mounted the high seat of his open barouche and drove through the winding streets, pointing out old Nutley Manor and the old millrace where weeping willows dipped down to the water. Mark Twain came on one of those visits; in the noisy Bunner living room he and Annie Oakley exchanged memories of London, Paris, and Rome. The Bunner children had dogs, parrots, goats, pigs—a household of pets. Years later they remembered how the tranquil "Missie" grew fiery when some boys mistreated a pet pig. In an instant her eyes changed and her voice lashed like a whip. Then she joined the laughter at one of Dick Munkittrick's humorous quatrains.

Nutley was a happy, harmonious, high-spirited place, with more laughter and more good talk than any other town in America. Its people were doing things of their own—writing, painting, composing —and sharing them with each other. They had come to Nutley from many backgrounds. Henry Goslee Prout could recall years of adventure in Egypt, surveying roads, planting a flagstaff on top of the Great Pyramid, serving with "Chinese" Gordon in the Nubian desert and the Sudan. Frederick H. Lungren had roved the deserts and mountains of the Southwest; in a studio above a leaf-strewn millpond he was painting the gaunt and golden country beyond the Rio Grande. Eaton Stone, the first man in America to ride four horses, stepping from one to another as they loped around the ring, had taken his circus from Mexico to Canada. Frank Fowler, with his quizzical eyes, long hands, and rumpled jacket, had studied in Rome and Florence and had won a medal in Paris in the year that crowds streamed to the Parc du Neuilly to see Annie Oakley in the Wild West. Now in his Nutley studio, while his wife worked out a passage on the piano, he was making sketches for a lavish fresco of "Music" and "Dance" for the ballroom of the Waldorf-Astoria. Nutley was in the country, but it was also in the midst of the world.

*　　*　　*

That winter the New York papers told of immense preparations at Chicago for the World's Columbian Exposition. On the night of October 12, 1892, on the lake shore at Jackson Park, fifteen thousand rockets had been shot "into the night zenith" to commemorate the discovery of America four hundred years before. A replica of Columbus's little flagship *Santa Maria*, built in Barcelona and towed across the Atlantic by the United States Navy, had been exhibited in New York harbor; then it was taken down the coast, across the Gulf, up the Mississippi, and through the Illinois canal to Chicago. Meanwhile at Jackson Park thousands of men milled over the winter shore—teamsters, carpenters, plumbers, plasterers, steelworkers, stonemasons, painters, sculptors, achitects. In offices and studios men revived memories of the academies in Paris, London, and Rome. "The greatest gathering of artists since the fifteenth century," Saint-Gaudens called it. They worked in mud and snow, amid cranes and derricks, among smoking engines and hissing boilers. Though the New York papers sniped at delay—resenting that Chicago had outbid New York for the exposition—on the trampled lake front rose a dream of colonnades and gateways, cupolas and towers, courts, terraces, and esplanades. Swamps became lagoons, alive with fountains, reflecting marble arches and the many-domed Court of Honor. A White City was rising out of the mire.

Nate Salsbury had asked for a concession inside the gates, proposing to make the Wild West an Exposition feature as it had been in London. When the commissioners refused, he leased fifteen acres adjoining the Fair Grounds. Now he had his own army of workmen laying out the show lot and building a horseshoe of covered stands to seat 18,000. Major Burke was promising the press an enlarged Wild West Company—five hundred people, with new performers and new spectacles in the arena. One of the first acts of Hoke Smith, Secretary of the Interior in Cleveland's Cabinet, was to grant permission for a hundred Indians to appear with the Wild West in Chicago. The papers told of a herd of buffalo coming from Montana and an international gathering of horsemen who would comprise a Congress of Rough Riders of the World. It would be the greatest season, Major Burke declared, in the annals of entertainment.

On mild March days Annie Oakley helped the yard man set out apple trees behind the house in Nutley. As the bare little whips went into the earth she made her own pictures of budding branches, white clouds of blossom, the green blur of new leaves, the red fruit of autumn; and her mind went back to North Star, to the orchard rows above the windy pasture. Her one quarrel with show life was that the season began before the apple trees had blossomed.

Frank Butler had a simple and persistent dream of strawberry vines and green berries ripening among the clustered leaves. He was a man deeply aware of seasons and weather. More complicated than Annie and more withdrawn, more inclined to reverie and reflection, he repeated verses in his mind while he spaced green plants along the straw-strewn garden rows. Though he lived a life of movement and change, he was never a restless man.

Both of them had a sense of future years in Nutley. Whenever they could return, life would be waiting there—the *clop-clop* of hoofs on the wooden bridge, carriages rolling through the streets in the long evening light, cycling parties on the River Road, the sound of lawnmowers on summer afternoons, the smell of leaf fires in the autumn dusk. They would come from trains and steamships, from show tents and hotels, and the house would be ready, with the river gleaming at the end of the street. Here their friends would find them —Denman Thompson, Elizabeth Custer, Langdon McCormick, the Salsburys, Johnnie Baker with his young wife and their small daughters. Here they would put down roots like the apple trees.

But when word came from Burke and Salsbury, telling of the big show lot across from the Exposition grounds on the lakefront, they forgot strawberry vines and apple blossoms. They were ready for the other life. Frank fitted shotguns and rifles into the worn gun case, while Annie aired the trunks and packed her costumes. After a last evening with the Nutley neighbors they boarded the train for Chicago.

CHAPTER 15

Wild West at the World's Fair

The existence of free land, its continuous recession, and the advance of American settlement westward explain American development.

—Frederick Jackson Turner

IN the second week of July, 1893, the American Historical Association met with the World's Historical Congress in morning and evening sessions at the Chicago Art Institute. On Tuesday evening, July 11th, after papers on the Union of Utrecht and the Relation of History to Politics, young Frederick J. Turner of the University of Wisconsin read an essay entitled "The Significance of the Frontier in American History." Through open windows the lake breeze came in warm and restless, the murmur of Michigan Avenue was a background for his words: "Up to our own day American history has been in a large degree the history of the colonization of the Great West. . . . In this advance, the frontier is the outer edge of the wave—the meeting point between savagery and civilization." A long whistle sounded, and out on the lake's darkness another excursion boat, blazing with lights, set off for Jackson Park and the World's Columbian Exposition.

Professor Turner read on: "Since the days when the fleet of Columbus sailed into the waters of the New World, America has been another name for opportunity, and the people of the United States have taken their tone from the incessant expansion which has not only been open but has even been forced upon them. . . . And now four centuries from the discovery of America, at the end of a hundred years of life under the Constitution, the frontier has gone, and with its going has closed the first period of American history."

While he spoke the sky to the southward glowed with a vast illumination. Trains hurried along the lake shore and people streamed out of the cars at Jackson Park. Across from the south gate of the Exposition, twenty thousand persons jammed the Wild West arena where the Pony Express raced around the ring, ambushed Indians swarmed after the Deadwood Stage, the emigrants pulled their wagons into a circle and made camp under the broken buttes.

Only the scholars heard young Professor Turner's essay and pondered its meaning, but millions of Americans had an instinctive knowledge of the significance of the frontier. They wandered through the greatest of all expositions—through endless exhibition halls, past the gleaming Court of Honor, the replicas of Columbus's three little caravels, the goddess of Liberty mirrored in the lagoon. Then they streamed across Stony Island Avenue to see the drama of the American past. Under the cardboard Badlands Indians raced after a herd of buffalo, covered wagons creaked across the plain. At that moment the frontier was disappearing, but its symbols were already fixed in American myth. The crowds did not need a historian to tell them that the frontier had a lasting claim on American memory.

At Sixty-seventh Street and Stony Island, adjoining the Midway Plaisance with its music and marvels, the Wild West had opened in an April downpour, four weeks ahead of the World's Fair, with ten thousand people cheering the Indians and cowboys, the sharp-shooters and broncobusters, and the hard-riding horsemen of seven countries. The company was enlarged—120 Indians, 75 cowboys, 50 Mexican vaqueros, 25 Argentine gauchos, scores of mounted Arabs, Cossacks, Chasseurs, and Lancers. Over the Wild West gateway a pictorial banner showed Columbus on his quarterdeck, "Pilot of the Ocean, the First Pioneer," balanced with Buffalo Bill on horseback, "Pilot of the Prairie, the Last Pioneer." The same design appeared on the Wild West letterhead for 1893. In his endless news dispatches Major Burke referred to the Wild West "at the World's

Fair Grounds." To millions of people Buffalo Bill's show seemed an official part of the Columbian Exposition.

Inside the gate five stuffed buffalo stood in a grove of transplanted poplar trees. Throngs of people passed the bison's glassy stare, seeking a glimpse of Buffalo Bill, Standing Bear, Short Bull, or Annie Oakley. According to Major Burke, who liked round numbers, every day twenty schoolteachers told Cody they had taught him arithmetic in an Iowa or Kansas schoolhouse; the Pilot of the Prairie smiled, nodded, and gave his manicured hand to the next in line. The crowd moved on, to Teddy Roosevelt's log cabin brought from the Dakota Badlands and to the bullet-scarred cabin, brought from Standing Rock, where Sitting Bull had been killed on a winter morning three years before. A weathered oxcart stood under the trees and a four-foot pair of steer horns hung over the doorway of the Roosevelt cabin. Beside Sitting Bull's cabin rose the Ghost Pole around which he had led the fatal Messiah Dance. Inside two stolid women, described as Sitting Bull's faithful widows, sold sweetgrass baskets and beaded moccasins.

In the scattered Indian camp visitors could stare at chiefs straight out of Western history. Sombre, massive Rain-in-the-Face was lame from a wound received in Custer's battle. Plenty Horses still carried in his body five bullets from the Battle of Wounded Knee. Kicking Bear and Short Bull had talked with the Paiute Prophet in Nevada and had brought the Ghost Dance to the Dakota tribes. Jack Red Cloud was the son of implacable old Red Cloud who had ambushed Captain Fetterman's troopers, driven the white men off the Bozeman Trail, and denounced the Indian Treaty of 1868—"The chiefs have sold themselves for another feast of crackers and molasses." Young-Man-Afraid-of-his-Horses had restrained his warriors from killing the commissioners who came to buy the sacred Black Hills.

On pay day the Indians left their camp to taste the pleasures of the Midway. Chief Standing Bear rode the giant Ferris wheel in his headdress of two hundred eagle feathers. Sioux and Cheyenne braves shouldered through the crowds, eating Crackerjack and drinking colored soda water. At the merry-go-round, where the steam organ was playing *Maggie Murphy's Home*, they mounted the painted ponies, and the engineer speeded up the turntable. With blankets flying they leaned over the horses, yelping *ki-yis* of delight.

In the big arena the Wild West held performances afternoon and evening. While the cowboy band played its opening medley, scores of riders worked into formation outside the gate. The band played the national anthem, the crowd sat down, the ringmaster's whistle knifed the air, and Buffalo Bill loped around the track on his cream-white stallion. He was forty-seven, his long hair thinning, his face lined with indulgence and dissipation, but he was still an imposing figure on a horse. From the parade ground his voice boomed out with its old authority: LADIES AND GENTLEMEN: PERMIT ME TO INTRODUCE TO YOU A CONGRESS OF ROUGH RIDERS OF THE WORLD. To a burst of music they appeared—an American cavalry troop with long-staffed guidons, a squad of British Lancers, a troop of French Chasseurs in blue coats and scarlet breeches, German Uhlans in gleaming helmets, booted Russian Cossacks, Argentine gauchos in sombreros and vivid serapes, white-robed Arab Bedouins, and American cowboys in leather chaps and faded shirts. While Buffalo Bill doffed his hat to the flags of all nations they circled the arena, men and horses of all colors, a World's Fair of horsemen. They galloped in concentric circles, in crisscross lines, in weaving patterns, and to a final fanfare they raced off to the wings. The arena was empty—except for a slender rider with a single star on her upturned hat. She curveted her pony in the center of the ring while the announcer gave the crowd a magic name, "the peerless woman marksman, the maid of the Western plains—Annie Oakley!"

She was thirty-three that season, but she looked seventeen. She still had her quick lithe movements, her girlish charm, her fine coloring that needed no makeup. While the band increased tempo she jumped off her pony and ran to the gun-covered table. Guns smoked in her hands and targets shattered in air. She shot on foot, on horseback, from a bicycle; she shot from both shoulders and behind her back. While six glass balls went up she turned a hand-spring and seized a repeating rifle; the six balls vanished. She caught her pony, leaped to the saddle, and raced away.

Then came a race between a Cossack, an Arab, a Mexican, an

Indian, and a cowboy, each on a horse from his own country. The Pony Express pounded across the prairie. As the rider dropped from his foaming horse, the saddlebags were thrown on a fresh mount. He leaped astride and the hoofbeats drummed away. A file of plains wagons was attacked by Indians, but the emigrants were saved by Buffalo Bill and his troopers. Following feats of horsemanship by the Rough Riders of the World, a hunting party of Sioux took after a herd of buffalo. Johnnie Baker did acrobatic shooting, Mexican vaqueros demonstrated the lariat, gauchos threw the bola, there was a bronco-breaking contest in which Frank Hammett, current King of the Cowboys, rode an outlaw horse across the prairie. After military formations, jumping, and acrobatic riding by the Congress of Rough Riders, the battered old Deadwood Stage was rescued again from whooping redskins. Though the show was more varied than before, it retained all the familiar features from Western history and folklore.

The final number, the Battle of the Little Big Horn, an enlarged version of "Custer's Last Stand," was most effective at night performances with artificial lighting. After a moment of silence and emptiness, floodlights showed an Indian village at the foot of colored buttes and ridges. For twenty thousand spectators it is daybreak on the Little Big Horn, with ponies picketed and fires gleaming. Through the stunted pines a scout approaches. Stealthy as a wolf he studies the camp and steals away. He returns with long-haired General Custer and his orderlies. They make a careful count of Indians and horses, but a wakeful young Sioux watches them ride away. In a burst of activity the Indians strike camp, catch their ponies, prepare for battle. The fight rages, Indians ringing the cavalry in a circle of running fire. One by one the troopers drop from the saddle, and at last Custer falls among his men. War whoops fade as the Indians ride away. The field is silent, men and animals in grotesque stillness, when Buffalo Bill reins his white horse above the body of Custer. He bares his head on the silent battlefield, and the show is over.

Despite the addition of the Congress of Rough Riders it was essentially the spectacle that Steele MacKaye had evolved for Madison Square Garden seven years before. The Pony Express, the wagon train, the Deadwood Stage, the steers and buffalo, the hard-riding Indians and cowboys, the feats of marksmanship—these belonged to the vanished frontier, but they would never grow old.

*   *   *

Steele MacKaye was in Chicago that summer with an undertaking of his own, a grandiose project that ended in resounding failure. After raising nearly a million dollars, he was erecting on the northern edge of the Exposition grounds the greatest theater in the world. The Spectatorium, he called it, a vast domed hall, half on land and half projecting into Lake Michigan. There he planned an epic pageant of Columbus, The World Finder, that would show in six acts on a forestage of water with twenty-five telescopic stages behind, the events of the great navigator's triumphant and tragic life. Musical background would be provided by three massive choruses and a symphonic orchestra. Young Walter Damrosch was engaged to direct the music, and Anton Dvorák was composing the score: for The World Finder he wrote parts of the New World Symphony. Twelve thousand spectators would watch the ships of Columbus sail into the water stage. They would see the Spaniards landing on the New World's shores: five carloads of tropical vegetation had arrived from Jamaica to convert a stage into the island of San Salvador. They would see the great navigator return to Spain in shackles and die in wretchedness at Valladolid.

While the early season crowds thronged Jackson Park, MacKaye feverishly pushed his architects and foremen. The vast theater took form on the lakefront. The orchestra was rehearsing, the choruses were assembled. But in June came reports of business failures around the country, and MacKaye's backers failed to produce the money they had subscribed. Carpenters came down from their lofty scaffolding, plumbers and electricians climbed up from their tunnels, teamsters dumped the last scoop-buckets of earth and drove their horses home. Steele MacKaye was left alone on the trampled shore.

He stayed in Chicago all summer, hoping that some miracle would bring the workmen back to complete his Spectatorium. Occasionally he visited the Wild West, watching the drama he had helped to shape. There was a welcome for him in every tent. Cody called for "a glass o' greetin'," Nate Salsbury showed him the attendance figures, Burke introduced him to the chiefs. His face might light up for a minute as he told Annie Oakley or Arizona John about his vast half built theater and his unproduced drama of Columbus. He walked through the Wild West grounds, feeling the frontier vitality around him, and then went back to the silent skeleton of the Spectatorium. No miracle had happened there.

To the Exposition came writers from the foreign press—from England, France, Belgium, Germany, Italy, Spain. After a tour of the halls of art and science, the exhibits of agriculture and industry, they found their way to the Wild West. They watched the drama of the plains, they drank with expansive Buffalo Bill, they toured the Indian village with Major Burke, and before they left the lot they called on Annie Oakley. A bed of flowers bordered her tent, geraniums and primroses flanked by tall-blooming hollyhocks. In front of the opening, like an extension of the tent floor, stretched a wooden platform where she sat in the shade of a tree. Inside were her couch and rocking chairs, her books and pictures, her guns and her banjo, her embroidery stand and dressing table. Her visitors had seen her shoot in Europe; they reminded her of past seasons in London, Paris, Rome, Munich, Brussels, Glasgow. They scribbled notes about her guns, her costumes, her homelike tent in the midst of the jostling show grounds.

With reporters, friends, visitors, Annie Oakley had company at all hours of the day. "She welcomes us royally," wrote Amy Leslie in the Chicago Daily News. "Her tent is a bower of comfort and taste. A bright Axminster carpet, cougar skins and buckskin trappings all about in artistic confusion. She has a glass of wine awaiting and a warm welcome." In that pleasant retreat the beautiful and vivacious Mrs. Nate Salsbury compared embroidery patterns with "the most remarkable markswoman of all time." Mrs. Cody (this was her only season with the show) brought her daughter Irma, then eleven years old and the Cody baby. They might be joined by the young wife of Johnnie Baker and busy "Marm" Whittaker, general housekeeper of the Wild West; when reporters appeared Marm Whittaker declared that Annie Oakley could shoot a fly a mile off. Irma Cody, a bright and handsome child, spent hours in Missie's tent; that summer Annie taught her to embroider, to find chords on the banjo, to ride a bicycle. Another frequent visitor was little Sammy Abdallah, a dark-eyed Arab boy, the son of a hard-riding Bedouin. He was five years old, always shy on his arrival at her tent but soon babbling in mixed Arab and English. When he grew sleepy he curled up like a dog and took his nap on her floor.

At the end of July Chicago's shrewd mayor, Carter Harrison, proclaimed a day of outing for the poor children of the city and asked the World's Fair officials to admit them free. When the request was denied, Major Burke saw an opportunity. The Wild West offered every child in Chicago a free ride on the Illinois Central to Sixty-third Street, a free pass into the show grounds, a free seat in the arena, and free candy and ice cream. "Waif's Day" found fifteen thousand children swarming over the grounds. Annie Oakley led a wide-eyed troop through the Indian village. They stared at feathered chiefs and blanketed squaws, they peered under wagons and into tepees. Out of a dim wigwam came a bright-eyed Indian boy. When Annie spoke he put his hand in hers and made the rounds with the Chicago children. He was Johnny Burke No Neck, the Sioux waif who had been found beside his dead father after the Battle of Wounded Knee.

In August the Wild West turned away thousands daily. Every fifteen minutes an excursion train pulled up at the World's Fair Station. The three-decked steamer *Christopher Columbus*, the only whaleback passenger vessel ever built, delivered thousands of people every hour at the Jackson Park dock, and twenty-five other steamers shuttled between the Fair Grounds and downtown Chicago. The World's Columbian Exposition had become the most successful of all World's Fairs, and the Wild West prospered with it. On Wild West Day, Cody led his grand parade through the Exposition grounds, around the Court of Honor, past the goddess of Liberty and the replicas of Columbus's fleet in the lagoon. Two hundred thousand people watched the frontier pass under the domes and towers of the White City.

At every performance celebrities sat in the Wild West boxes and were presented to the audience: the Duke of Veragua, a direct descendant of Columbus, and his brother the Marquis of Barboles; an international company of naval officers; the Princess Infanta of Spain and her husband Prince Antoine; the Duke of Seramonte; the Prince of Teave and his party; the royal Italian commissioners to the Exposition. There were churchmen, actors, writers, mayors of American and foreign cities, state governors, United States senators, members of Parliament. Prince Roland Bonaparte renewed acquaintance with the Wild West; four years before, in Paris, he had brought a committee of French anthropologists to visit the Indian camp. Now Prince Roland, inveterate president of the French Geographical Society, asked the cowboys about locations in Colorado and New Mexico where he could investigate cliff dwellings. Another French visitor was M. Benoit Constant Coquelin of the Comédie-Française; a few years later he would tour the United States with Sarah Bernhardt. M. Bartholdi, the sculptor of "Liberty," stood in his place while the cowboy band played the *Marseillaise*. Cardinal Gibbons and a party of fifteen churchmen filled the center boxes on a day in early September. On another day came a Hoosier delegation led by Governor Claude Driscoll of Indiana, ex-President Benjamin Harrison, and James Whitcomb Riley.

Generals were common figures in the stands, but a special event was made of the visit of General Nelson A. Miles and his wife and a party of twenty-five officers from Fort Sheridan. For that performance Cody rode a bay gelding given him a few years before by General Miles. After the show there were food and drink in Cody's spacious tent and a reunion of old plainsmen. In 1876 General Miles (he was known as "Bear Coat" among the Sioux) had met Sitting Bull on the windswept prairie north of the Yellowstone—the mustached general on a white horse at the head of his troops, Sitting Bull in full headdress sitting bareback on a painted mustang with his hunters behind him. The meeting ended in battle. General Miles had already defeated the Cheyennes, Kiowas, and Comanches; in that year he defeated the Nez Percés and the Sioux. Ten years later he crushed Geronimo's Apaches in the desert of Arizona. He had received grateful tribute from the legislatures of Kansas, Montana, Arizona, and New Mexico. He knew about the disappearance of the frontier.

*   *   *

In the summer of 1893 they came to Chicago from near and far from the crossroads of the Middle West and the capitols of Europe. Many visitors made long journeys, but the most strenuous traveling was done by nine Western ranch hands who engaged in the Great Cowboy Race. It was an idea originated by a Nebraska editor and first promoted by a publicity agent for the Exposition; at news of it Major Burke groaned with envy and self-reproach. Then he climbed aboard, announcing that the race would end at the gateway of the Wild West grounds and that Buffalo Bill would present the winner with $500 and a Colt revolver inlaid with silver and pearl. It began to look like a Wild West feature.

On the afternoon of June 13th the prairie town of Chadron, Nebraska, swarmed with people. They had come in on horseback, in buckboards and rattling farm wagons, from the Niobrara sand hills and the coulees of Chadron Creek, even from the Black Hills over the Dakota line. Four thousand were there, according to the *Chicago Tribune*, and that would have emptied all of Sioux, Sheridan, and Box Butte counties. They streamed through Main Street and milled around the pillared veranda of the Blaine Hotel, where the nine riders drew into line and were photographed for *Harper's Illus- trated Weekly*. Editor Jim Hartsell of the Chadron weekly paper pushed up the hotel steps and made them a short speech: "Gentle- men, the time to start the great cowboy race from Chadron to Chi- cago has arrived. Pay strict attention to the rules governing the race; also the laws of the states through which you pass. Take good care of your ponies and sustain the renown of the city of Chadron, the State of Nebraska, and the great West." The town marshal, standing in for Governor Lorenzo Crounse who regretted that he could not be on hand, raised a gleaming revolver presented for the ceremony by the Colt company. At the crack of the pistol the horses shuffled off. They had a thousand miles to go. The crowd guessed that the winner would arrive at Chicago in something between twelve and eighteen days.

The last rider out of town was Doc Middleton, a roving Western character with a lurid reputation. Now forty-five, with a furrowed face and grizzled hair, he was said to have spent his youth in Texas and come to Nebraska as a fugitive from justice. There he became the leader of the Pony Boys, an outlaw band operating from the Black Hills. He had been a gambler, cattle rustler, road agent, Indian fighter. (He would die in jail in Douglas, Wyoming, in 1913.) Once, according to legend, he had made a famous ride, pounding two hundred miles from Crow Buttes to Long Pine Barracks ahead of a band of Sioux. Now he was a family man, hoping to pick up some prize money for another lengthy ride. But he was in no hurry at the start. After the others had jogged over the first bare ridge he was still lounging in the saddle, shaking hands with his well-wishers, making bets on the time of his arrival in Chicago. He leaned down to his wife and two children and then waved a hand to his friends. "Boys, I'm the last to start, but I'll be first in Chicago." It would be a reunion when he pulled up at the Wild West grounds, for Doc Middleton, billed as the Black Hills Desperado, had traveled with Buffalo Bill in 1886-1887. As he loped out of Chadron he looked like a winner.

One well publicized contestant had failed to appear for the race. She was Emma Hutchinson from Denver, a cowgirl who became the favorite of the Chicago newspapers as soon as she announced her plans. They gave a colorful account of her background: born in LaCrosse, Wisconsin, she had grown up in Montana where she rode the range like a veteran cowboy. Once she brought a string of horses through 450 miles of rough country in seven days of stormy weather. She had ridden bucking horses in cowboy contests and won races from scouts and Indians. The horse she would ride to Chicago, said the papers, was a noted outlaw which only she could manage. In Denver she gave a statement to the press: "I'll leave Denver a fortnight before the race, toughening up my horse by stints of twenty-five miles a day to the starting point at Chadron. I expect to win. In long rides I start off very easily and will probably be left far behind when we start. But look for my pony to cover ground when we get to

Illinois. I'll rub him down each night and sleep in the stall to keep him from being 'salted.' He will get oats but very little hay. If he is fagged on the last days I'll begin to give him whisky. I expect to win by endurance and foresight."

After this announcement Emma Hutchinson dropped out of sight as completely as if Major Burke had created her in his fancy. Some sizable bets were placed on her, but she never appeared in Chadron or Chicago and was not heard of again.

But the press agents had other material. They kept the columns filled day after day while the riders crossed the prairies of Nebraska and clattered through the towns of Iowa. The contestants had sober names—Dave Douglas, Emmet Albright, Jim Stephens, Charlie Smith, John Berry, but the papers called them Snake Creek Tom, Cockeyed Bill, Rattlesnake Pete, and gave each one a past of hairbreadth escapes from Indians, rustlers, and murderous outlaw horses. Two Sioux Indians were reported among the riders, He Dog and Spotted Wolf, both from the Rosebud Agency, but they dropped into limbo along with Emma Hutchinson.

The rest of the contestants jogged on across the plains and prairies. Rules required them to register at stations at Long Pine, O'Neill, and Wausau in Nebraska; at Sioux City, Galva, Fort Dodge, Iowa Falls, Waterloo, Manchester, and Dubuque in Iowa; at Freeport and DeKalb, Illinois. All the riders except Joe Campbell of Creede, Colorado, had two horses, one on a lead rope.

Slim George Jones of Whitewood, South Dakota, the youngest rider, led the race at the end of the second day, arriving in Gordon, Nebraska, with the long shadows of sundown. Next day Jim Stephens, Doc Middleton, and Joe Gillespie galloped through town. "The rest," said the papers, "are either lost in the sand hills or laid up with fatigue." After six days Doc Middleton had pulled ahead. When he reached the Missouri River he had but one horse; the other had gone lame near O'Neill, Nebraska, and had been left at Coleridge. While he stopped to water his horse and talk to a knot of admirers, a rattle of hoofs came up behind him. Joe Gillespie loped past on a sorrel pony, with a gray gelding on the lead rope. Soon Jim Stephens went by, waving his hat with its rattlesnake band.

The riders crossed the Missouri on a ferry and were cheered by a waiting crowd at Sioux City. They spent the night there, a hot night followed by a hot, windless morning. Doc Middleton decided to rest his horse for half a day. Before noon Emmet Albright, Charlie Smith, and John Berry registered at the Sioux City station. Two days later Berry was in the lead, passing through Webster, Iowa, with Stephens and Gillespie two hours behind him. In three more days, just as Sunday morning church bells were ringing on the Mississippi bluffs, a small man in dusty, sweat-stained clothes clattered into Dubuque on the North Cascade Road. Sunday schools emptied at news of the first rider in the Great Cowboy Race. The children of Dubuque watched John Berry, riding a brown pony and leading a bay, take his animals to a livery stable for a rubdown while he ate stewed chicken at the hotel. At noon he rode across the high bridge over the Mississippi, escorted by a swarm of children and dogs.

As John Berry crossed to Illinois, "Rattlesnake Pete" rode into Dubuque. He had left one horse in Sioux City, and now he rode a big roan, General Grant. Pete fed him oats, then reached into the saddlebag for the horse's dessert—dried beef. While he was tightening his cinch, Joe Gillespie pulled up, his face dark with a week's dusty beard. They crossed the bridge together, mentally calculating the miles to Chicago.

Two mornings later, on the stony pavement of Sixty-third Street at the south end of Jackson Park there was a brittle clatter, lighter than the stamp of teams and cart horses. A shout went up and crowds gathered. People swarmed out of the Midway and the Exposition grounds. John Berry had finished the ride begun far out on the plains of Nebraska thirteen days and sixteen hours before. When he slid down from his saddle in front of Cody's tent, he wasn't as tall as his wiry bronco. He looked around at the stuffed buffalo under the trees, at the Indians shuffling up from their camp and the Wild West performers coming out of the cook tent. They all shook his hand. Then the dusty cowboy looked up at beaming, booming Major Burke and at Colonel Cody, a little puffy-eyed with sleep. They sent his horse to the stable and took winner Berry to a late breakfast.

Afterward John Berry told reporters about his last night's ride:

"I left DeKalb at 11:05. Fed and watered at a farm between Elburn and Lodi. Took the straight St. Charles Road and struck Mayville around 7 A.M. Came into Chicago on Madison, Jackson, Ashland Avenue, 22nd Street, and Michigan Avenue, asking the way to the World's Fair Grounds. I didn't like all this pavement for my horse. My horses were furnished by John D. Hale of Devil's Tower Ranch in Wyoming. Both good horses. I left Sandy sixty miles out of Chicago and came in on Poison."

Reporters were still talking to Berry when Emmet Albright rode in on a dun pony with a black mare trailing; he was the only man to finish with two horses. Joe Gillespie and Charlie Smith arrived in mid-afternoon. Doc Middleton and Rattlesnake Pete came in after dark, complaining that they had lost their way in the suburbs of Chicago.

To allay the concern of the Humane Society, Buffalo Bill himself examined the horses and pronounced them all sound and fit. Albright's dun bronco bit a Wild West wrangler, and Poison aimed a kick at admiring Major Burke. Joe Gillespie's sorrel mare Betty Shafer tried to bite solicitous John G. Shortall, president of the Illinois Humane Society. Cody declared that there was more abuse of horses in the city of Chicago than on the Western range, and cited the cowboy, rather than the Humane Society, as the horse's best friend.

The next day, before prizes were awarded, the air was charged with rancor. Reporters watched warily for six-shooters while they scribbled rumors about contestants riding on freight trains and taking their horses off to register at the stations. A farmer in Iowa was said to have seen a cowboy riding in the tail of a wagon leading two horses on tether. One rider was accused of ending the race on a horse that had never been west of the Missouri. At this point stubby John Berry, not a talkative man, made a statement to the press: "There was a combination put up to beat me. But I walked my horses half time the first two days so they could finish strong. Some say I rode in a wagon but they are liars."

After a day of wrangling the contestants rode into the crowded arena to a fanfare of music. The prize money was divided among the five who had finished the run, and Major Burke made a speech about the character of the cowboy, the city of Chadron, the State of Nebraska, and the epic empire of the West. If the Great Cowboy Race was a fiasco, Arizona John did not seem to know it.

*   *   *

Years afterward Annie Oakley recalled the summer of the World's Fair as vaguely unreal, like something dreamed or read about. There was the Wild West make-believe with its cardboard buttes and bluffs, its stuffed bison, its transplanted frontier life; and around it the greater make-believe of the Midway Plaisance and the Grand Court of Honor. Crowds, music, carnival, from April to October. The kaleidoscopic Midway brought far places of the world into jostling nearness—Old Vienna with cobbled streets and lilting music, the gray walls of Blarney Castle rising above the Irish village, camels swaying out of Cairo Street, the Russian village with its horse fair, the German village enclosing a feudal castle, a cluster of tents from Lapland with the Lapps sweating in their furs, a walled Hungarian village with dancers whirling to wild gypsy music, a bamboo Javanese village cool and tranquil with a water-wheel turning in a green glade and a lookout on a platform keeping watch for tigers. Through the crowds on the long boardwalk passed natives of Siam, India, China, Japan, tall Russians from the steppes, black pygmies from Africa. Jim Corbett who had knocked out John L. Sullivan punched a bag in an exhibition hall. Edison's miraculous new phonograph gave out words and music in a concert room. A banner advertised a Congress of Beauties from twenty lands. Tom-toms throbbed for a tribal dance in the African village, Turkish musicians kept time for whirling dervishes, a Torture Dance went on in the Algerian Theater. There were Hindu jugglers, Chinese fire-eaters, Persian sword-swallowers. Overhead, high above the bands and orchestras, the barkers and vendors, the wheel chairs, sedan chairs, and miniature railroads, a tightrope walker streamed fireworks from his hands and feet. In the center of the long Plaisance rose the enormous lighted Ferris wheel, carrying 1,300 people high above the roar of the Midway and the glare of the White City. From the crest of the circle there was a far view over the dark lake and the night prairie.

After the evening performance in the arena it was dream-like to stroll through the Exposition grounds—down the avenues of the state and foreign pavilions, past the plazas, fountains, and lagoons. From the bandstand young John Philip Sousa turned to the ebbing crowd and their voices joined in *Old Folks at Home*. Venetian gondolas, with a gondolier singing *Santa Lucia*, drifted over the lagoon, past the illuminated "Liberty," around the huge MacMonnies Fountain with its many-colored waters, under the high stern of the *Santa María* with the ghost of Columbus at the rail, past the wooded island glimmering with thousands of Japanese lanterns.

Beyond the esplanade excursion boats blazed on the black water, and at the lake's edge rose the gaunt framework of MacKaye's Spectatorium. It looked, said a Chicago newspaper, like the skeleton of some great extinct animal cast up by the dark and ancient lake on the lighted shores. It had cost $850,000 to plant the deep foundations, to dig the conduits and tunnels, to raise the empty shell. In September it was sold to a wrecking company for $2,500. Soon it would vanish, and five months later feverish, dynamic Steele Mac-Kaye would be dead.

September brought a haze over the lake and a languor over the lavish Fair Grounds. It brought a kind of sadness to the Wild West. A triumphant summer was ending; six million people had passed through the gates; would there ever be such a season again? Nate Salsbury walked the lot thinking about next year; his eyes were tired and his beard was flecked with gray. Major Burke was restless as a buffalo bull, but the ring was gone from his voice as he talked of the great next season at Ambrose Park in Brooklyn. Cody sat in his tent, drinking with old Pony Bob Haslam. The immortal plainsman was showing his mortality; downtown in the Palmer House or in the Gold Coast mansions his eyes lit up with the excitement of bare-shouldered women and convivial admirers, but in his tent at midnight under the yellowing leaves of the maple grove he drank his whisky like a tired and lonely man. He had made a fortune this season. Back in North Platte he would pay off the mortgages of five churches, and that winter he would invest many thousands in a printing plant in Duluth, a Wisconsin cereal company, and a reclamation project in Wyoming. Gullible, generous, childishly believing that money would flow like a fountain, he would begin to dream of fortunes in Arizona copper mines.

Something was ending in September, 1893, while yellow leaves drifted down on the grand lagoon and paint began to peel from the domed pavilions. From across the country came news of economic crisis, rumors of strikes and lockouts, a growing anxiety and unrest. Hundreds of banks were closing their doors, thousands of firms were suddenly bankrupt, one out of every four American railroads passed into the hands of receivers. Half the people of Pittsburgh were in want. In New York and Boston strikers were patrolling silent factories, and militiamen were patrolling the strikers. On one September day in Chicago 22,000 waited for food tickets at the Kopperl relief agency. Even in frontier Denver times were desperate; a relief camp spread along the South Platte riverbank, people slept on the barracks floor and at meal time a thousand men shuffled into line. In Massillon, Ohio, fiery Jacob Coxey proposed that the federal government launch a $500,000,000 public works program; soon he would lead his ragged army over the roads to Washington. While floodlights still illumined the Court of Honor and the band played *Oh! Susanna, don't you cry for me!* men gathered in Chicago soup lines and shivered in the first chill of autumn. The City Hall was opened and homeless people slept in the corridors.

At the end of summer the foreign commissioners to the Exposition left Chicago for a tour of the Dakota wheat fields. In the Red River Valley they saw the vast Dalrymple farm with wheat to the sky. Forty-two mechanical binders were at work, a dozen steam threshers spouted grain and straw in a 25,000-acre field. Frederic Remington, along on a journalistic assignment, was amazed at the transformation of the country where he had once ridden with scouts and cavalry. "The immensity of the wheat fields in Dakota is astonishing to a stranger. They begin at the edge of town and we drive all day and we are never out of them. On either side they stretch away as far as the eye can travel."

In Oklahoma the opening of the 6½ million acres of the Cherokee Strip sent thousands of home seekers into the Indian lands. On the morning of September 16th bugles shrilled, guns sounded, and an army of men on horseback, in cart, wagon, buckboard, and carryall raced over the prairie; and America's last great body of arable land ceased to be public domain.

Only the scholars at the World's Historical Congress had heard Professor Turner describe the end of the frontier, but all America felt the difference. At Jackson Park at the end of October there was tension in the air when the sunset gun boomed its last salute and all the Exposition flags came down. (They came down from half-staff because Mayor Carter Harrison had been shot by an irate citizen three days before.) Within a few months Chicago would be paralyzed by the great railroad strike. Governor John Peter Altgeld, who as a young Chicago lawyer had drawn up the partnership of Cody and Salsbury in 1883, would refuse to muster Illinois troops to protect trains from strikers' violence. Then President Cleveland would order two thousand federal troops to Chicago. So in 1894 the Seventh Cavalry, Custer's regiment, would ride through the streets of Chicago, throwing a guard around the railroad shops and terminals. General Miles at the head of his men might recall his meeting with Sitting Bull on the plains of the Yellowstone and his pursuit of Geronimo through the harsh valleys of Arizona. Hearing the troops sing Garry Owen while protecting the property of the Pullman Company and the New York Central, he would have his own thoughts about the passing of the frontier.

One of the headquarters tents, London, 1887. Albert Scheibel, secretary; Nate Salsbury, general manager; Jule Keen, treasurer; John M. Burke, press agent. Photograph of Annie Oakley at right.

A group from the Wild West at Mannheim, Germany, 1890.

North Platte
Jan. 19th 91

My Dear Annie

I received your nice Christmas Card. And would have acknowledged it before but I've been off to the war. Just got back to day. I heard a thousand soldiers out. the war is over. but Pawnee is so stuck on it he wont come away. I think he is going to marry a squaw. Old John Nelson got scared out and run away & never stoped until he got here to North Platte.

Well my dear little Bird Pretimy cried when I first heard of your death. then I got to thinking it over & made up my mind it was not so. Cabled Frank but recd no answer. & knew full well if our Annie had died. Frank would have cabled me. Will be glad to hear from you when ever your birth day come & hear. W. C. is all N.Y. —

Love to you & Frank.—
Col.

Letter from Cody to Annie Oakley. (Courtesy of Mrs. Annie Fern Swartwout). The Indian War referred to followed the death of Sitting Bull and culminated in the Battle of Wounded Knee. The report of Annie Oakley's death was occasioned by the death of a concert singer who had taken the name.

BELOW: Annie Oakley's Christmas Card. Glasgow, 1891. (Courtesy of Mrs. Annie Fern Swartwout).

Annie Oakley's
A Christmas Greeting

"LITTLE SURE SHOT."

CHRISTMAS IN THE WEST.

CHRISTMAS IN THE EAST.

CHAPTER 16

The Long Show Train

Why hasten the advent of that threatening day when
the vacant spaces of the continent shall all be filled, and
the poverty and discontent of the older States shall find
no outlet? —BRYCE: *The American Commonwealth*

BEFORE they had unpacked their trunks in Nutley, the neighbors
were calling. Some of them had been to the World's Fair and had
seen Annie Oakley in the Wild West arena, but that is not what
they talked about. They were all full of the same thing—the Nutley
Charity Circus.

In New York thousands of unemployed were standing in bread
lines and sleeping in fifteen-cent lodginghouses; in Philadelphia and
Baltimore crowds gathered at relief stations; the Boston Common
was full of restless, jobless men, and the police drove a mob from
the Massachusetts State House. Every day hundreds of homeless
men were climbing out of boxcars in the freight yards of Newark
and Jersey City. Even in tranquil Nutley the mills had closed and
families were cold and hungry. "Now is the time," wrote the editor
of *Harper's Weekly*, "for devising means of relief, for saving the
worthy poor from suffering and death from starvation and exposure."
To provide funds for a Red Cross relief organization, the citizens of
Nutley would hold a charity circus. H. C. Bunner had proposed it,
all his neighbors had responded, and now plans were under way.

Around the Bunner fireside, in Eaton Stone's jumbled living room, at the Butler house on Grant Avenue, at Munkittricks' and Fowlers and Fields', they talked about the talent they could enlist in Nutley the sequence of skill and slapstick in the program, the advertising that would bring people from Newark, the Oranges, Jersey City, and New York. The date was set in March, before Eaton Stone would take his horses on the road and Annie Oakley would begin rehearsal for the new Wild West season. H. C. Bunner served as press agent while J. H. Bailey, in the red coat and silk hat of a ringmaster supervised rehearsals. "The performers were amateurs," the New York papers said, "with one or two brilliant exceptions."

In the final week of March, 1894, Eaton Stone's big white riding barn was gay with bunting, bright with electricity, noisy with a circus band. Special trains brought visitors from New York, Paterson, Passaic, Orange, and Newark. They streamed up the hill and crowded into the makeshift arena. While the Nutley amateur band played an opening medley, they bought peanuts from Henry Cuyler Bunner in a vendor's white coat and cap. After a parade of costumed performers, led by flag-bearers carrying the American flag and a Red Cross banner, Ringmaster Bailey introduced Nutley's acrobatic rider Eaton Stone. A short, lithe man in cream-colored tights loped around the ring on a white horse. When he took a standing position, the horse lengthened stride. Eaton Stone crouched, spread his arms, and turned a back flip, to the delight of the crowded stands. While he rode off, the ringmaster announced that Eaton Stone was the first American equestrian to do a back somersault on a galloping horse. After a burst of fanfare the Orange Athletic Club went through an acrobatic sequence on the mat, the parallel bars, the giant rings and the trapeze. An amateur boxing demonstration was accompanied by antics of clowns. The National Turnverein of Newark went through some precision exercises, and Eaton Stone's riders jumped barricades around the ring.

Then came the feature of the show. "One of the fair dwellers of Nutley," wrote the reporter for *Harper's Weekly*, "is Miss Annie Oakley—she needs no introduction to the public. Her fame as a rifle and pistol shot circles the globe. Miss Oakley has cultivated a most remarkable grip from shaking hands with princes, great men and crowned heads, but she will always remain a true little American, who can hit with her rifle anything you want to mention at any distance whatsoever. Miss Oakley stood on the back of a galloping horse going at full speed about the ring and broke glass balls thrown in the air, with the result that she kept up a continual shower of broken glass. This was the first time that Miss Oakley ever tried this feat in public."

The show went on with a fencing act, a ladder act, and Mr. Guy Ward's fox terrier jumping from one loping pony to another. Edward Loyal Field, known to the public as an etcher and engraver, appeared in a red and gold suit as iron-nerved Herr Hagenbeck, cracking a whip over a circle of stuffed animals. There was a final exhibition of trained horses, including Monte Carlo and Magic, two of Mr. Marsh Young's thoroughbreds.

After the final grand review the people of Nutley streamed down the hill with their visitors and cheered while the train pulled out. Up in Eaton Stone's barn H. C. Bunner and Frank Butler were counting money. The Nutley Red Cross chapter was assured.

A few weeks later, in a charity exhibition at the Nutley Gun Club, Annie Oakley broke one hundred clay birds in less than seven minutes. After that demonstration H. C. Bunner wrote in her autograph book:

It was a pleasant day
As near the first of May
As days come in pleasant April weather,
That Miss Anna Oakley shot
Her hundred pigeon pot
When the record and the clays broke together.
And may all the days she knows
As through the world she goes
Be as lucky for her all time through,
As that pleasant day in spring
When she showed us she could wing
One hundred birds in minutes six and seconds thirty-two!

*   *   *

In April, 1894, the Wild West began rehearsals at Ambrose Park in South Brooklyn; the season opened on the 12th of May. They had a twenty-four-acre lot near Bay Ridge on the shore of New York harbor, with a covered grandstand seating twenty thousand. It was an airy open ground served by tram lines, bus lines, and the Thirty-ninth Street ferry which used a new fleet of boats for the Wild West season. In Annie Oakley's dressing tent a sea breeze fluttered the curtained opening and brought the whistle of ships from the Narrows. But this year the Butlers lived as much at home as on the show grounds; on fine days they commuted from Nutley by bicycle and harbor ferry.

The season began under a cloud. A threat of smallpox led Nate Salsbury to order a general vaccination. In one day four hundred Indians, riders, teamsters, and roustabouts were inoculated, old Marm Whittaker (who always had to taste medicine before the Indians would take it) assuring every Sioux and Cheyenne of the harmlessness of the doctor's needle and baring her arm to show that she had submitted before them. When four hundred arms stiffened and swelled, the Wild West action faltered. In the heat of Custer's battle Indians dropped their rifles and clutched at itching arms; cowboys rode their horses gingerly with left arms dangling. Salsbury asked the doctor how long the inoculation sores would itch and burn; then he improvised a new act that vaccination could not hinder, and Major Burke promptly filled the newspapers with a novelty offered by the Wild West. It was tame enough—an Indian wedding in which a frontier missionary joined in matrimony Miss Holy Blanket (*Tasina Wakán*) and Mr. High Bear. The bride had an Indian maid of honor, hooded in a new blanket and wearing a necklace of bear's claws. Glum-looking High Bear was accompanied by a best man in the person of Frank Hammett, champion bronco-buster. The ceremony was witnessed by four scowling cowboys—bowlegged John Frantz, sandy Angus McPhee, leathery old Gus Uhle, and Jim Mitchell with his perpetual sun squint and drooping mustache. When the wedding was over High Bear and Holy Blanket shuffled off toward the Badlands, the cowboys mounted horses and loped into the distance, and all the smallpox scabs were still unbroken. In Annie Oakley's tent Marm Whittaker scolded about Indians who were covered with scars from the torture of the Sun Dance but complained of their vaccinated arms.

In this halfhearted season Annie Oakley wore her brightest costumes—a new cowboy hat with a gold star on the upturned brim, a powder-blue blouse and a short skirt of cadet flannel, blue leggings and soft black shoes. Sometimes she added a sportive innovation to her performance—missing a shot, pouting so expressively that ten thousand people could read it, then shrugging her shoulders and racing around the table to change her luck. With one gun after another she broke the targets that sprayed up from rotating traps. She rode a bicycle around the ring, shooting glass globes out of the air. With guns smoking on the table she leaped onto her pony and flashed around the ring. Back in her tent Frank bathed her aching shoulder and frowned over the fiery vaccination.

By midsummer the Wild West had recovered its fire and dash, but the crowds were small. At an informal banquet on the grounds Annie Oakley was honored by the New York press. After the others had spoken, she stood at the end of the long table. "I wish it were a bicycle or a banjo or how to shoot—rather than a speech—but really to tell the truth I guess the press has made me famous. . . . I would like to knock a few years off my age, for to tell the truth I am nearly twenty-eight." She made a girlish face of despair, and every reporter could have believed she was eighteen. It would have been harder for them to believe, or for her to say, that she was in her thirty-fifth year. To the reporters and the public she was still the little girl of the Western plains—"lithe and airy as a fairy . . . nerves of steel on a galloping horse and modest charm in a drawing room . . . sparkling conversation, a delightful manner. . . . her trigger finger is finer than the hairspring of a watch, her eyesight as clear and accurate as the finest field glasses." There was a report that she would star in a new play on the English stage during the coming winter. Another paper announced that she would go to Paris at the end of the season.

Throughout the lean summer Major Burke kept the reporters working. He arranged a press conference with Annie Oakley on the value of shooting for women. It provided outdoor exercise, Little Sureshot declared; it gave a woman the rewarding company of dogs and horses; it developed judgment, self-confidence, composure, self-possession. A week later he arranged another conference on the riding of bicycles, which was a national pastime in the 1890's. Women reporters gave a detailed account of Annie Oakley's cycling costume: a tan and white skirt hooked at the knee into a pair of blue leggings, a bolero jacket with rickrack braid on collar and cuffs, a trim jockey cap to keep the hair in place. They described her as a model of vigorous modern young womanhood. "Every day Annie Oakley rides from 39th Street, Brooklyn, to her home in New Jersey, five miles distant," wrote an inaccurate reporter. Another had her riding twenty miles daily—"sitting very straight, breathing deeply and regularly as she pedals without fatigue."

In September Frederic Remington renewed acquaintance with the outfit. For a week he hung around the camp, drinking with Cody, playing poker with the cowboys, sketching the Indian lodges and the ponies in the corral. While he was there another veteran arrived. General Guy Vernor Henry, lean, lined, leathery, still carried scars from the Badlands; he had been shot through the face while fighting the Sioux in the Rosebud Mountains. Major Burke assembled the Indians and troopers and had a photographer snap the two visitors with the Wild West around them.

That was good publicity, but something better was coming. On September 24th Major Burke took Colonel Cody, Annie Oakley, and five Indians across town and across the Hudson to a Lackawanna railroad train. They got off at Orange, New Jersey, and went on in two livery carriages to rural West Orange. In the long low Edison laboratory at the foot of Orange Mountain they were taken to the "Black Maria," a square black room with sunlight streaming between black curtains on the glass-paned ceiling. Here Edison and his colleagues had taken motion pictures of dancing bears, fencing contests, and Gentleman Jim Corbett sparring with a punching bag. While one of Edison's men cranked the stilted kinetograph, Annie Oakley went through a shooting pantomime, Lost Horse stamped out the Buffalo Dance, Cody and Short Bull conversed in sign language

nd the Sioux shuffled around the room in a war dance. A few weeks
ter the first of all Western motion pictures was exhibited in a dark
oom at 1155 Broadway.

On October 6th, at Ambrose Park, the cowboy band played
Auld Lang Syne, and a disappointing season was over. The Butlers
vent home to a quiet winter in Nutley, Cody joined his drinking
ompanions in Chicago before going on to Nebraska and Wyoming,
Major Burke went on the road to plan a tour for 1895. Salsbury, dis-
ouraged by the season and troubled by Cody's disregard of personal
nd business problems, went home to Long Branch, New Jersey.

Tired and troubled as he was, Nate Salsbury still burned with an
nner energy. That winter his restless mind evolved a new show—
n all-Negro musical drama which would gather up the history and
olklore of the South. By midwinter he had an organization working
nd a dramatic sequence planned. *Black America* opened at Ambrose
'ark in April, with a cast of 620 Negroes. Against a lighted back-
round showing Abraham Lincoln, Uncle Tom's Cabin, a pillared
lantation house and magnolia gardens, the entire company marched
nd sang in a grand opening. The program, modeled on the Wild
West, began with a scene from African jungle life, moved to the
lantation fields of the South, cotton picking, a cotton gin, loading
f baled cotton on the wharf—all done with rich native music and
nterspersed with musical tableaus. The spectacle played to large
udiences at Ambrose Park, then in Boston, Philadelphia, Baltimore,
nd Washington. But in Washington Salsbury fell ill. He was taken
:o his home at Long Branch, and without his management *Black
America* began to fall apart. After two weeks of confusion, discord,
nd increasing turmoil, the show was disbanded. The equipment went
)ack to Ambrose Park for storage, the Negroes went home. Nate
Salsbury had hoped to take the spectacle to Europe to show the
Old World another of the folk traditions of America.

*   *   *

For the Wild West 1895 was a strenuous year. For the first
time since 1885 they played a full season on the road. Seven hundred

people in two long show trains covered ten thousand miles between
April and October. Nate Salsbury had given up his office as business
manager, though he retained part ownership of the show. When the
season opened in Philadelphia, he left his Deep South exhibition to
spend a few days on the Wild West lot. It was good to see his
friends, to breathe the mingled smell of horses, harness, hay, canvas,
rope, paint, and dust, to hear the teamsters swearing and the reporters
asking for news. But his voice was husky and he walked with a cane.
A few weeks later he was sitting in a wheel chair at his home on the
New Jersey shore. Long Branch was a festive place; it had gambling,
horse racing, trap shooting, and a colony of actors—Mary Anderson,
Arthur Byron, William Collier, Maggie Mitchell, Oliver and
Katherine Byron. But Nate Salsbury saw little of his friends that
summer. He watched the surf tumbling on Monmouth Beach and
in his mind he followed the Wild West from town to town, from
state to state, on its long Midwestern tour.

The grueling schedule—131 stands in 190 days—was laid out by
Salsbury's successor, the hard-driving circus man James A. Bailey.
Under his management the Wild West changed character. Side
shows were added, with barkers shouting about freaks, marvels, and
monstrosities. Plumes and spangles appeared on the parade harness
and the wagon wheels were painted red. There was talk of a steam
calliope to replace Bill Sweeney's veteran cowboy band. That year
the Barnum and Bailey Circus featured the famous Duryea motor
wagon that had won the first road race in Chicago; thinking of that
competition James A. Bailey looked wryly at the old Deadwood
Stage.

On barns and walls and signboards Bailey billed the Wild West
as a "Congress of Marvels." He had a taste for baboons and elephants
and would gladly have traded the Pony Express for anything from
the Antipodes. Meanwhile Cody was indifferent to the show, except
for its financial statements. He was living lavishly, taking over whole
floors in hotels for his friends and followers, entertaining chorus girls
in his private car in the second show train. When they played in
Cleveland a reporter wrote: "Colonel Cody is one of the wealthiest
men in the West. In Wyoming he has leased 3,000 acres from the

government, and 2,000 men are now digging canals for water that will make it fertile farms. He is the owner of many stage lines, has hotels in half a hundred towns in the West, owns two newspapers."

In these years Cody was served by a devoted valet and butler who would remain with him for a decade. Alfred Heimer, a German immigrant, had read of Buffalo Bill in the Old Country, before he knew a word of English. On his arrival in America he went to see the Wild West at Ambrose Park, and soon afterward he became a waiter at the Opera Hotel near Union Square, a haunt of show people in the Nineties. There he met Colonel Cody. In the spring of 1895 he began his service as butler in Cody's private car, "Number 50." Heimer was a shrewd, discreet, loyal, self-effacing manservant whose one aim in life was to please the princely colonel. He traveled in Number 50 till it was burned in a fire at the Wild West winter quarters in Bridgeport; then he was installed in a new car which the Wild West bought from the Pennsylvania Railroad. Originally called "Mayflower," it had been built for the opera singer Adelina Patti; now it was renamed "Cody." It had four staterooms, living room, dining room, kitchen, and like Number 50 it was perpetually stocked with drink. When the great plainsman came in from rescuing the emigrant wagons, Heimer was ready with his dressing gown and slippers, his whisky and cigars. Cody was jaded. "As a fellow gets old he doesn't feel like tearing about the country forever. I grow very tired of this sort of sham hero-worship sometimes."

But to Major Burke the Wild West was still magic. Now he had an able publicity agent, Dexter Fellows, but only Arizona John could write a Wild West blurb that was also a testament of faith: "What we are doing is educating people. The Wild West symposium of equestrian ability has done more for this country than the Declaration of Independence, the Constitution of the United States, or the Life of General Washington. Its mission is to teach manhood and horse sense. We are not traveling to make money but only to do good." He believed all this, and so for him the Wild West never grew stale. When they opened a two-week run in Chicago, a reporter noted: "Major Burke stood in his old place by the entrance to the grandstand and watched the performance with as deep and profound an interest as though he had not seen it 7,368 times by actual count.

And it still fascinated young boys and old men; it still lured crowd
in city, town, and village. Bailey called it "An Ethnological, Anthro
pological, Etymological Congress—Greatest Since Adam"; but i
was the bucking broncos, the whooping Indians, the feats of marks
manship and horsemanship that filled the stands.

During the 1895 season the artist Charles Shreyvogle traveled with
the show. Nate Salsbury had brought him to the lot in Philadelphia
he was given a bunk in the cowboys' car and the run of the grounds
He set up his easel in the corral, in the Indian camp, at the end o
the arena. All summer he painted Indians, horses, cowboys; in th
Wild West lot he sketched scenes from the Indian wars of a decad
past. With Cody for a model he painted "The Last Drop." Tha
picture promptly became famous and it added a feature to th
show in future seasons: under converging spotlights in the empt
arena Buffalo Bill pantomimed the painting which showed a lon
trooper kneeling at a desert spring and giving his horse the last dro
of water in his hat. Western folklore was still growing in the dust
show grounds.

*   *   *

One season was like another—1895, 1896, 1897; they blurred to
gether in memory. After an opening two weeks in the huge nev
Madison Square Garden, the show trains pulled out of New Yor
for the long road tour. New England, Pennsylvania, Ohio, Indiana
Illinois, Michigan, Wisconsin, Iowa, Missouri, Kentucky, Virginia
Mud, dust, wind, heat, cold. Pastures, race tracks, ball parks, fair
grounds. The state capitals, the county seats, the lake, river, an
prairie towns. Then, on a chilly day in October, the band playe
Home, Sweet Home while they ate a last meal in the cook tent
and the season was over.

A few times and places remained vivid in memory. In Cincinnati
where Colonel Cody's parents had been married in a vanished hous
at Fourth and Pike streets, a baby buffalo was born and named fo
the city. For old times' sake Annie Oakley and her husband wante

o visit Shooter's Hill, the onetime *Schuetzenbuckel* at Fairmount,
out they had to pack their guns and board the long show train for
Hamilton, where the advance crew was already on the grounds beside
the Miami and Erie Canal. In Chicago, in June of 1896, they opened
the largest indoor stadium in the world, the huge new Coliseum on
Sixty-third Street, near the site of the Wild West camp of the
World's Fair season. Mayor Swift welcomed the Wild West, and for
this occasion Major Burke announced a new feature—an animated
tableau of Rosa Bonheur's painting "The Horse Fair." In September,
1896, for the first time since its organization, the Wild West toured
beyond the Mississippi. There was a Western feeling in the Iowa
towns where sunburned farmers tied their teams to miles of hitching
racks and crowded into the dusty show grounds. In October they
crossed the Missouri—it was Annie Oakley's first sight of the Western plains—and the Wild West came home to North Platte where it
had been first assembled thirteen years before.

For the homecoming special trains on the Union Pacific brought
thousands of Nebraska people. Cody was as delighted as a boy, and
the whole outfit was in a festive mood. They put on a crackling,
hard-riding, high-spirited show, and then took a day off before
moving on to Lincoln. It was a blue and golden day, October 13th,
with the tawny autumn plain stretched out like a tranquil ocean.
Cody drove a happy crowd out to Scout's Rest Ranch, three miles
north of town. When they swung into the lane a flag was rippling
from a tall flagpole and horses whickered from the corral. As Annie
Oakley stepped down, Irma Cody came racing across the lawn. Cody
tried to point out everything at once—he had seven thousand acres
here, horses and cattle, a herd of deer and a small herd of buffalo.
He led his visitors to the corral where his favorite horses had been
brought in from the range. Reluctantly he turned back to the house.
There were three big connecting parlors decorated with antlers, elk
and buffalo heads, bearskins and Indian rugs, photographs of Wild
Bill, Jack Crawford, and Major Frank North, pictures of hunting
scenes and Indian battles. On the way back to North Platte he kept
looking over his shoulder at the long lift of the land. He talked
about his Dismal River Ranch, a hundred miles north in the big

empty country, where there wasn't a railroad or even a wagon roa
in a day's travel. But now there was a schedule to finish up—
Lincoln, St. Joseph, Leavenworth, Kansas City.

In 1897 the long show trains visited Canada for the first time sinc
1885 when Sitting Bull had stolen the headlines from Cody. I
Quebec they played on the Plains of Abraham, looking over th
gray roofs and spires of the old French city. After the Ontario towr
they made another stand at the Chicago Coliseum. When Am
Leslie of the *Daily News* called at Annie Oakley's dressing room t
revive memories of the World's Fair, she found the markswoma
"darning Mr. Butler's hose, every stitch as neat as a pigeon sho
from her pet gun." After the performance in the arena she reporte
that Annie Oakley's rifle was "as shiny and steady as ever and he
chic activity as captivating."

In the same issue of the *Daily News* appeared an obscure not
about unrest in Cuba. The "Cuban Revolutionary Party," swolle
by unemployment on the sugar plantations, was attempting to resis
the harsh government of Spain.

CHAPTER 17

End of the Road

It is worthy of note that their present and sixteenth annual tour will be signalized by a magnitude, interest, value and perfection even surpassing previous efforts and splendid successes. As indicated by the published programme of performances, the result is such an historical, martial and equestrian triumph as but one man could organize and but one country produce.

—*Buffalo Bill's Wild West*, 1899.

BY the following spring Cuba had come to fill whole pages of the American press. In February the battleship *Maine* had exploded in Havana harbor, and while newspapers headlined REMEMBER THE MAINE! shrewd Major Burke hurried down to Cuba with some Wild West contracts in his handbag. On opening day, March 30, 1898, a color guard of fifteen Cuban troopers led the Wild West street parade; in Madison Square Garden the Stars and Stripes hung beside the Single Star of Cuba. The printed program explained that these Cuban campaigners, having fought under gallant General Maceo, were on leave while their wounds could heal; their hearts were still with Gómez and García while they doffed their wide palm hats to American applause.

Ringmaster J. J. McCarthy, in brown suit, brown derby, and luxuriant brown mustache, called the roll of the Cuban veterans: One was described as having seven wounds, another had fought in fifty battles, one had a single leg, one dangled an empty sleeve, one wore a saber wound across his face, one was the only man alive who knew where General Maceo was buried, one had escaped from grim Morro Castle. At the name each man cantered around the ring on a pony, shouting *Cuba Libre! Viva Cuba Libre!* When Martínez with one arm and Delgado with one leg passed the stands, the crowd roared *Cuba Libre!* in what the *New York Journal* called "a hurricane of applause."

The Wild West had grown martial for this martial season. After the grand review came an exhibition drill by veterans of Captain Thorpe's 5th U.S. Artillery. Men from the 6th U.S. Cavalry were added to Cody's "Congress of Rough Riders." The *New York World* for April 3rd showed long-haired Buffalo Bill leading a band of Indians against the troops of Spain; he was quoted: "I could drive the Spaniards out of Cuba with 30,000 Indians. With that many Indians on their wiry ponies I do not think the Spaniards would last more than sixty days in Cuba." On the same day the *New York Daily News* reported: "The spectacle of the Wild West is particularly suited to the martial spirit that has suddenly blazed up in the breast of Americans." The next day President McKinley read to his Cabinet a proposed message to Congress advising a declaration of war. War was declared on April 19th.

On April 25th Major Burke informed the press that Buffalo Bill (who had recently been given the rank of brigadier general in the Nebraska National Guard) would report within a week to General Miles for active service in the conflict with Spain. Headlines: BRIG. GEN. WILLIAM F. CODY WILL COMMAND A REGIMENT IN CUBA. READY TO START IMMEDIATELY.

In Washington two weeks later the Wild West street parade was reviewed by General Miles from the steps of the War Department. At the Mount Vernon Hotel, Cody told reporters that he had been riding Duke, a horse presented him by General Miles after the Battle of Wounded Knee, and that Duke seemed to recognize the general as the parade moved past. Nothing was said about a regiment in Cuba. On May 16th, at Trenton, the crowd had prolonged cheers for Buffalo Bill, and again the papers said, "Any day he may be sent to war." The Wild West camp sounded like a cavalry post: bugles summoned the company to meals, to the corrals, to saddle; drums and bugles set the tempo for the street parade.

Rain followed the show through New England; for two days they were mired in mud at Hartford. Then the weather cleared for a swing through New York and Pennsylvania. For a month Cody's wife and daughter Irma joined the camp—to be with the colonel before his departure for the war. In Kalamazoo he told reporters that his heart was at San Juan Hill and that he still expected the call to action. In mid-August, during a run at St. Paul, Burke announced a telegram from General Miles suggesting that Cody remain in America during the current negotiations for peace. In Iowa in the last week of August, after the brief war with Spain had ended, Buffalo Bill gave the newspapers a statement: "I have been in every war since I was old enough, but this one, and I did all I could to get into this. . . . It is probably due to the fact that General Miles did not lead the Santiago campaign that I was left behind."

But a triumph was coming. That summer the Trans-Mississippi Exposition brought great crowds to Omaha, and its culminating event was the appearance of Buffalo Bill's Wild West. On the morning of August 31st, "Cody Day," the commanding plainsman led his Congress of Rough Riders to the main gate where he was escorted into the thronged stadium. On behalf of the people of Nebraska, Governor Holcomb welcomed him to his home state. Old Alexander Majors, the weathered wagon-master who had given young Bill Cody his first job, stood on the flag-draped platform and made a speech:

"Gentlemen and my boy, Colonel Cody (laughter)—can I say a few words of welcome? . . . Gentleman, forty-four years ago this day this fine-looking physical specimen of manhood was brought to me by his mother—a little boy nine years old—and little did I think at that time that the little boy that was standing before me, asking for employment of some kind by which I could afford to pay his mother a little money for his services, was going to be a boy of such destiny as he has turned out to be. (Applause) In this country we have great men; we have great men at Washington; we have men who are famous as politicians in this country; we have great statesmen; we have had Jackson and Clay, and we had a Lincoln. We have men great in agriculture and in stock growing, and in the manufacturing business, who have made great names for themselves, who have stood high in the nation. We had a Barnum in the show business. Next, and even greater and higher, we have a Cody. (Tremendous applause) He, gentlemen, stands not at the head of the showmen of the United States of America, but of the world. (Great applause) Little did I think this, gentlemen, at the time this little boy came to me, standing straight as an arrow; and he came to me and looked me in the face, you know, and I said to my partner, 'We will take this little boy'—Mr. Russell was standing by my side—'and we will pay him a man's wages because he can ride a pony just as well as a man can.' He was lighter and could do just the same service, just as good service of that kind, when he was a little boy, just nine years old. I remember when we paid him $25 for his first month's work; he was paid in half dollars, and he got fifty of them. He tied them up in his little handkerchief, and when he got home he untied the handkerchief and spread it all over the table." (Laughter)

COLONEL CODY—"I have been spreading it ever since."

MR. MAJORS—"And he is still spreading it. Now, gentlemen, this is an occasion when a man does not want to hold people long. I could say so much to you on any other occasion, when there are not tens of thousands of people waiting and anxious to see the wind-up of this thing. This occasion can never happen on this globe again. The same number of people and the same conditions and circumstances never will occur here on earth again. This is the biggest thing I ever saw, and I was at the World's Fair, and I have been at the expositions in London, in Edinburgh, Scotland, and in New York. Bless your precious life, Colonel Cody."

The old wagon-master was followed by Senator Thurston who called Cody "the best representative of the great and progressive West. . . . You have not been a showman in the common sense of the word; you have been a grand national and international educator of men."

Cody was ready with a response which showed the hand of Major Burke: "How little I dreamed in the long ago that the lonely path of the scout and the pony express rider would lead me to the place to which you have assigned me today. . . . I have sought fortune in many lands, but wherever I have wandered the flag of our beloved State has been unfurled to every breeze. From the Platte to the Danube, from the Tiber to the Clyde, the emblem of our sovereign State has always floated over the Wild West. . . . The whistle of the locomotive has drowned the howl of the coyote, the barb-wire fence has narrowed the range of the cow-puncher, but no material evidence of prosperity can obliterate our contribution to Nebraska's imperial progress."

With that, the speechmaking ended and the Wild West took over the arena with a hell-for-leather show. But the ceremonies were not forgotten. In future Wild West programs Major Burke included an account of the great day at Omaha:

"In 1883, the year of its organization and upon a much less comprehensive and colossal scale than it has since attained, Colonel Cody presented his now world-famous 'Wild West' at Omaha. Fifteen years later, on the 31st day of August, and on the same spot previously occupied by his arena, he again appeared, and this time as the invited and honored guest of the State of Nebraska and of the great Trans-Mississippi Exposition. There were gathered to enthusiastically and proudly welcome him some thirty thousand people, including the most prominent officials and political leaders of Nebraska and her representative pioneers and business men. Although within the period of a decade and a half his name had grown to be a household word in every land, he had become the most widely known and lionized man of his generation, had met with continuous ovations from applauding millions in both Europe and America, in which the mightiest of rulers, the most renowned of soldiers, the most distinguished of statesmen and diplomats, the first of savants, and the beauty, wealth, power and culture of the world had participated, yet to him 'Cody Day' was infinitely and inexpressibly the most gloriously gratifying triumph of his memorable life, involving the highest compliment ever paid by any sovereign state, community or association to a private citizen."

After the triumph at Omaha the Wild West moved on across Nebraska to Colorado Springs, Pueblo, Trinidad. Under the front range of the Rockies, with the Spanish Peaks against the sky, they set up at Trinidad on September 10th. At noon the sky turned gray and a bitter wind swept the arena. They played in a whistling blizzard and that night they loaded in a driving snow. The show trains whistled, turned their taillights to the storm, and began the long pull across Kansas. At Kansas City, Cody's head was swimming; he fainted three times during the afternoon performance. While the night show went on, he was taken to his car in the Missouri Pacific yards, then to St. Joseph's Hospital. "Pneumonia," the doctor said.

A week later he rejoined the outfit in Joplin, Missouri, pale and shaken but still anxious for attention. He received reporters in his most splendid dress—a diamond flashing from his silk neckerchief, in his checked waistcoat a gold watch from the Prince of Wales, cuff links of silver buffalo heads set with rubies and diamonds, the gift of Grand Duke Alexis of Russia. He did not mention the Spanish-American War.

But the next year, 1899, the Wild West featured the "Battle of San Juan Hill," along with riders from the Philippine and Hawaiian Islands and groups of "aborigines" from the West Indies. With the growth of American imperialism the show exhibited an imperial theme, demonstrating "the hand of progress and the conquering march of civilization under Old Glory's protecting folds." On opening night in Madison Square Garden the band played *The Star-Spangled Banner* and *Rule Britannia*. In the boxes were General Miles, Mrs. Elizabeth Custer, Governor Theodore Roosevelt, Chauncey Depew, and the recent war heroes "Fighting Bob" Evans, Rear Admiral Phillips, and Captain Higginson. Before the performance Governor Roosevelt shook hands, in a public ceremony, with Troopers McGinty and Isbel, veterans of San Juan. McGinty was the little bronco rider whose antics had cheered his comrade in Cuba. Tom Isbel had fired the first shot at Siboney, where American troops went ashore in the face of Spanish fire, and carried seven bullets in his body. Thirteen other veterans of Roosevelt's Rough Riders appeared with the show. Wrote Major Burke, "The Wild West presents the history of the country, from the times the frontier was in the East until it vanished in the sunlight of the Golden Gate."

The Battle of San Juan Hill was enacted by five hundred men. Detachments of Rough Riders, the 24th Infantry and the 9th and 10th Cavalry, Grimes's Battery and García's Scouts were all represented; Indians played the role of the Spanish troops. Against a silhouette of palm trees and rolling Cuban hills the scene opens quietly, with men lolling on the grass. A pack train moves up, its Cuban outriders in baggy white uniforms, broad belts, palm leaf hats. An order is shouted. Men get to their feet and begin marching to the tune of *A Hot Time in the Old Town Tonight*. Gunfire explodes and they begin the attack on the Spanish fort at the summit of San Juan Hill. Smoke and blaze of powder, threshing of horses and men, the wounded carried off, a quaver of bugles, a surge of khaki-clad men. From the fort Spanish colors come down and the Stars and Stripes ripple in the wind. The crowd roars and Major Burke beams at the men in the press box. San Juan Hill had replaced Custer's battlefield as the climax of the show.

There was a long tour from Maine to Texas in 1899, and in 1900 a strenuous schedule through the East and the Midwest. In fine summer weather the Wild West trains pulled through Darke County, Ohio, and unloaded at Greenville. Early in the morning of July 25, 1900, Annie Oakley's mother and sisters drove in from the country; they had lunch in Annie's tent and sat in a box for the afternoon performance. There was so much to talk about that Annie Oakley did not ride in the parade down Broadway, but all Greenville came out to Armstrong's pasture to see her. After her act, while twenty thousand watched and listened, lawyer Charlie Anderson, a Darke County man who had grown up in Ansonia, presented a silver cup: "To Miss Annie Oakley, From Old Home Friends of Greenville, Ohio. July 25, 1900."

She looked around at the cheering stands. It was all changed since a country girl had come in to Greenville in muddy shoes and a skirt beaded with cockleburs. There was a face she would have liked to see. But Frenchy La Motte's shop was now a clothing store, with no pile of peltry at the doorway and no chair beside the stove.

*   *   *

Sometimes the years seemed long. After the night performance, while the train got under way, Annie stretched out in the stateroom while Frank made tea; his hair showed gray as he bent over the spirit lamp. Sometimes in the rhythmic midnight darkness they talked about retiring. But they had talked that way before, and every spring the pull of the show and the thought of another season's earnings sent them on the road again.

But 1901 was different. Cody was growing old; his voice had lost its ring and his thin hair and goatee were almost white. In place of the storied chiefs of past seasons, the Indian camp was headed by impassive Has No Horses, glum Iron Tail, boyish Sammy Lone Bear, shrunken old Flat Iron. Now Johnnie Baker was a thickset man in a derby hat, a widower, with a cigar tilted in his mouth. He had given up shooting for the post of "arenic director." Major Burke, acting as general manager, had a new advertising director, the veteran circus man Louis E. Cooke; in Madison Square Garden his five children Virgiline, Vivian, Viola, Victor, and Vulcan kept bursting into Annie Oakley's dressing room. Annie Oakley was forty, with lines gathering about her mouth and eyes, and her husband's hair was gray.

Nineteen hundred and one—a new century—the world was changing. It was a time of billion-dollar trusts, of extravagances, disasters, crimes, sensations. The liner *Celtic* with nine decks above the water had arrived in New York harbor. The New York Central was tunneling under Park Avenue and the Flatiron Building was climbing twenty stories into the sky. The first automobile show had opened in Madison Square Garden, and horses took fright from auto wagons in the streets. Financial scandals rocked the city governments of Philadelphia and St. Louis. Through the New Jersey courts went the notorious Barker-Keller case, Mr. Barker having shot the Reverend Mr. Keller for assaulting Barker's wife. James Gorden Bennett bought the fabulous yacht *Lysistrata* and staffed it with a crew of a hundred men. President McKinley, shaking hands with a line of people between the Fountain of Abundance and the Court of Lilies at the Buffalo Exposition, was assassinated by a young factory worker who did not believe in government, marriage, or religion. By

"Hertzian waves" Marconi signaled the letter S across the Atlantic. The Wright brothers, testing glider wings on the sands of Kitty Hawk, were planning to build a flying machine. At the beginning of the new century the frontier past seemed distant.

That spring Nate Salsbury was on hand for rehearsals at Bridgeport. Though thin and worn, he was in better health than in recent years. He walked the lot with his restless stride and his mind working. The old Western episodes were still the heart of the show, but times were changed, and Barnum and Bailey, advertising the Greatest Show on Earth, had new troops of aerialists and an enlarged menagerie. That year the Wild West added two extravaganzas, an exhibition by a regiment of Royal Northwest Mounted Police and the "Maze of Nations" in which two hundred riders moved through an intricate pattern of circles, stars, and revolving wheels. Another novelty was provided by a crew from the U.S. Coast Guard: from an imagined beach a cannon fired a life line to a floundering vessel across the arena. Over the stretched line the survivors rode, one after another, to safety above the imagined waves. This was the way, declared Ringmaster McCarthy, in which in the year 1900 four thousand lives were saved on the Atlantic coast. In the street parade, following the scarlet and blue file of the Northwest Mounted Police, the coast Guard men rode in a lifeboat on wheels. The Wild West was changing.

Another innovation was the spectacular enactment of the Storming of Tientsin. Recreating the scene of the recent Boxer Rebellion, detachments from Britain, France, and the United States stormed the ancient walls of the Chinese city and tore down the Chinese standard. For this act the Wild West Indians reluctantly donned padded tunics, straw hats, and sandals to play the part of the beaten Chinese. Mark Twain saw the opening performance at Madison Square Garden, but the fierce old humorist stamped out of the hall during the attack on Tientsin. In the February number of the *North American Review* he had published a bitter defense of the Chinese patriots who vainly tried to resist foreign encroachment.

In mid-April the long show trains pulled out of New York and swung west. In Dayton, Ohio, on May 23rd, a party from Greenville came to see Annie Oakley, and Major Burke made a grandiose announcement: At the end of the season Buffalo Bill would launch at Cody, Wyoming, the Cody Military College and International Academy of Rough Riders. Burke still believed in his hero, but Cody was chiefly concerned about the money that was needed to extend his copper mines at Oracle, Arizona, the supply of liquor in his private car, and the chorus girls who sat in his show box and rode in the Deadwood Stage.

They swung back east for an engagement at Buffalo on the grounds of the Pan-American Exposition, with Frederic Remington's bronze "Bronco-buster" in the gateway. Above the Badlands scenery rose the Tower of Light, 409 feet high and faced with 35,000 light bulbs. On opening night in Buffalo the Wild West's old friend General Miles shared a box with the notorious Apache chief Geronimo, who, according to the papers, had recently been converted to Christianity.

West again in the humid weeks of summer, across the Mississippi to the great corn-covered prairies. They played the corn-belt towns of Iowa and the mule-trading towns of Missouri, and at the end of August they headed back through Kentucky and West Virginia. Annie Oakley, who never got tired, or almost never, was tired now. Each night she checked off another day on the railroad calendar in their stateroom. In the arena her smile flashed white and her hair fell dark to her shoulders, but as she listened to the clicking rails and waited for sleep to come there was a distant ringing in her ears. Sometimes Frank had to speak twice before she answered; twenty years of daily gunfire had affected her hearing. Perhaps it was time to put the guns away. Nate Salsbury was in a wheel chair, staring at the breakers on a New Jersey sea beach. Cody sat drinking in his palace car. Major Burke kept talking about times past; now Dexter Fellows met distinguished visitors and led reporters over the grounds. The Wild West was changing, changing. Perhaps they *should* retire.

On October 28th, at Charlotte, North Carolina, twelve thousand people passed through the gates for the evening performance, an excellent late-season crowd. Cody was in a genial mood, riding Old Pap, doffing his hat not once but three times to the cheering stands.

It had been a long and tiring season, but now the whole outfit was relaxed. There was one more stand, at Danville, Virginia; then *Auld Lang Syne*.

They loaded in Charlotte at midnight, a clear crisp night with a Hallowe'en tingle in the air. In their carriage Annie and Frank rode through the sleeping streets, past the heavy tread of the draft horses and the big gray show wagons with their lanterns swinging. When they left the carriage their steps crunched on cinders beside the train. The last night. Even the horses seemed to know it, standing quiet in the two long stock cars behind the locomotive. In the darkness a wrangler whistled softly as he rolled down the canvas to protect the animals from drafts. Tomorrow . . . the last show . . . then *Home, Sweet Home*.

The stateroom was warm, the beds were turned down, and a plate of sandwiches was on the little table. It was good to lie in bed, hearing the muffled voices outside, feeling the lurch and movement of the train. The rails clicked faster. The lights of Charlotte dropped behind. Then darkness and the steady humming of the rails.

The show train left Charlotte in three sections. Two and a half hours later, as the second section neared the scattered lights of Lexington, a headlamp bore down the single track. With a thunderous crash two locomotives met. For a moment the night was filled with rending iron and splintering wood. For another moment there was only a hissing of steam in the darkness. Then came the screams of horses and the cursing of men.

In their blind and shattered stateroom Frank Butler called, "Annie! Annie!" At last his hands found her. He carried her, swaddled in bedclothes, out of the ruined car. She opened her eyes when a light flared up like lurid sunrise.

"I can walk, Jimmy. I'm all right."

With his arm around her they made their way past the wreckage where John Frantz and Gus Uhle, their faces harsh in the red flares, were aiming rifles into the twisted horse cars. They saw Old Eagle, the star ring horse, lying grotesquely on the wrecked engine cab. They saw the white, staring eyes of a mule, and the wild bronco Dynamite crumpled over the engine coupling. Someone loomed up beside them. It was Cody in his purple dressing gown, his thin white hair streaming and his face looking older than anyone had ever seen it. He said in a strange voice, "There's Old Pap." The horse twitched, and Cody turned to John Frantz. "Give me that rifle, son."

Frank caught her as she swayed on the cinders. He carried her back from the red flares, away from the dying hiss of steam. He stumbled over crossties toward a blinding headlight where the last section of the show train stood panting in the dark.

CHAPTER 18

The Closed Gun Trunk

Guns put away for months should have the inside of
the bore coated with grease and the outside coated lightly
with gungrease or vaseline. The gunstock should be
rubbed with a small piece of sheepskin dipped in linseed
oil.

—Major Charles Askins: *Wing and Trap Shooting*

AT home in Nutley in the corner bedroom with five windows
showing the bare trees and the gray November sky, Frank told her
again. As the show train left Charlotte, freight train Number 75
was running south from Greensboro. The conductor of Number 75
missed a telegraphic order, and beyond Lexington the engineer
opened the throttle. The freight crashed head-on into the northbound
show train. No one was killed, though four trainmen were injured.
In the mangled wooden stock cars a hundred Wild West horses
were crushed to death. Old Pap and Old Eagle, Dynamite and
Dusty, the mules, the ring horses, the roping and cutting horses—
they were all buried in a huge pit in a Carolina cornfield. Major
Burke couldn't think of any statement for the newspapers. Cody had
gone back to Nebraska, an old and shaken man. Just two horses
went on to winter quarters at Bridgeport.

Sitting up in bed, Annie Oakley asked for a mirror and her brush
and comb. But when he had brought them she only stared.

"Jimmy—my hair is white!"

He took away the mirror. "You're just catching up with me."

More than her hair was changed. Internal injuries, the doctor said, had paralyzed her left side. A few days, perhaps, at the hospital. But it was months in St. Michael's Hospital in Newark, and repeated operations, before she was home again. In pale spring sunlight she watched the budding trees outside her windows. When she left the house she wore a brace on her leg and stabbed the ground with a cane. She got to the garden the first day; then to the end of the block on Grant Avenue; then to the river. That spring the Passaic was out of its banks, with floods swirling through the streets of Passaic and Paterson. She stared at the hurrying water and dragged herself back home.

At first she walked like a child taking the first uncertain steps, with Frank holding her. Then she walked alone, her knuckles clenched white on the cane. As the summer passed, her body grew lean and firm and her warm smile came back. On a visit in Highfield Lane she turned a sudden cartwheel and swung the cane like a rifle to her shoulder.

But could she shoot again? At home she stared at the closed gun trunk and tried to picture a flying target. Could she ever shoot again?

On autumn days Frank tramped off to the marshes with a gun on his shoulder, and she took her daily walk through falling leaves along Basking Creek and the Yantacaw. On a windy afternoon when crows cawed in the bare walnut branches she passed the Nutley Gun Club. Something stopped her there. As she waited, hearing the bang of gunfire beyond the gate, the blood throbbed in her ears. At last she went inside. She lifted a gun. For thirty years that had been the most familiar object in the world—the long dark barrel, the smooth solid stock, the checkered handgrip, the curving trigger guard. Now it seemed strange. She weighed it in her hands, held it to her shoulder, drew the sights together. She lowered it again. She was returning it to the stand when she saw the attendant's eyes.

Her braced left leg went forward, her weight balanced lightly "Give me a target."

The disk flew up and out, and the gun went to her shoulder. Her trigger finger pressed.

"Dead!" cried the attendant.

*   *   *

At Atlantic City, on November 12, 1902, while wind whipped the water into whitecaps and surf roared on the sand, the curtain went up at Young's Pier Theater on Langdon McCormick's melodrama *The Western Girl*. To millions of people the Western girl was Annie Oakley. With dyed hair and fringed costume she played Nance Berry in this "startling picture of the wild west." It was a heavy role, with Nance Berry dominating the action in a Western main street, a Mexican music hall, the Canyon of the Colorado; in the final holdup scene she saved the life of the young lieutenant and put the Silver Creek bandits to rout. With rifle, pistol, and lariat Annie Oakley kept the play going—to Scranton, Hoboken, Camden, New Haven, Gloversville, Rochester, Syracuse, Louisville. When the troupe broke up it was spring in the Ohio Valley. Annie and Frank had a holiday in Darke County, forgetting the holdup of the Silverwood Coach and the bandits of Silver Creek.

It had been a reassuring season. White-haired Annie Oakley could still look young beyond the footlights. With a catch in her step and new lines in her face, she could still dominate a stage. She could shoot a falling target and throw a loop around a running man. Even in a flimsy melodrama she could hold an audience until the curtain fell. She was still a professional.

But it was a sad season too. After a transcontinental tour the Wild West returned to New York and was loaded aboard ship for a long engagement in England. Cody was tired and complaining. Nate Salsbury lay in bed above the bare New Jersey sands, his thoughts following the Wild West across the winter ocean to a new season at Earl's Court. On Christmas Eve, at his home in Long Branch, Nate Salsbury died, and to Annie Oakley it was like the loss of a father. The Wild West opened in London the day after Christmas with flags at half-staff and the cavalry draped in crepe. On that day Nate Salsbury was buried in Woodlawn Cemetery, New York, and a heartbroken actress played *The Western Girl* in Camden, across the river from Philadelphia.

* * *

In time she found a friend to take the place of Nate Salsbury-
a hearty, generous, and lifelong friend. Eventually she made him tl
custodian of her personal papers and the administrator of her estat

She first saw him in New York when *The Wizard of Oz* opened
the new Majestic Theater on Columbus Circle in 1903. The Oz stor
as told by L. Frank Baum, began, "Dorothy lived in the midst of tl
great Kansas prairies. . . . There was a great cornfield beyond the fenc
and not far away she saw the Scarecrow, placed high on a pole
keep the birds from the ripe corn. . . . Its head was a small sack stuff(
with straw, with eyes, nose and mouth painted on it to represent
face. An old pointed blue hat that had belonged to some Munchk
was perched on its head, and the rest of the figure was a blue suit
clothes, worn and faded, which had also been stuffed with straw
That was the scene when the curtain lifted. The scarecrow hung (
a stile—a painted face under a tattered hat, shapeless dangling fe(
two huge white gloves tied to straw-fringed sleeves with ragged bo
of binder twine. It hung grinning and lifeless until the Kansas g
finished her song and went over to release it. Then the limp figu
came to life. In a burst of grotesque dancing it covered the stag
left and right, front and back, from wing to wing. That was Ann
Oakley's first sight of Fred Stone.

She saw *The Wizard* again and again—first at the Majestic, a ye
later at the Academy of Music on Fourteenth Street, still later at tl
New York Theater. By that time Fred Stone had married a girl
the cast, Arlene Crater of Denver, and the Stones and the Butlers we
firm friends. Over late supper at Rector's or Delmonico's they e
changed talk of shows and circuses, of people and places; they trad(
memories of wind-blown Western towns and garden parties
London. Like the scarecrow, Fred Stone had come from Kansas ar
had gone on to a world as wonderful as the Land of Oz. He was a
actor from childhood. When trains came through Wellingto
Kansas, carrying soldiers to the Indian wars, young Fred Stone spre;
an old carpet on the cinder track and did acrobatic tricks for tl
troops. He left school at the fourth grade. At fourteen he travel(
the prairie states with Berry and Sealer's Wagon Circus. He learn(
tumbling, juggling, tight-rope walking, acrobatic dancing; he join(

a variety troop and toured the country; he played in Cripple Creek, Colorado, with the creek rushing under the theater floor, and in the Palace Theater in London to Queen Victoria and the Prince of Wales. Once in Kansas he had seen a young Cherokee with a bow and arrow hit a quarter in a split stick at sixty feet. But his father told him about an Indian who could shoot an arrow through a finger ring while it was in the air. Fred Stone's head went back and his homely face broke into the famous scarecrow smile. Could Annie Oakley do that?

The Red Mill opened in 1906, with Fred Stone and his old vaudeville partner Dave Montgomery playing Kid Connor and Con Kidder, two young Americans stranded in Holland. When the show closed for the summer Fred Stone persuaded the Butlers to move into his rambling house at Amityville, Long Island. His brother-in-law Rex Beach had promised to take him bear hunting in Alaska, and Fred wanted to learn marksmanship. Every day Annie Oakley instructed him in shooting, and between sessions at the traps she taught him to throw a rope. There were horses in the stable, along with two baby buffalo that Fred had found at the horse market. That Amityville farm was almost like the Wild West.

On an August day when the house overflowed with actors, writers, musicians, and newspapermen, Fred demonstrated his new skill. With Frank Butler throwing targets, he scored a run of twenty. Then he handed the gun to white-haired Annie Oakley, who looked as gentle as Whistler's mother, sitting in a lawn chair in the shade. Frank tossed out five targets. Her gun swung up. Onetwothreefourfive—they shattered in the air. Mason Peters, a New York reporter, mopped his head with a handkerchief and turned to his host. "My God, Fred, was that your mother?"

In his autobiography, twenty years after her death, Fred Stone wrote: "There was never a sweeter, gentler, more lovable woman than Annie Oakley."

* * *

After an Ohio visit the Butlers brought back to Nutley a sturdy brown-haired, wide-eyed girl, Annie's favorite niece. Fern Campbell lived and traveled with them for parts of the next six years. From her aunt she learned two arts, shooting and sewing, and from her uncle she heard stories of far travels with Buffalo Bill's cowboys and Indians. In the winter of 1912, at Leesburg, Florida, they hunted the woods and swamps of the flat inland country, and when spring came they thought about Buffalo Bill, old tired, disheartened, starting one more "final" tour with a show controlled by strangers.* Then came a letter from a new show with a familiar-ringing name, Young Buffalo Wild West, offering a season's contract to Annie Oakley. It was spring and Annie felt like being on the move. The contract was generous and their bank account was low. In Nutley their house had been sold to Joseph Stirratt and rented to the Munkittricks. Again they packed the costumes and the guns. They were ready for the road.

They joined the show at Peoria, Illinois, and began a tour that crossed the Midwest, swung up into Canada, and moved down the coast. It was a familiar life—horsemen and Indians, steers and buffalo, the trampled show grounds, the straw-strewn corral, the roar of voices as Annie Oakley splintered targets in the arena. It was like past seasons. Coming out of her dressing tent she half expected to see Nate Salsbury or Major Burke, and in the dark grounds at midnight she could imagine a deep voice humming: "Tenting tonight, tenting tonight, tenting on the old camp ground."

In October they played at Cambridge, Maryland, on the shore of Chesapeake Bay. Perhaps it was the season; perhaps it was the light on the water, or the wild geese going over, or hunters coming in from the marshes with bales of black muskrat pelts. Frank said, "Missie, here's a place I'd like to live."

The show moved on, but they remembered the easy, friendly, un-hurried town, with wharves and canneries lining Cambridge Creek and spacious old houses facing High Street from their groves of magnolias, mimosa, and crepe myrtle trees. Frank wrote to a Cam-bridge lawyer and to a real-estate man. At the end of the season they were back again, buying a house on the shore of Hambrooks Bay at the mouth of the Great Choptank River. Their windows looked out

* Buffalo Bill's Original Wild West made its last tour in 1913 and was sold at auction in Denver on August 21st; but in that year Cody was appearing with the Sells Floto Circus, owned by a flamboyant Denver newspaper man

at oyster boats passing and a ferry plodding across from Oxford; at night they heard bell buoys clanging in the tide.

They bought an Irish setter, a bright-eyed black and white puppy, and named him Dave for Fred Stone's partner Dave Montgomery. A son of California Bell Boy, a field trial winner, Dave was an ardent hunter; even on the porch of the cottage he would point for quail. On December days they tramped the fields and tidal flats and came home with bulging game bags. The winter evenings were long and tranquil, Dave asleep on his rug at the fireside, Frank reading aloud while Annie stitched at her embroidery hoop.

To that quiet household came a visitor—a seasoned, quiet-spoken man, George Widows of London, who twenty-five years ago had written Annie Oakley a pathetic letter and sailed for Africa. He had stayed in Africa all those years, and now he brought a gift as large as a gun trunk. It was a collection of horns from the veldt, more than twenty pairs ranging from the tiny horns of the diminutive water deer to handsome fluted eland horns and straight gemsbok horns as long as walking sticks. George Widows was curious about America. After showing a set of pictures of Africa, he wanted to know about the United States—Where did the West begin? What kind of country did the Indians inhabit? How did the South differ from the North?

From Chesapeake Bay he set out to see America, but a few weeks later, in Florida, he fell ill and died. Annie Oakley prized the trophies he had brought from the heart of Africa. Eventually those exotic horns were hung in a Darke County farmhouse.

*   *   *

That winter Frank Butler dipped into the deep well of memory. Other times, other places, the enduring days, the remembered people. He was a hunter, often alone in the frosty marshland, along the empty shore, in the bare woods where winter was coming. More composed than Annie Oakley, never restless for change, he was a man of memory and feeling. Wherever he went he wrote sentimental verses about the weather and the seasons—

> I was sitting at my window
> Just at the close of day—

or love poems to Missie, after many years of marriage—

> Her presence would remind you
> Of an angel in the skies—

He had a liking for rhythm and meter. Even when he wrote in prose there was cadence in his language, like the swinging stride of a hunter across a stubble field.

On a gray afternoon when the Choptank was blurred with snow and the bell buoys sounded faintly, he sat at the desk till daylight waned at the window. Dave was lying on the floor, his legs twitching in some dream of his own hunting, while Annie showed a length of feather-stitching to her niece. At last he stood at the window and looked out at the falling snow. Once he would have been out in this weather; now the gun trunk was closed and he was content to range the woods and marshes of the past. He went back to the desk and turned up the lamp. What he was writing touched all the unforgotten seasons, and it ended with the October dusk in Shropshire when beacons burned in honor of the Queen. In the blue remembered hills he was afield again.

As the day darkened and the fire grew bright, Annie put her sewing down. In the quiet room Frank read his reverie. He called it "A Hunter's Dream."

A hunter now old and gray sat musing on his sports of long ago, of the days when he was young and of the dogs and guns he had owned . . . and sighed because his hunting days were o'er. He slept and dreamed that he followed once again Diana to the rock ledge and timber thick, the home of the grouse. His dog by his side he follows the ledge mid the timber tall. . . . Thus in his dream he hunts again the partridge on the mountainside as he did in days now past and gone.

Then from the mountainside he passes over the hills to the familiar fields where the call of the quail is heard. . . . The tumbling

"The Custer Charge," Ambrose Park, 1894, showing Brooklyn
beyond the forks of the Yellowstone.

The Deadwood Stagecoach, in London.
Buffalo Bill standing, John Nelson
on the box.

Sitting Bull and Buffalo Bill
"Foes in '76—
Friends in '85"

Annie Oakley after her medals were put away.

waters to him are singing, the trees beneath the gentle breezes blow, and the rocks their moss-gloved hands extend to the friend of long ago. . . . His dog is off and quickly circles the stubble field to see if they are feeding there, then stops, sniffs the air . . . and stands there pointing, proclaiming there they are! The covey flushes, two shots, a bird for each in turn; the dog awaits the word—Hi on! Thus in fancy he hunts the quail over the hills and stubble fields of long ago. . . . By fancy led to the burnt heather of the marsh for that bird of flight the English snipe, he presses on, the dog to the windward passing, better to sniff the air of the old marshland. . . .

While he read, the dog at the fireside stretched and woke. He lifted his ears and thumped his tail while the birds were being scented.

Then the old hunter wakes and sighs because these days have passed forever.

CHAPTER 19

Pinehurst

TO Annie Oakley home meant many things—a cabin in the Ohio woods, a tent on the show grounds, a hotel room in a hundred cities, a house in New Jersey, a cottage on Chesapeake Bay. For seven winters it meant a rambling hotel in the North Carolina pine woods.

In 1915 Annie Oakley and Frank Butler joined the staff of the Carolina Hotel at Pinehurst, Frank in charge of the skeet range and Annie to give exhibitions and shooting lessons. It was a life of guns, dogs, and horses, and of relaxed and congenial people. In the gun room or on the sunny terrace they talked about guns, golf, and game birds with John Philip Sousa, John Bassett Moore, Walter Hines Page, John D. Rockefeller. They exchanged Ohio and Indiana memories with Booth Tarkington, and Frank Butler quoted homely verse to the author Edgar A. Guest. Sousa was an excellent trapshooter, banging away alternately with Annie Oakley; the others brooded about their golf.

To the ladies from Philadelphia, New York, and Boston in their tailored shooting jackets, Annie Oakley explained the parts of a gun and the value of sport-shooting. Marksmanship, she observed, calls upon both body and mind—body in handling the weapon, mind in exercising judgment when aiming and firing. From this sport a woman can learn confidence and self-possession, nerve and judgment—all useful qualities in daily life.

She had them begin by aiming a light rifle, 22-caliber, unloaded. They aimed, dropped the gun to the waist, raised it to the shoulder, sighted the target—over and over. Then the shotgun. For beginners a light 20-bore was best—"Some of my best scores in the field and at traps were made with a 20-bore"—and it was best to use a light load until the shooter became accustomed to the recoil. A good marksman need not have a black-and-blue shoulder.

Then she showed them the shooter's stance, his balance, his swing. She demonstrated—the left hand grasps the stock, not too tight but firmly. The cheek touches the wood, not presses, just meets it snugly. If the cheek does not snuggle to the wood the mark will be overshot. . . . Lead the target. Always lead a moving target. To hit a flying target the gun must be kept moving while the trigger is being pressed. . . . At eighteen yards from the trap the target reaches the high point of its arc and begins to fall. A marksman does not wait for the fall. He finds his lead and smashes the bird still rising, just before it has reached the height of its climb.

When she sat on the veranda, Annie Oakley was a white-haired woman, slight and birdlike, fifty-five years old, but coming out of the gun room with Dave at her heels she was young again. She wore tweeds, laced boots, a soft hat with a blowing feather, and she carried a gun as though it were a part of her. The targets sailed up, the gun swept to her shoulder, the birds vanished in a puff of dust. At a sign from Frank Butler, Dave ran to his stand and sat up while Frank balanced an apple on his head. When she fired, the apple fell apart and Dave trotted along the gallery for approval. Frank threw brass disks in the air and she dented them, one after another, with rifle bullets. Around Pinehurst, it is said, there are still some brass dollars showing Annie Oakley's mark.

Twice a week they hunted with the hotel guests, but the best hunting was their own. Ahead of them Dave came to point, tail out, ears alert, muzzle lifted. They came up softly, guns half raised. With an exploding noise the November turf flew up; but it was not turf, it was quail, flying with full speed at the first wing-beat. They scattered, climbed steeply, with a rushing of wings. At the gunshot the dog was off. He trotted back with the game held gently in his mouth.

Some things never grow stale—the gray sandhills streaked with pine, the chill November air, clumps of scrub oak among the tawny fields of sedge grass, the swiftness of the birds, the creak of saddle

leather and the rocking rhythm of a horse's stride, the excitement
skill, and obedience of the dogs. Some things take you back. A gir
in baggy boy's clothing roaming the Darke County woods had learnec
about game birds as well as marksmanship. Quail will fly straight fo
an opening in the trees. When a branch looms ahead they can dodge
with blinding speed, scattering like wind around it. A grouse wil
seek cover; you must outguess him and be ready for his rushing flight
If there is a break in the forest cover, be sure you are on the far side
of the old rail fence, commanding the opening he will find. He can
drop from a bare tree as swift as sight; he can skim like a bullet ove
the ground. Doves fly out of a grain field or a patch of ragweed
swooping and swerving in unpredictable pattern. You wait then
holding your gun for their straightening flight. It all came back in
a day afield.

The next day the skeet range and the ladies in their tailored jackets
"After mastering the singles you are ready for the double targets
Twin targets are not two birds at the same time but one after th
other. Consider only the first target until it is smashed, then giv
attention to the second. The shooter who thinks about both at once
will miss them both. Concentrate on the first target, the outgoer
before giving any thought to the incoming bird." Most of the ladie
would never learn, but the lessons went on.

Pinehurst was a congenial, self-contained community, a little ou
of the world, with tallyhos, victorias, and wagonettes clopping aroun
the village market place. It had four hotels, a clubhouse, two gol
courses, a skeet and target range, kennels and stables. To keep th
guests occupied there were gymkhanas, golf tournaments, shootin
matches, horse shows, dances at the Carolina Hotel and the Holl
Inn, plays in the Carolina ballroom. Every season at the Sandhi
Fair, Annie Oakley gave a shooting exhibition to a crowded galler
In Pinehurst plays she took the leading role, whether it was an India
maiden or an English dowager. She always had a part in the spring
time performance of the Pinehurst minstrels, organized by Charli
Baxter, the station agent and telegraph operator.

A rumbling little trolley car ran from the hotels to the golf link
On the nine o'clock trolley a small, slightly stooped man with a pin

and wrinkled face was always the first to enter. He greeted young
Karl Abbott, who collected fares, with a shy smile—"Have you
change for a half-dollar?" offering a silver dollar neatly cut in half.
It was Mr. Rockefeller's morning joke. At shooting exhibitions Karl
Abbott proudly carried Annie Oakley's ammunition.

*   *   *

Harry Priest, manager of the Carolina Hotel, owned a summer
hotel at Newcastle-by-the-Sea, three miles from Portsmouth, New
Hampshire. In the summer of 1916 he took the Butlers to the Hotel
Wentworth as instructors in trapshooting. Frank Butler, a big silent
man in a gray Norfolk jacket and russet shoes, trailing his white-haired
wife into the dining room, seemed a pathetic figure to the Wentworth
waitresses and bellboys. It was obvious that he lived off the career of
his wife, and it was back-hall gossip that Buffalo Bill had tricked them
out of their savings. The gossip was not true, but Frank Butler, once
full of Irish laughter, had been overtaken by an Irish gravity. He was
a lonely man, talking occasionally about his years on the stage and
their travels with the Wild West, recalling bygone hunting seasons,
reaching for the irrecoverable past. Once they had been the guests
of princes, now the hotel help smiled at them. But no one laughed
when Annie Oakley stood on the target range beside the hotel golf
course. With no apparent aim she smashed the pigeons—full-flight,
quartering, across wing, single and double targets. When Frank
threw out a golf ball she dribbled it toward the green with pistol
fire. That summer she broke the Wentworth Gun Club record with
a perfect score of 100 successive targets. When the gallery applauded,
Frank Butler smiled as though the handclaps were for him. No man
was ever prouder of his wife.

*   *   *

They were at Pinehurst in January, 1917, when newspaper headlines carried a reverberating name. BUFFALO BILL DIES IN DENVER.
Just two months earlier the shaky old showman had made his final

public appearance at Portsmouth, Virginia, with Miller's 101 Ranch Show, riding in a phaeton because arthritis and prostate trouble made it a struggle for him to mount a horse. That winter he was a lost man. Divorced from his wife, his money gone, his ranches in Nebraska and Wyoming in the hands of strangers, he went to the home of his sister on Lafayette Street in Denver. There he died on a cold January morning. He had been all but forgotten, but death made him famous again. On a gray winter day a long procession moved from Lafayette Street to the Colorado capitol, and Buffalo Bill lay in state, in a bronze casket with a glass top, under the lofty gold-leaf dome. Outside stood his horse Isham, the saddle empty, the reins hanging loose. A company of troops from Fort Logan made a guard of honor while thousands filed past the coffin banked with flowers from every state in the nation. In the balcony a military band played *Tenting on the Old Camp Ground.*

North Platte wanted his grave; Cody, Wyoming, wanted it; both had claim to the memory of Buffalo Bill. But Denver got it. After weeks of wrangling, while the body lay in a Denver mortuary vault, the grave was dug in Denver's Mountain Park. On the 3rd of June another procession wound up the switchbacks of Lookout Mountain, and Buffalo Bill was buried while the shadows crept over the endless plains. At Pinehurst, thinking of the irrecoverable past, Annie Oakley wrote a farewell that Major Burke—he died before the year was over—would have approved: "Goodbye, old friend. The setting sun beyond the western hills will pay daily tribute to the last great pioneer of the West."

*   *   *

When America entered the war in 1917 the newspapers recalled that Annie Oakley had once shot a cigarette out of the mouth of the Crown Prince of Germany, now Kaiser Wilhelm, and they deplored that her aim had been so accurate. She was sent on a tour of American training camps to give rifle demonstrations for the troops. Frank threw targets and Annie smashed them. Dave sat up with an apple on his head, like the son of Wilhelm Tell, and she punctured it. Then Dave went to work for the Red Cross. Spectators were asked to let the dog scent currency, which they hid within a range of a hundred feet. When Dave located the money it was donated to the Red Cross. That summer "Captain" Dave earned thousands of dollars for the fund.

Annie Oakley was growing older, but she remained miraculous with a gun. Season after season she won matches and established records. In the spring of 1922 at Pinehurst, shooting from sixteen yards, she broke a hundred clay targets in succession.

The summer of 1922 they spent at Fred Stone's country place on Long Island. Annie taught the Stone daughters to shoot and ride, and from drawling Will Rogers, who lived across the road, she learned new tricks with a rope. In August she made her last public appearance on a target range. At the Mineola Race Track, Fred Stone staged a rodeo for the benefit of the Occupational Therapy Society and its rehabilitation of wounded war veterans. Four thousand high-spirited spectators filled the grandstand as Annie Oakley and Fred Stone led the clattering parade. The Lambs Club sponsored an acrobatic act. Madison Square Garden sent an exhibition prize fight. The Friars Club produced a Western melodrama written by George M. Cohan and staged by William Collier. After riding and roping contests, Annie Oakley broke her last targets. The show ended with a memory of the Wild West—a battered stagecoach drawn by a six-horse team rumbled around the ring. A band of painted Indians went whooping after it until plainsman Fred Stone led his cowboys to the rescue. The stagecoach had an authentic history; it had been brought from Dakota by Joseph P. Kennedy and presented to Fred Stone for his charity show. A year later Fred Stone gave it to the Smithsonian Institution.

*   *   *

In the autumn of 1922 the November wind felt cold as winter and the thought of snow brought no exhilaration. Annie Oakley was past sixty; a little anemic, the doctor said, and the best prescription was a warm winter in Florida. They sailed from Philadelphia on the

Essex of the old Merchant and Miner Line, a pleasant voyage with the ship creaking comfortably in the long Atlantic swell. There were two dogs now, Dave and Lad; every day Annie walked them on the sun deck in the bracing air. Off Cape Hatteras the Gulf Stream brought a warm wind from the south. They kept inside the current and the coast slipped past—the low line of Smith Island with the white lighthouse lifting, the Cape Fear River opening in the dense green shore, Cape Romain and Raccoon Key, then the wide Georgia marshes in the sun. They swung into the St. Johns River between the low Florida shores. At the dock in Jacksonville, friends were waiting in a motorcar to drive them to Leesburg in Lake County. The air was soft, the sun was warm, birds sang in the pine woods. They were talking about the dogs and the hunting when the car struck a soft place in the road. It turned over. For weeks Annie Oakley lay in a hospital bed with a fractured hip and a shattered ankle. She would never hunt again.

She came out of the hospital in a wheel chair. There were weeks in bed in the hotel, and then weeks on crutches. At last she traded the crutches for a cane, but the steel brace remained on her leg. Frank hunted that winter, more to tell her about it than for any other reason. On a Sunday in February, 1923, he took the young dog to the woods. On the hotel porch Dave lay at Annie's feet; he had a lame shoulder and for him, too, the hunting was over. The afternoon shadows grew long and bullbats began calling from the woods. Restlessly the dog watched for Frank to appear; at last he trotted down the road to meet him. A car swung out of a side street. Brakes screamed and the dog lay still in the road. When Frank came, Annie Oakley was alone. They buried Dave in the pine woods behind the hotel.

That spring, while the days grew longer, Frank Butler sat for hours at his writing desk, frowning over a growing sheaf of pages. One day he came back from a printer's shop and handed Missie a bound folder with the dog's photograph under the title—The Life of Dave —As Told by Himself. The story began: "Now that I am getting on in years and not hunting anymore, I have decided to write up my life and dedicate it to my many friends." Dave had made friends every where he went—in Maryland, at Pinehurst, in New York, in New Hampshire, in army camps across the country. In his life story he told about his friends and about himself. He recalled the running of field trials in Maryland, and hunting seasons in North Carolina and Florida. He told how on a Florida creek bank a rattlesnake had struck at Missie, who fired a pistol from the hip and shattered the wedge-shaped head. He told how, having gone lame, he watched beside his mistress, their hunting done.

Frank had copies of that story to mail to all Dave's scattered friends.

*   *   *

Three years more they stayed at Leesburg. Annie Oakley would never have another dog or another horse, and she would not hold a rifle in her hands. But she held things in her mind. Not the street parade and the cheering arena—deeper things. Spring in Darke County. Swamp lilies in the slough, wild honeysuckle at the fence rows, blue flag and yellow flag on the borders of Swamp Creek, wild plum and haw trees blossoming in the woods. In April of 1926 they took the train to Ohio.

CHAPTER 20

Home to Darke County

> It won't be many years before the timber will be
> thinned out so that wild game will be scarce. Go into the
> county in any direction and you will see gangs of men
> burning down trees so as to get them out of the way.
> Timber is an awful nuisance in Darke County.
>
> —GEORGE W. CALDERWOOD: *Darke County Boy*

It was spring in Dayton, the maple trees fuzzy with catkins and dandelions yellow in the grass, when the taxi crossed the Great Miami, went out Salem Avenue, and turned into Lexington. It stopped at Number 706. When Frank carried her up the steps and the door swung open, Annie's smile reassured her sister, Mrs. Emily Brumbaugh Patterson.

Propped up in bed with a bunch of jonquils on the little table, she heard children's voices outside, the whirr of lawnmowers, a streetcar rumbling at the corner. Emmie came in twenty times a day with a letter or a tray or a cup of tea, and with some recollection of Darke County or of the nieces and nephews now scattered from Michigan to Oklahoma. Frank came every day, bringing flowers, papers, magazines, telling about the man he had met at breakfast or the boy he talked to on the streetcar, reading letters from New York, New Jersey, and Florida, then going back downtown to the Miami Hotel.

For Annie Oakley that spring was curiously mingled with other springs. When she took the embroidery hoop from the table, her hands fell into familiar rhythms and her mind went back. Spring in Darke County—meadow larks singing across the swamp, squirrels chattering in the oaks, wild roses at the fence corners, Sweet William pushing through the winter leaves, dogwood shining in the under-forest. Her mother had cooked "spring medicine" on the kitchen stove—three spoons of sulphur, three spoons of wild honey, one spoon of cream of tartar (Annie Oakley carried the recipe in her note-book for forty years), but the best tonic was spring itself, blue sky and south wind and the white clouds changing. Spring in New York when the huge arena seemed close and imprisoning, when the foun-tain jetted in Madison Square and ships whistled from the harbor. Spring in London, the ring of horses' hoofs on the wet streets past Kensington Gardens where the sheep were grazing. Spring in Paris, spring in Scotland, spring in New Jersey. Spring over Chesapeake Bay, the light on the river, oyster boats tugging at the wharf, and barefoot Negro boys raking shells on the shore.

One day Frank brought a caller, and again her mind went back. He stayed all afternoon, walking up and down with his hands jammed in his pockets, then tilting in the rocker, the coarse wing of hair falling down his forehead, leaning toward her: "You remember, Annie, that little glass-eyed pony, Dopey, we had on Long Island? . . . Remem-ber when Fred got tangled up in that rope he was spinning? . . . Remember when Dorothy fell off of Bootlegger and you got her right back on before she had time to be scared? . . . Remember—"

Annie Oakley had come from Woodland, Ohio, and Will Rogers had come from Claremore, Oklahoma, and they both remembered the beginnings. After winning a roping and riding contest, young Will went to the St. Louis Fair where Colonel Zack Mulhall was putting on a Western show. He pushed the hair out of his eyes. "Now they got a new name for it—rodeo." Colonel Mulhall got together a cow-boy band and toured the state fairs, taking bets that his musicians could rope and tie a steer faster than anybody on the grounds. "Me and Jim O'Donnell had to produce—mostly Jim." Will showed his sheepish grin. "There we'd sit in the band, me with a trombone I couldn't make a sound on."

He paced the room again, hands in his pockets. He picked up his big hat and twirled it on a finger. They looked at each other, the white-haired woman against the pillows and the sunburned man in his rumpled clothes. He said: "I'll see you in the fall. I'll be back this way. I'll stop in. Likely you'll be up and around by then."

The next day she wrote a letter to Leesburg. Her old saddle was there—as familiar as anything in the world—the wide pommel flaring out before it drew into the horn, the horn raked forward and the knob covered with half-inch leather, wide skirts to the stirrup straps, double horsehair cinches, rawhide latigo thongs front and back. A Navajo blanket went with it, red with white zigzag stripes, and a silver-mounted bridle. As she pictured it she could feel the rocking of the horse and hear the leather creaking, she could see the horses in the corral standing nose to rump swishing flies, she could smell the tanbark on the grounds and hear the Colonel booming: "Light down, Missie. There's coffee in my tent."

Frank was puzzled about the letter. Why did she want her saddle?

"Not for me. I want them to fix it up and send it to Dorothy Stone. Will reminded me—I want her to have the saddle."

A week later Frank opened a newspaper on the bed and pointed to Will Rogers' column. He went to the window while she read it.

This is a good story about a little woman that all the older generation will remember. She was the reigning sensation of America and Europe during the heyday of Buffalo Bill's Wild West show. She was their star. Her picture was on more billboards than a modern Gloria Swanson. It was Annie Oakley, the greatest woman rifle shot the world has ever produced. Nobody took her place. There was only one. She is bedridden from an automobile accident a few years ago. She for years taught the fashionable people at Pinehurst, N. C., to shoot. America is worshiping at the feet of Raquel Meller, the Spanish lady. Europe talked the same of Annie Oakley in her day. I want you to write her, all you who remember her, and those that can go and see her. Her address is 706 Lexington Avenue, Dayton, Ohio. She will be a lesson to you. She is a greater character than she was a rifle shot. Circuses have produced the cleanest living class of people in America today, and Annie Oakley's name, her lovable traits, her thoughtful consideration of others, will live as a mark for any woman to shoot at.

She looked up from the paper. "That's like Will."

"Still getting clippings," Frank said. "I'll put it in the trunk."

She thought of the trunk full of clippings, photographs, programs, letters, and now she wanted them sorted and put in order. Frank Butler didn't have a heart for that; it seemed like the end of things. In June he advertised for a secretary, and a college girl, on vacation from Miami University, fifty miles away, came to the hotel. She went through that pile of papers, lingering over pictures of Indians and horsemen, sorting yellowed letters and faded clippings, wondering at the datelines: New York, Naples, Cincinnati, Charlottenburg, Kalamazoo, Paris, Munich, Montreal, Barcelona, Greenville, Windsor Castle.

When the doctor said "pernicious anemia," she wanted to be back in Darke County. Now the North Star farmhouse belonged to strangers, but Annie Oakley's niece, Bonnie Blakeley, lived in the village of Ansonia, eight miles north of Greenville. There she lay in the long days of summer, occasionally a wagon creaking past, a load of hay leaving wisps on the arching maple branches, wheat trucks droning to the elevator, the smell of timothy and clover blowing in the windows. From her bed she answered many letters, and the letters touched memories that made her want to set down the life pattern that had gone far from Darke County and come back to it again.

She began an autobiography, writing in sentimental and inaccurate terms, dating her birth six years later than the fact and changing her childhood name: "I was born August 13, 1866, in Patterson Township, Darke County, Ohio, a short distance from the village of Woodland (now called Willowdell) and christened Phoebe Ann Oakley Mozee." She covered thirty years in a sketchy narrative that mingled her own memory with the inventions of the press agents. The story stopped at the autumn of 1890 when the Wild West made its cheerless winter camp near Strasbourg on the Rhine. She was too tired to write more.

By the end of August she needed a nurse. Her sister Hulda came down from Ferndale, Michigan, and found a place in Greenville. Two family friends, teachers in Greenville, Kate Broderick and Harriet Zemer, had a roomy frame house on Third Street, between Walnut and Oak. There Annie Oakley lay in a big four-poster bed, with a

nurse's cot nearby. Her friend Hazel Grote lived on the next street.
Dr. Husted and Pastor Wessel looked in every other day. In that
airy room she heard the last sounds of summer, the fading chorus of
locusts and katydids, and she watched the coming of fall. Green
branches changed to yellow, yellow leaves turned scarlet. Through
the windows came the bittersweet tang of leaf fires, and the trees
stood bare against the sky.

Lying languid and clear-minded just two blocks from where she
had brought her bundled furs to Frenchy La Motte, it all came back
—the children's voices taunting *Moses Poses!* in the orphanage; cold
bare dressing rooms smelling of grease paint and talcum powder,
covered with frayed posters and scribbled messages; nights on the
show lot when the horses munched their hay and a sleepless cowboy
played a homesick tune on a mouth organ; hunting in Shrewsbury,
Norfolk, and the Black Forest; riding the midnight ferry with a wind
blowing in from the sea; sitting in a gray hotel room remembering
yellow lamplight across the fields of home. It all came back, happy
and sad, painful and exciting, and she didn't want any of it different
from the way it had been.

From her bed she bought two burial lots in the country cemetery
at Brock; now beech leaves would be drifting over the graves in the
withered grass. Frank Butler, seventy-six, tired, troubled, slow-moving,
was reluctant to think about a burial place, but she had always been
the deciding one. She asked for a packing box for the clippings he had
sorted. Around her on the bed she made them into bundles which
Frank tied together. She wanted them to go to Fred Stone—at his
Globe Theater address.

Frank had a little disordered notebook scribbled with names and
street numbers along with notes on ammunition, recipes for dog
food, a list of "high hands in poker." Before he could find the address she read it from the brown leather book on her table. After
the package was gone she went on turning the worn pages, drawing
the past around her in those names and places: Mrs. Nate Salsbury,
Elizabeth Bacon Custer, Louis E. Cooke of the Continental Hotel in
Newark, the Steward of the S.S. *Essex*, Miller Brothers 101 Ranch,
people in Boston, Newtonville, Newton Center, in Newark, Nutley,

East Orange, in New Rochelle, Amityville, and Port Washington. She closed the book and came back to the present, which could not last much longer.

She wrote: "Bonds in box 300 at the National Newark and Essex Banking Company, Newark, N.J. Notify Spencer S. Marsh, vice-president. My bonds are all in the Trust Department. My will is in the box in the vault. $24,000 of securities held for F. E. Butler. He to have the interest during his life and the disposal of principal at his death. . . . His will to the same stock is in the same box with my will. *All* is at the National Newark and Essex Banking Company, Broad Street, Newark, N.J." She read it over and signed "A. O. Butler." It was good to have that done.

In the streets of Greenville, Frank Butler scuffed through drifts of colored leaves, a tired and distant man. Sometimes he wandered out a country road and came back with a bunch of bittersweet, a burst milkweed pod, or a clump of asters faded to their final smoky blue. Missie always liked the wild things best. On a wet and windy afternoon his deliberate steps paused at the landing. He coughed, and came up with a slower tread. When he was in the room she had made up her mind again; he must go to Florida before the cold winds of November. She was firm and cheerful, telling him what clothes to take, insisting that he pack the gun trunk; in the South he would be his old self again. He objected, he would wait till they both could go. Then a spell of coughing shook him.

If she knew it was their last day together, she did not let him feel it. She kept him remembering—the bright and windy day just fifty years ago when she had stood with a gun shaking in her hands at a shooting club in Cincinnati. What made her tremble so? Not the strange place and the strange people. Not the money her brother-in-law had bet on her shooting. It was the tall smiling man in a feathered hat and a belted jacket. She was a girl in a homemade blouse who could not even read the sign beside the target range, but she wanted him to think her rare, gifted, and exceptional. No wonder her hands shook—her whole life was changed that day. What would she have done without him? She would have come back to Darke County, she would have lived her life on a back road somewhere without ever knowing what the world was like. How had Annie Moses of North Star township become Annie Oakley? Frank Butler had made her over. She reached out to his big-knuckled hands. "You know, Jimmy, you really reared me. You brought me up."

The next day he was on the train to New Jersey, planning to take care of business at the Newark bank before turning south. There were old friends in Newark, but when he was there he felt too tired to see them. What would he do in Florida? How could he pass the winter, alone? At last he telegraphed the niece, Fern Campbell, who had lived with them as a child. She was with her mother in Detroit, doing publicity work for hotels. She could not join him at once, but she urged him to come to Detroit while she arranged to take him south for the winter.

In Detroit his breath was short and shallow and his hands would not stop shaking. He stayed in his room, waiting for word from Greenville. It came on the third day of November: Annie Oakley had died in her sleep.

Day after day he sat staring through his own grayness at the gray roofs and the gray November sky. Then he stayed in bed. Outside, the traffic poured between Royal Oak and Detroit, and the sky was smudged with the smoking factories of Hamtramck. They had played in Detroit, at the Recreation Park, in September, 1885, their first season with the Wild West. Then the world was large, alive, and alluring, full of promise and discovery. Now it was empty, empty.

*   *   *

On Broadway in Greenville, just off the Main Street corner where farm wagons once lined the hitching rack, stands Schmerman's Jewelry Store. Now a fountain bubbles in the open square, but the grim old town hall stood there in November, 1926, when an engraved loving cup—*To Annie Oakley, from the people of France, Exposition Universal, 1889*—was being fitted with a silver cover. It stayed on a shelf in Schmerman's back room, among silent clocks, tarnished table ware, and broken jewelry, until Annie Oakley's ashes were brought back from a Cincinnati crematory. When the ashes were sealed in, Hazel Grote took the cup to her home on East Main Street, beside the bridge over Greenville Creek. Two days later Pastor Wessel of the Lutheran Church read the funeral service in the Grote living room. No reporters were admitted, though press wires were carrying the name of Annie Oakley across the country. Then the silver cup was put on a shelf in a bedroom closet.

Annie Oakley's ashes stayed in the Grote house during the gray weather of November, 1926. On the 23rd, twenty days after her death, Frank Butler died in Detroit. His body was brought to Greenville. On Thanksgiving Day there was a second funeral in the house by Greenville Creek. A few cars drove out, through Pikeville, Beamsville, and Dawn, past the wheat stubble and the cornfields with their dry leaves clashing.

In the Brock cemetery two stones of russet marble stand together.

ANNIE OAKLEY	FRANK BUTLER
1926	1926
At Rest	At Rest

On that Thanksgiving Day the pastor read: *In the midst of life we are in death—* A shower of beech leaves came spinning from the dense grove across the road. They found a resting place under leaning headstones. *Grant to us who are still in our pilgrimage—* Over the north ridge a shotgun roared, drowning the words of the burial service. *The grace of our Lord be with you, the peace of God keep your minds and hearts—* The pastor closed his book and walked away. The little company filed past the graves, got into their cars, and drove back to Greenville. A cold wind rattled the cornstalks around the little cemetery. From the north the gun sounded again, faint with distance. Darke County had changed, but there was still good hunting around Woodland and North Star.

*   *   *

Eleven years later, on the 150th anniversary of the Ordinance of the Northwest Territory, Greenville decorated for the celebration.

Schmerman's window displayed another loving cup, presented to Annie Oakley by the people of Greenville in the summer of 1900, along with her photographs, her medals, the jeweled opera glasses given her by Queen Victoria, Buffalo Bill's rifle, and the war bonnet of Sitting Bull.

Greenville is like countless county-seat towns between Pennsylvania and Kansas. There was the commonplace Midwestern street —farmers coming in with loads of yellow corn, mud-stained trucks and faded sedans jutting from the curb, a freight train clanking out of sight, baskets of apples and rows of pumpkins outside the redfront grocery, ruled tablets and colored pencils in the window of the Five and Ten, mackinaw coats and gumshoes in J. C. Penney's window, stiff mannikins wearing stiff cloth coats in the Palace Store. The ugly town hall made an island in the north end of Broadway; on the drab stone courthouse a stone Justice stood unnoticed above the passing people. But there was a spell in Schmerman's window. It took you to Old Fort Laramie and the Little Big Horn, to Madison Square Garden and the Chicago Midway, to Windsor Castle and the Bois de Bologne. It took you to Buffalo Bill's grave above the plains of Colorado, and to the old stage road twisting up to Deadwood City.

They stood around the display window. "My old man remembers when she was a bare-legged girl up in the country." . . . "I saw her at the World's Fair. She gave me a ticket to Buffalo Bill's show, good any time, anywhere." . . . "My uncle used to throw wood blocks for her to shoot at." . . . "I was there when they gave her that cup on the show grounds in Armstrong's pasture. I can recollect that day." . . . "She brought dressed game to Charlie Katzenberger and muskrat hides to Frenchy La Motte. I remember when his shop was right here."

In the northern townships of the county, Swamp Creek wound through the woods and marshes. It found its way to the Stillwater River, and to the Great Miami, and the Ohio, and eventually to the Mississippi and the Gulf. In winter the little creeks of Darke County froze like iron. Years ago, on a sudden sunny day in March, Annie Moses had watched the ice go out—stillness turning into movement, silence breaking into sound, the water running away to distant places. The things in Schmerman's window meant the restlessness, the escape, the winning.

"She used to hunt game birds on my cousin's farm. There was lots of timber in Darke County then."

Acknowledgments

ALTHOUGH her name has found a permanent place in American folklore, the life story of Annie Oakley has not been generally known. With the help of a number of people I have followed her from her childhood in Ohio, through her association with Buffalo Bill and the years of free-lancing which followed, and back to Ohio at the end. While she was with Buffalo Bill's organization, the Wild West grew into a spectacle of Western history and scored its great success in America and abroad. Inevitably the story of Annie Oakley is also the story of the Wild West; I have given especial detail to that setting and to those seventeen years of Annie Oakley's life. Though I have used a narrative method, occasionally imagining details of action and dialogue, all the persons, situations, and events in the narrative are drawn from real life.

For help in following the course of Annie Oakley's life I am indebted to a number of persons. Mrs. Annie Fern Swartwout of Greenville, Ohio, Annie Oakley's niece and herself a biographer of Annie Oakley, has generously given me access to records and documents, and has answered a number of my questions from her own memory of Annie Oakley and Frank Butler. Mrs. Rebecca Salsbury James of Taos, N.M., has answered numerous questions and has taken notes for me of conversations with the late Harry Tarleton, one-time tent attendant of Buffalo Bill. Miss Ina T. Aulls, Head of the Western History Department of the Denver Public Library, has guided me to a wealth of records and photographs in the Western History Room of the Denver Library. Stewart H. Holbrook has generously shared his enthusiasm for Annie Oakley and has put me in touch with several persons who knew Annie Oakley and her husband. Richard J. Walsh of the John Day Company, New York, a biographer of

Buffalo Bill, helped me to find answers to some persistent questions.

A writer on any aspect of Americana soon incurs a debt to librarians and directors of historical societies. I am grateful for assistance of various kinds from many of these generous and resourceful people. I should like to express my thanks to Miss Alice Lee Parker and Miss Virginia Daiker of the Library of Congress; Sylvester Vigilante of the New York Public Library; Donald C. Holmes, Chief of the Photo-duplication Service of the Library of Congress; Mrs. Mary Jester Allen, Director of the Buffalo Bill Museum, Cody, Wyo.; Paul Angle, Director of the Chicago Historical Society; Robert W. Bingham, Director of the Buffalo Historical Society; Russell Reid, Superintendent of the State Historical Society of North Dakota; N. Orwin Rush, Director of the University of Wyoming Library; Miss Lois M. Fawcett, Head of the Reference Department, Minnesota Historical Society; Miss Ludie J. Kinkead, Curator of the Filson Club, Louisville; Miss Ellen T. Harding of the Louisville Free Library; Miss Ethel Hutchins of the Cincinnati Public Library; Miss Florence M. Gifford of the Cleveland Public Library; Mrs. Depew Head of the Ohioana Library, Columbus; H. M. Orcutt, Director of the Toledo Public Library; Miss Kathleen Moore of the Greenville Public Library; Mrs. Margarite Stoltz, Curator of the Darke County Museum; and my University colleagues John E. Dome, Director of Audio-Visual Service; L. S. Dutton, Reference Librarian; and E. W. King, Director of Libraries, at Miami University.

For assistance with details of informaton I wish to thank Judge Frank Zahn of the Standing Rock Jurisdiction, Fort Yates, N.D.; Mrs. Lucy K. Priest of Franconia, N.H.; Mrs. Draper Howard and Mrs. Eugene Plunkett of San Francisco; Mr. R. C. Brummer of Portland, Ore.; Mr. Harry D. Kirkover of Camden, S.C.; Colonel John R. Simpson of Englewood, N.J.; Dr. O. O. Fisher of Detroit; Mrs. Fred Stone of North Hollywood, Calif.; Mr. W. R. Coe of New York City; Mr. W. S. Campbell of Norman, Okla.; Miss Esther B. Mooney of New York City; Mr. Michael Harrison and Mr. A. R. Van Noy of the Los Angeles Corral of "The Westerners"; Mr. Frazer E. Wilson, historian of Darke County, Ohio; Mr. Harold S. Latham of The Macmillan Company, New York City; Mr. Harry Chenoweth,

Mayor of Nutley, N.J.; Mr. Eddie Botsford, onetime cowboy with the Wild West, of Littlefield, Tex.; and two of my friends and former students, Kenneth L. Jay of Casper, Wyo., and Richard Rentz of Greenville, Ohio.

To my wife, Marion Boyd Havighurst, who made hundreds of pages of expert and nearly legible notes in library reference rooms and frequently took to the road with me on Annie Oakley's trail, I offer, once again, my heartfelt thanks.

WALTER HAVIGHURST

SHADOWY HILLS
OXFORD, OHIO
January, 1954

INDEX